Achieve IELTS 2

English for International Education

Student's Book

UPPER INTERMEDIATE – ADVANCED

Band 5.5 to 7.5

Louis Harrison
Caroline Cushen
Susan Hutchison

Marshall Cavendish
Education

Map of the book

Language study	Pronunciation	Achieve IELTS	Expressions
present tenses: stative, transitive and intransitive verbs present perfect, present perfect continuous describing change	sentence stress	predicting	names and spelling meeting people importance
asking for information negatives referring to numbers	saying electronic addresses	negative words describing charts	finances and purchases
comparatives and superlatives past simple and past continuous comparing and contrasting	contrastive stress	language repair comparing data	asking for repetition correcting yourself
present and past passives describing processes purpose stages and sequences	linking: vowel to consonant	matching headings with paragraphs / topic sentences describing a process	encouraging someone
road directions present, present continuous, past, present perfect and future passives location describing changes in a city	linking with /w/ and /j/	listening to lectures	asking for more information
will, going to, modal verbs, be (about) to phrasal verbs introductions, main points and conclusions	linking with /r/	buying time discussion	consoling someone
past perfect third conditional agreeing and disagreeing adding information concession	intonation in third conditional sentences	true / false / not given problem / solution essays task 2 titles	(un)certainty
information clauses formal definitions reasons and results	intonation in relative clauses	signposting in lectures	talking about shopping talking about objects
would and used to reporting speech exemplification	word stress	mind maps in task 2 time limits referring to gender	talking about responsibilities talking about other people
reporting verbs rephrasing and giving alternatives	elision	understanding views and attitudes	suggesting offering to pay
phrasal verbs multi-word verbs future continuous, future perfect adverbs of certainty and attitude cohesion	symbols and numbers	timed writing interrupting	talking about the weather interrupting and continuing
inversion adjectives for people and things	reformulation and checking	listening and note-taking	talking about studying talking about feelings talking about plans

Introduction

Test overview; *Achieve IELTS* survey

A candidate
examiner
task card
notepaper/notes

B speaking
reading
writing
listening
grammar
pronunciation
vocabulary

1 Label the picture with the words in A.

1.1 **2** Listen to three students and answer the questions.

	student 1	student 2	student 3
1 Why did they take IELTS?			
2 What did they find most difficult?			
3 What did they find most enjoyable?			
4 What score did they get?			

3 Talk about your reasons for taking the test.

Now say which skills in B are your strengths and weaknesses in English.

4 Read the passage and complete the table.

test module	content	tests
listening	four parts – 1 and 2 based on social situation; 3 and 4 in educational situation	1 a _____ b _____ c _____
2 _____	three passages	3 a _____ b _____ c _____ d _____
writing	4 a _____ b _____	a ability to organise, present and compare information b how well they answer the question c linking, vocabulary, grammatical accuracy
5 _____	three parts	6 a _____ b _____ c _____ d _____

International English Language Testing System (IELTS)

IELTS is made up of four modules: Listening (30 minutes); Reading (60 minutes); Speaking (about 15 minutes); Writing (60 minutes). The listening and reading modules test the candidates' understanding of English; the writing and speaking modules test candidates' production of English. In general, each module gets more difficult as it goes on. There is a choice of academic and general training modules for reading and writing, depending on whether you are taking the test to enter university or for other reasons like work or training.

The listening test has four parts. Parts 1 and 2 are based on social situations in or around an educational setting. Parts 3 and 4 are based on educational situations like seminars and lectures. Parts 1 and 3 include two or more people, parts 2 and 4 have only one speaker. Candidates hear the listening passages only once. It tests the candidates' ability to listen for specific information like numbers and words, to listen and take notes and to understand and summarise a passage.

The reading test has three passages which come from magazines, journals and newspapers. Candidates are tested on their ability to understand main points, find specific information, transfer information from a passage to a chart or diagram, and to understand the attitude of a writer.

In the writing test, students are asked to write a report about a graph or chart in part 1 and to write a discursive essay in part 2. In part 1, candidates are marked on their ability to organise, present and compare information. Alternatively, candidates may be asked to describe a process or describe changes over a period of time. In part 2, candidates are marked on four things. Firstly, how well they answer the question – how relevant their main points are, if they give examples to support these and if their opinion is clear. Secondly, how well the information is linked and put into paragraphs. Thirdly, if a wide range of vocabulary is used accurately. Finally, if a wide range of grammatical structures is used accurately.

The speaking test has three parts. In part 1, the candidate answers general questions about themselves. In part 2, the candidate is given a topic to speak about for two minutes. In the last part, the examiner and the candidate have a short discussion. Candidates are marked on fluency – how confidently they speak in English; their range of vocabulary, how good their grammar is and finally, their pronunciation.

5 **Look through *Achieve IELTS* and find activities to improve and practise …**

1 your vocabulary.

2 your grammatical accuracy.

3 your exam skills.

4 speaking test part (a) 1, (b) 2, (c) 3.

5 listening …
     (a) for specific information.
     (b) for main points.
     (c) and taking notes.
     (d) and completing diagrams.

6 reading …
     (a) for specific information.
     (b) for main points.
     (c) and transferring information.
     (d) and understanding attitude.

7 writing …
     (a) about a chart.   (b) an essay.

8 pronunciation.

Exchange

❶ Work in pairs. Ask each other the questions.

1 How do students usually fund their education in your country?

2 What do you know about scholarships?

A United States of America
United Kingdom
European Union

❷ Read the passages and match the scholarships with the places in A.

Chevening programme

The Chevening programme consists mainly of postgraduate courses. Chevening scholars are placed at a wide range of higher education institutions throughout Great Britain. Scholars from all over the world choose where to study in one of two ways. Some carry out their own research on where to study, others get advice from the British Council. Most Chevening scholarships are awarded for study on Masters programmes, although we do support a small number of PhD awards. Undergraduate study is not funded under Chevening.

Fulbright Scholar program

Each year some 800 people from around the world receive Fulbright Scholar grants to study in the United States. Under the Visiting Fulbright Scholar Program, scholars apply in their home country for Fulbright awards. In many countries, scholars are expected to show that they have got a place at a university in the United States as part of the application process to be eligible for an award. Applicants usually include a letter of invitation from the university in their application materials.

Erasmus for students

Have you ever wanted to get to know a different culture, study at a foreign university, meet new friends, learn another language, all at the same time? Then *Socrates / Erasmus* may be what you are looking for. The *Socrates / Erasmus* programme offers applicants the possibility of studying abroad in another European country for a period of between three and twelve months. *Erasmus* is a European Commission exchange programme that helps students in European countries to study for part of their degree in another country. You may receive a study grant and you will not have to pay university fees. In addition, your studies abroad will be recognised at your home university.

Education and Culture
Socrates
Erasmus

Now read the passages again and answer the questions.

1 Which programmes are for any nationality?

2 Which programme is mainly for Masters degrees?

3 Which is only for European students?

4 What do students need to show before they can apply for a Fulbright scholarship?

3 Read the passages again and match the words in B with the definitions.

1 having the right qualifications or abilities to do something
2 to provide money to an institution or pay for a course
3 an amount of money often given to someone for a particular purpose
4 a person who applies for something
5 a person who studies an academic subject

B grant
scholar
eligible
fund
applicant

4 Work in pairs. Discuss which questions applicants may be asked in an interview for a scholarship in the UK.

1 What qualifications do you have?
2 Why are you applying to take the course?
3 Do you like travelling?
4 How you do you think you will benefit from taking the course?
5 How far is it from your country to the UK?
6 Why do you want to study in the UK?

Now write two more questions that could be asked.

◁2 **5** Listen to an interview and complete the application form.

◁2 Now listen again and answer the questions in activity 4.

Express yourself: names and spelling

Decide which expressions we use for (a) spelling names and (b) talking about names.

that's c with a dash underneath it _____
You can call me Chris if you like. _____
G with a line above it _____
people call me Liz _____
the u has two dots above it _____
It's short for Christopher. _____
i without the dot _____

◁3 **Now listen and practise.**

APPLICATION FORM

(1) Family name:
(2) Other names:
(3) Title:
(4) Status: ☐ single ☐ married ☐ divorced ☐ widowed
(5) Address for correspondence:

Izmir

Where are you currently working?
Aegean University

Course applied for:
MSc Biomedical Science

Academic background:
Qualification first degree – subject (6) _____
Qualification (7) _____ – subject Bioengineering

6 Work in groups. Students A and B, turn to assignment 1.1 and interview Student C. Student C, answer the questions.

Now change roles.

Language study: present tenses

7 Study the examples and explanations.

> *we **say** words the same way we **write** them (1) they **live** in Izmir (2) I **work** at the British Embassy (3)*
>
> We use the present simple to show that something is generally true (1), situations we think will continue for a long time (2), and things that happen regularly (3).
>
> *I'm **working at** The Aegean University (1) I'm **applying** for a scholarship for several reasons … (2) At the moment I'm **studying** English and I'm **learning** Spanish too. (3)*
>
> We use the present continuous to talk about a temporary situation (1) or to talk about something happening now (2). We often use the present continuous to talk about courses (3).
>
> *Where did you **hear** about the course? I **saw** the course advertised in the British Council library. (1) I **see**. I **understand**. I **think** that's all. (2)*
>
> We do not use some verbs with the present continuous, such as verbs that describe senses (1) or thought / understanding (2). We call these *stative* verbs.
>
> *Hello, **come** in. Let's **start**.*
>
> Some verbs do not need an object. These are intransitive verbs. Common intransitive verbs are: *appear, arrive, come in, go, happen, occur, start, take place, wait.*
>
> *I'll just **repeat** that. Please **take** a seat. Why do you **want** another degree?*
>
> Other verbs need an object. These are called transitive verbs. Common transitive verbs are: *bring, give, prefer, report, send, repeat, take, want.*

Now correct the mistakes.

1 A: Do you live in Izmir too?
   B: Yes, I am living in Bornova in a small apartment.
2 A: My first name is Luis.
   B: I'm sorry, could you repeat?
3 A: Bioengineering is really three subjects together – engineering, medicine and biology.
   B: I'm thinking I understand.
4 What course do you take at the moment?
5 A: Do you want a coffee or a tea?
   B: Thanks, cold water I'd prefer.

8 Work in pairs. Ask each other the questions.

1 Why are you studying for IELTS?
2 Which country would you like to go to?
3 Would you like to study abroad? Why (not)?

Listening

IELTS tasks:
table completion;
diagram completion;
multiple-choice questions

❶ Work in pairs. Discuss what new students need to know on the first day of a course.

❷ Read the table and find words which mean …

1 finding your way around
2 a place where an event happens
3 a person or organisation who gives money to a person for a period of time
4 a restaurant at university
5 the person in charge of a university.

1.4 Now listen to a conversation and complete the table.

ORIENTATION DAY 5 OCTOBER

a.m.	event	time	person / people	venue
	meeting at International Office	9.30	International Office administrator	International Office
	greeting new students	10.00 – (2) _____	Vice-Chancellor Mayor	(1) _____
	sponsor's meeting	11.15	British Council representative	(3) _____
	departmental meeting	12.00	(4) _____	departmental office
	(5) _____	1.00 – 2.00	departmental staff	refectory
p.m.	(6) meeting _____	2.30 onwards	international students	main hall

1.4 ❸ Listen again and label the plan.

Now answer the questions.

1 Who will welcome the students to the city?
2 Why is it important to meet the representative from the British Council?
3 What will Professor Heanue tell them about?

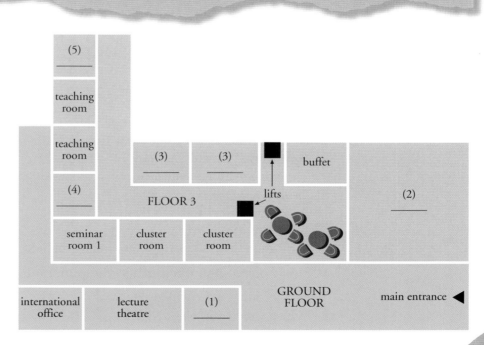

Express yourself: meeting people

Read the expressions and underline the stressed words.

Let me introduce myself …
Perhaps you could introduce yourselves.
Nice to meet you.
Pleased to meet you too.
It's a pleasure to meet you.

1.5   **Now listen and practise.**

4 Complete the sentences with *Do* or *Don't*.

STUDY SKILLS

1 _____ make a study plan. ☐
2 _____ be late or miss lectures. ☐
3 _____ ask your lecturer if you can record the lecture. ☐
4 _____ review your work frequently. ☐
5 _____ throw away handouts. ☐
6 _____ forget to do homework. ☐
7 _____ be prepared to work on your own for a lot of time. ☐
8 _____ think about information and form an opinion about it. ☐

1.6   **Now listen to a talk and tick the things you hear.**

1.6 **5 Listen again and choose A – C.**

1 Students need to be good at …
  A time management.
  B laboratory work.
  C listening.
2 With deadlines, students need to …
  A put them into a calendar or diary.
  B leave things to the last minute.
  C be realistic.
3 It is important to attend lectures as …
  A the lecturer will test the students.
  B students get extra materials in lectures.
  C students can remember information more easily.
4 *Critical thinking* is …
  A remembering facts and figures.
  B part of the course.
  C reading information and forming an opinion about it.

6 Work in pairs. Ask each other the questions.

1 Which things in activity 4 do you do?
2 Which would you like to do?
3 Which things can help you on this course?
4 Which other things can help prepare you for IELTS?

Speaking

IELTS tasks:
part 1 –
introduction

1 Match the words in C with the definitions.

This kind of person …

1 prefers to do things by themselves and can work without other people. _____ ☐
2 arranges and plans activities carefully. _____ ☐
3 is interested in something and really wants to succeed. _____ ☐
4 does not allow anything to stop them from succeeding. _____ ☐
5 admires people because of their personal achievements. _____ ☐
6 is good at thinking quickly and clearly. _____ ☐

C determined
independent
intelligent
motivated
organised
respectful

1.7 Now listen to a conversation and tick the words you hear.

Express yourself: importance

Read the phrases and underline the words that mean *important*.

other characteristics are more significant   *I think that's absolutely essential*
It's really important to be organised   *the vital thing is motivation*
Organisation and motivation are fundamental to good learning
the crucial factor is determination   *isn't intelligence the main thing*

Now work in pairs and check your answers.

Pronunciation

2 Circle the stressed words in the phrases in *Express yourself: importance*.

1.8 Now listen and practise.

3 Work in groups. Discuss the questions.

1 What other qualities do good students have?
2 What are the most important qualities?
3 Which qualities do you have?

4 Put questions and statements A – F into 1 – 3 below. If necessary, look back at the reading passage on page 5.

A Describe a teacher who taught you.
B In your opinion, how far are universities like large corporations?
C What is your favourite subject at school or college?
D What is the role of education in today's society?
E What sort of things do you like to do in your spare time?
F Describe something you have won that is very important to you.

1 Speaking test, part 1: _____
2 Speaking test, part 2: _____
3 Speaking test, part 3: _____

Now ask the other students in the class questions for speaking test, part 1.

D enthusiastic
lazy
motivated
spoilt
bright
hardworking
demanding

E cope
entrepreneurial
impressive
philanthropy
recruit

Reading

❶ Put the words in D into groups.

1 positive characteristics
2 negative characteristics

Now match the words in E with the definitions.

1 giving money to people without any conditions in order to help them
2 to deal with a situation or problem successfully
3 to find new people to join an organisation or institution
4 having the ability to set up successful businesses
5 having a strong effect on people

Achieve IELTS: predicting

Before you begin to read a passage, try to guess what it is about from the title, charts, tables or pictures, or other information you see like names and numbers. Try to think about what you already know about the subject. Predicting the subject of a passage and what you already know about it will help you understand the passage better.

Now read the passage and answer the questions.

1 What or who does the title of the passage refer to?
2 What do (a) 800,000 (b) 13 (c) £50,000 (d) £1.2 million refer to?
3 What information do the charts give?

❷ Read the passage again. Choose the most suitable headings for paragraphs A – E.

i   Increasing competition and new opportunities
ii A worldwide university
iii Differences in higher education systems
iv Advantages of internationals students for UK universities
v   What international students need
vi Marketing education
vii Differences in fees and grants

Now read the passage again and answer the questions.

1 Why do British universities like international students?
2 What effects are international students having on universities in Britain?
3 What does Middlesex University want to become?
4 Why are international students demanding?
5 What does Westminster University look for when they are giving grants?

GOING GLOBAL
how international students are changing western university life

A Universities love overseas students – they are clever and hardworking, they bring different cultures to seminars and student life and they pay their way. In Britain, universities are getting ready to enrol more overseas students. The British Council has published a report predicting that overseas student numbers could soar to more than 800,000 by 2018. In 2002, figures put the total at 270,000 international students out of two million students in UK
5   higher education and it is clear that this influx will have an enormous impact on universities and colleges. These students bring welcome fees, of course, but they are also likely to be extremely bright students who inject new cultural influences and bring changes to the old systems. Their demand for vocational subjects such as business, biotechnology and computing, rather than traditional academic subjects, is affecting what is taught as well.

B The impressive expansion of foreign students has already changed higher education. Up to now it has been the
10 modern universities that have been most entrepreneurial when it comes to selling themselves abroad. The London School of Economics took that route several years ago – less than half its students are British. Overseas student numbers, including European Union students, rose from 198,000 in 1996 to 270,000 by 2002. During this time the number from China (not counting Hong Kong) jumped more than tenfold to nearly 32,000, and numbers from India went up from 2,300 to 10,900. In contrast the number of Malaysian students fell by nearly half from 18,000 to
15 10,200, reflecting their government's efforts to educate more of its young people at home, as well as competition from Australia, Singapore and the USA. But as the Asian tiger economies expand their own universities, the good news for places like the London School of Economics is that there are more and more graduates looking to improve their qualifications or to pursue research in their subjects.

C At Middlesex University, the vice-chancellor has told staff: 'We will
20 move from being primarily a large domestic regional university, mainly focussed on expanding at undergraduate level, to being to a greater extent a global university, with a culturally and internationally diverse staff and student body, based in London'. Middlesex University is recruiting students by providing information
25 points in home countries with people who have experience of the British system. It has 13 offices around the world, with another about to open in Mumbai – a sign of the growing Indian market.

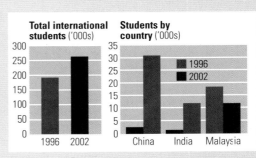

D At its London neighbour, Westminster University, where overseas students make up almost a quarter of its full-time student population, Colin Matheson warns that international students should not be seen as a cash cow. 'Word of
30 mouth is still the most important recruiter and if a university is only interested in money and doesn't value them as contributing to the internationalism of the place, then it is soon found out,' he says. He points out that international students are demanding customers – after all, their families in India or China are paying up to £50,000 to put them through a three-year undergraduate degree or between £16,000 and £20,000 for a Masters. Many will not only need English language support but other help in coping. 'In some cultures it is not normal to question the lecturers
35 or even to speak in class,' says Mr Matheson.

E The great majority of overseas students are postgraduates – they are not taking places away from home undergraduates and in fact are helping to subsidise the education of young British students – something the international students are becoming increasingly sensitive about. They see themselves paying a lot more than home students. Westminster University now gives grants worth £1.2m a year, most of them to overseas students.
40 'It started as philanthropy but it has had an effect on our marketing,' comments Mr Matheson. Awards range from £1,000 off fees to a complete package worth up to £20,000 including visa and flights. The university looks for academic excellence, financial need and confidence that the student will return to their country and contribute there.

3 Find words and phrases in the passage which mean ...

1 to increase rapidly (paragraph A)
2 multiplied by ten (paragraph B)
3 containing many different things (paragraph C)
4 a good source of money / income (paragraph D)
5 to pay some of the cost of something so that it can be sold to another person at a lower price. (paragraph E)

Language study: present perfect and present perfect continuous

4 Study the examples and explanations.

> *The British Council **has published** a report ...*
> *Overseas student numbers, including European Union students, **have risen** ...*
>
> **has / have + past participle**
>
> We use the present perfect for events that started in the past and are still relevant in the present. We often use the present perfect to talk about news, figures and trends and experiences.
>
> *The impressive expansion of foreign students **has already changed** higher education.*
>
> We can use words like *already, before, yet, since* and *so far* with the present perfect.
>
> *it **has had** an effect on our marketing*
>
> Verbs that have an irregular past tense form often have an irregular past participle.
>
> *numbers from India **have been going** up*
>
> **has / have + been + verb -ing**
>
> We use the present perfect continuous to refer to an activity or event that started in the past and continued over a period of time to the present. We use the present perfect continuous to focus on the length of time of the activity or event. When we refer to temporary situations we can use either the present perfect or the present perfect continuous.

Now complete the sentences with the correct form of the verbs in brackets.

1 There _____ a 13% increase in overseas students into the UK since 1996. (be)
2 Where _____ you _____? I _____ here for twenty minutes. (be / wait)
3 The cost of a UK visa _____ a lot. (increase)
4 Professor Heanue _____ the same seminar for the last ten years. (give)
5 I'm worried about Tao – he _____ a hard time recently. (have)

5 Work in pairs. Discuss the questions.

1 Has education in your county been changing? How has it changed?
2 Do many students from your country study abroad? Why do you think this is?

Writing

❶ Look at the charts and say what each one describes.

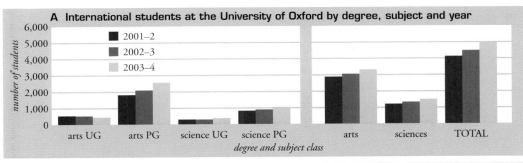

A International students at the University of Oxford by degree, subject and year

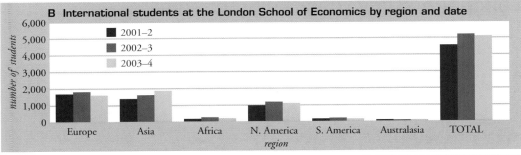

B International students at the London School of Economics by region and date

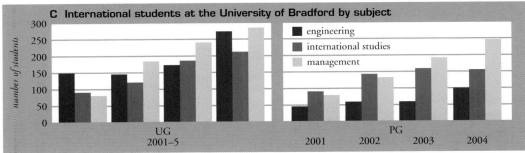

C International students at the University of Bradford by subject

Now match the paragraphs with charts A – C.

1 The vertical axis gives the number of students while the horizontal axis shows the division of students by year and is sub-divided into undergraduate and postgraduate students. On the right-hand side of the second chart are subjects taken: engineering, international studies and management.

2 The bar chart shows the number of international students over three years. It gives the type of degree, undergraduate or postgraduate, and the kind of course they took – arts or sciences. The overall short-term movement has been towards a noticeable increase in international students, particularly in postgraduate arts students from just under 2,000 in 2001 to nearly 2,500 in 2003.

3 Let's look at this trend in more detail by examining international students going there by region. We can see that the general trend for students entering the University from Africa, South America and Australasia stayed relatively steady at roughly 200 over the years between 2001 and 2004. Students from North America and Europe also dropped from the level of 2003 to reach just above 1,000 and just under 2,000 respectively by 2004. The figure which bucks this trend is in students from Asia, which rose strongly between 2001 and 2004.

2 Read the paragraphs again and decide which ...

1 introduces the chart and gives the general trend.
2 describes the information in the chart in more detail.
3 explains what the chart shows.

3 Read the paragraphs again and find words and phrases which mean ...

1 line at the bottom or at the side of a chart or graph (paragraph 1)
2 divided into smaller parts (paragraph 1)
3 easy to see (paragraph 2)
4 in relation to other information (paragraph 3)
5 to be different from the average trend. (paragraph 3)

Language study: describing change

4 Study the examples and explanations.

*The **overall short-term** move the **general** trend for students*

We use words like *overall*, *short-term* and *general* to talk about trends and changes.

describing trends	
current, present, recent, general	
long-term, short-term	
upwards, downwards	trend, change, move(ment)
growing, rising, increasing, noticeable	
overall, underlying	

*a noticeable **increase** in international students students from North America also **dropped** the general trend ... stayed relatively **steady***

We use words and phrases like *increase*, *drop* and *stay steady* to describe the movement of trends. We can use the words and phrases in blue as nouns or verbs.

increasing numbers		decreasing numbers	
rise	**jump**	**slow down**	**drop**
increase	shoot up	**fall**	**crash**
climb	rocket	**decrease**	collapse
go up		**plummet**	decline

no or little change	movement up and down
remain stable	fluctuate
level off	
stay the same / steady	
rise and fall	

*students from Asia ... **rose strongly***

We use words like *strong(ly)* to show the degree or speed of change.

degree of change	speed of change	
dramatic	very	dramatically
severe	extremely	quickly
strong		slowly
significant		
noticeable		gradually
slight		steadily
gentle		

Now look at the charts and complete the report.

Charts A – C show the number of international students in a number of English-speaking countries and in the UK. Pie chart A shows the destinations of (1) _____ by country in 2002. We can see that the major destination for the majority of international students is (2) _____ with 57% of the share of students. The next most popular destination is the United Kingdom with almost a quarter of international students, followed by Australia and Canada with around 10% each and finally New Zealand with (3) _____ .

Line graph B gives us the breakdown of the number of international students in the UK between 1995 and 2004. There has been a(n) (4) _____ in international student numbers. In 1995 numbers were around 125,000 and this (5) _____ to 300,000 in 2004.

When we compare the percentage of international students in the UK to students from the UK (home students) in bar chart C we can see a(n) (6) _____ from 1995 – 2000. In 1995 international students made up just over 6% of students in the UK. This (7) _____ to over 12% in 1999 and (8) _____ at around 12%.

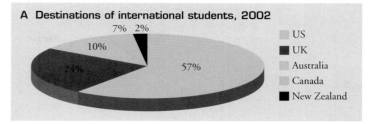

A Destinations of international students, 2002

7% 2%
10%
24%
57%

US
UK
Australia
Canada
New Zealand

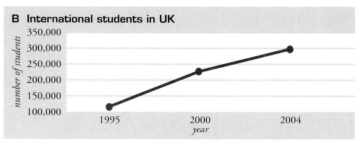

B International students in UK

number of students

350,000
300,000
250,000
200,000
150,000
100,000

1995   2000   2004
year

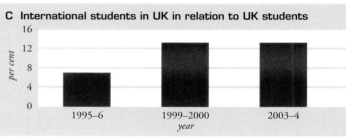

C International students in UK in relation to UK students

per cent

16
12
8
4
0

1995–6   1999–2000   2003–4
year

5 **Read the question and underline the key words.**

> *The charts show the number of international students in the USA by subject and country.*
>
> *Summarise the information by selecting and reporting the main features, and make comparisons where relevant.*
>
> *Now write a report. You should write at least 150 words.*

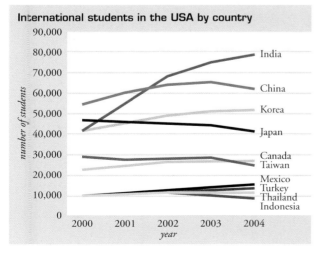

International students in the USA by country

number of students

90,000
80,000
70,000
60,000
50,000
40,000
30,000
20,000
10,000
0

2000   2001   2002   2003   2004
year

India
China
Korea
Japan
Canada
Taiwan
Mexico
Turkey
Thailand
Indonesia

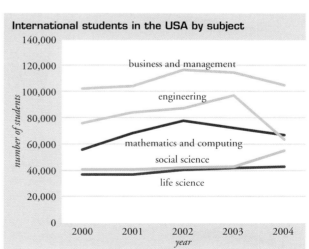

International students in the USA by subject

number of students

140,000
120,000
100,000
80,000
60,000
40,000
20,000
0

2000   2001   2002   2003   2004
year

business and management
engineering
mathematics and computing
social science
life science

Money

Opening an account

1 **Work in pairs. Ask each other the questions.**

1 Do you try to save money or do you like to spend it?
2 What are the advantages and disadvantages of spending and saving money?
3 When you pay for something, do you prefer cash or credit card?

2 **Match the words in A with the pictures.**

A cheque (book) _____
cash point _____
debit card _____
statement _____

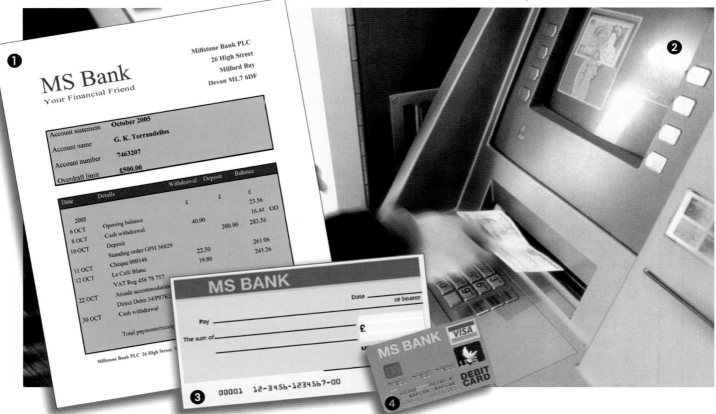

Now work in pairs. Say how often you use the things in A.

3 Read the bank statement and decide what the words in B mean.

4 Read the text and complete it with the headings.

Banking services   Ways of banking   What to look for

B deposit
overdraft limit
withdrawal
balance
account

Choosing your bank

When you want to open an account, don't walk into the first bank you see. There are many things to consider before you open an account with a bank. The most important things are:

1 _____

☐ the interest rates on the current account.
☐ the overdraft facilities.

2 _____

☐ Does the account pay interest when it is in credit?
☐ What is the limit on your interest-free overdraft?
☐ Can you receive a credit card immediately?
☐ What is available with the student package (including savings account, and direct debit)?

3 _____

☐ Is there a branch of the bank in the student's home country?
☐ Do they provide a free / local rate telephone banking service?
☐ Do they have online banking services?
☐ Can the bank send an e-mail alert if you are near your overdraft limit?

🔊 **1.9** Now listen to a conversation and tick the things the student advisor talks about.

🔊 **1.9** **5** Listen again and choose A – C.

1 The student heard about the bank from …
A an international student.
B student services.
C a bank's student advisor.

2 The interest on the current account is …
A 0%.
B 1.5%.
C 4%.

3 You can change the personal identification number …
A when you want to.
B the first time you use the card.
C if you tell the bank you want to change it.

4 The number for telephone banking is …
A 08457 440 440.
B 08547 004 004.
C 08457 004 004.

Now work in pairs and discuss the questions.

1 Which account has the best interest?
2 What is *direct debit*?
3 In which ways can students manage their accounts?
4 Do you have similar banking systems in your country?

6 Read the form and answer the questions.

1 Which two addresses does the bank want?
2 Which contact numbers do they ask for?
3 Why do you think they want an e-mail address?

1.10 **7** Listen to a conversation and decide if the statements are true or false.

	TRUE	FALSE
1 The student advisor needs to see the student's university card.	☐	☐
2 The student's handwriting is difficult to read.	☐	☐
3 The advisor asks for his middle name.	☐	☐
4 He is in the second year of his course.	☐	☐
5 He would like the bank to give his details to other businesses.	☐	☐

1.10 Now listen again and complete the form.

International student application form

1 Personal details	Title	(1)
	Forenames (first name(s))	(2)
	Surname (last name)	Li
	Date of birth	12 06 1984
	Your country of residence	China
2 Home address (overseas)	House no. or name	2 F
	Street name	Kai Yuen St, North Point
	Town / City	Hong Kong
3 Address in UK	Hall of residence	(3)
	House no. or name	11B
	Date of arrival	(4)

If you have a preference to where all correspondence should be mailed, please indicate.   Home (overseas) ☐   UK ☑

4 Contact numbers	Home no. (overseas)	00 852-2565-6892
	Mobile no.	(5)
	UK no.	01274 235650
	e-mail	(6)
		(7)
5 University details	Course date	start 09 2006 / end (8)

(9) Undergraduate ☐   Postgraduate ☐

(10) If undergraduate, which year are you in? 1 ☐   2 ☐   3 ☐   4+ ☐

6 Your information   Telephone marketing (11) Y / N   Other marketing   (12) Y / N

Do you want your details passed on to our other bank businesses? (13) Y / N

Pronunciation

1.11 **8** Listen and notice how we say the letters and symbols.

han.li@bradford.ac.uk   www.hsbc.co.uk/online-banking   han_21@yahoo.co.uk

1.11 Now listen again and practise.

Language study: asking for information

9 Study the examples and explanations.

I'm sorry?
And you are an international student at the university?

> We can make a sentence into a question by making our voice rise at the end of the sentence.

Is there a branch of the bank on or near campus?   *Yes, there is. / No, there isn't.*
Do they have online banking services?   *Yes, they do. / No, they don't.*
Can you receive a debit card immediately?   *Yes, you can. / No, you can't.*

> **auxiliary verb + subject**

> The questions we ask depend upon the information we would like. For simple answers we use *yes / no* questions.

What's that?   *How long have you been there?*   *How can I do that?*

> ***wh-* word + verb + subject**

> We use *wh-* questions to ask for more detailed information.

I'd like to ask you a few details   *Could you tell me how that works?*

> We use *Can you / Could you tell me ... ?*, *I'd like to know ...*, *I'd like to ask you ...* to ask for detailed information politely. Information questions have the same form as sentences.

Now put the words in each question in order.

1 been you in this country have long? _____
2 can where find nearest the cash point I? _____
3 how money can I from abroad transfer? _____
4 office is this international the? _____
5 is what date of your birth? _____
6 you open tell could how to a savings account me? _____

10 Match questions 1 – 6 in activity 9 with answers a – f.

a It's on the campus, in the Students' Union.
b The third of January 1980.
c No, I haven't.
d There are three ways to do it.
e Just fill in this form and we'll open it right away.
f Yes, it is.

11 Work in pairs. Student A, ask Student B questions and complete the form in activity 7. Student B, answer Student A's questions.

Now change roles.

C payment
transaction
purchase
cash flow
bankruptcy

Reading

1 Work in pairs. Discuss what the cartoon is about.

2 Match the words in C with the definitions.

1 when a business or a person has no money
2 money you give to pay for something
3 the money a business takes and spends to keep operating
4 to buy something
5 the process of buying something

3 Read the passage and complete the sentences with a – i.

1 Credit cards are better
2 Smart cards in Hong Kong
3 In the US the use of cheques is falling
4 The main advantage of smart cards is
5 Consumer spending rose because

a cash machines were introduced.
b the ability to store information.
c for payments between countries.
d people prefer to use direct debit.
e can be used for tickets and fast food.
f that they are able to replace cash.
g people could take out money 24 hours a day.
h for small and large amounts.
i because banks are charging people more to use them.

4 Do the statements agree with the information given in the Reading Passage? Write ...

TRUE if the statement is true according to the passage.
FALSE if the statement is false according to the passage.
NOT GIVEN if the statement is not given in the passage.

1 Banks today still have the same structures as five hundred years ago.
2 North America has become a society that does not use cash.
3 Tax rates could be lowered as a result of a reduction in crime.
4 Smart cards can carry computer programs.
5 In the 1980s people became more responsible with money.

5 Read the passage again and find words which mean ...

1 to put equipment in a place where it is ready for use (paragraph C)
2 very important and long-term (paragraph D)
3 relating to the basic characteristic of something (paragraph D)
4 a system in a country or organisation that carries goods or information (paragraph E)
5 something that advertises a special product or event. (paragraph E)

THE CASHLESS SOCIETY

A If a banker from fourteenth-century Italy used a bank today, he would probably still be able to recognise the banking system. Twenty-first century banking is still more a product of the past than the present and customers are becoming impatient. Payments made through banks can still take three or four days to clear and cross-border payments can cost up to 25% of the amount sent. Credit cards are a little better as an
5 easy means of payment especially across borders, but for merchants and consumers they are expensive both for very small payments and for very large ones. The pressure for banks to change is certainly here.

B In the future, whispering into your wristwatch or waving your mobile phone could be enough to start a transaction – from paying a newsagent, downloading digital music, buying a train ticket, sending cash to a relative or trading shares. In Finland you can already pay for a car using your mobile. In Japan 650,000
10 electronic purses known as *Edy* cards are in circulation and can be used at around 2,100 stores in the Tokyo area. In Hong Kong, you can walk through ticket barriers and buy fast food with your *Octopus* stored-value (smart) card. In Hong Kong there are about 8.6 million of these cards in circulation with more than 95% of citizens using the cards, making Hong Kong the world leader in e-cash.

C The US too is much closer to becoming a cashless society than many people realise. Credit and debit card
15 purchases in the US make up most of all retail transactions. Card scanners are installed in parking meters, fast-food restaurants and unstaffed petrol stations. The use of cheques is declining as banks charge higher fees for using them, in an effort to encourage consumers to use debit cards and direct debit bill payment. The percentage of consumer purchases made with cash or cheques has fallen from 80% in 1994 to 66% recently. There are already 6.2 million smart cards in North America and this is predicted to rise to
20 nearly 40 million by 2007.

D The immediate effects of a cash-free society could be profound and fundamental. Theft of cash would become impossible – bank robberies could not happen. Attacks on shopkeepers, taxi-drivers and cashiers would end, the streets would be safer, security and insurance costs would fall. Unpaid taxes could be collected, and as a result tax rates could be lowered. The real advantage of smart cards, however, is not
25 the ability to replace cash, but the information they can hold in addition to this. They can store data, making them ideal to use as security passes to office buildings or ID cards. They can store medical information so that in an emergency a hospital would have all the information they need about you. Scientists are even proposing computer chips the size of a grain of rice placed under the skin to carry this information. Given these benefits, why is the cashless society a lot further away than many people have
30 predicted? The problem is not a technological one – the technology to replace cash exists today.

E There are several reasons why the cashless society has not yet arrived. Firstly, the economic infrastructure for debit and credit cards is already in place, making it difficult for e-cash cards to enter the market. Secondly, the cost of introducing these smart cards is estimated at $15 billion worldwide and what is more, the consumer is not necessarily looking for a new way to pay. Furthermore, making society cash-
35 free has other consequences. Starting from the early 1980s, consumer spending rose with the introduction of cash machines which allowed consumers to withdraw cash around the clock. Secondly, personal bankruptcies rose dramatically as people had easier access to credit: people's cash flow became invisible and people became irresponsible with their money. Thirdly, in France smart card fraud rates were very high. Lastly, companies will be able to follow the consumer's spending patterns, analyse this and target
40 them for sales promotions. Although every month brings closer the dream of a cashless society, no new scheme has found the best way forward yet.

Language study: negatives

6 Study the examples and explanation.

> **There are several ways of making a word negative.**
>
> | *un-* | *Unpaid taxes could be collected, **un**staffed petrol stations* |
> |---|---|
> | *in- / im- / il- / ir-* | *peoples' cash flow became **in**visible, Theft of cash would become **im**possible, people became **ir**responsible with their money …* |
> | *-less* | *the cash**less** society has not yet arrived* |
> | *-free* | *The immediate effects of a cash-**free** society could be profound* |
>
> Also: *mis-, non-, de-, dis-.*

Now decide how to make these words negative.

legal   understand   wire   tax   decisive   responsible
manage   stress   motivated   important   relevant   precise
hope   calculate

7 Complete the sentences with the correct form of some of the negative words from activity 6.

1 I think this tax bill must be a _____ , I paid my tax last week.

2 I can't believe you spent your grant already: you're _____ with money.

3 Don't be _____ , make a decision.

4 John's not doing much work at the moment, he's a bit _____ .

5 You can buy laptop computers _____ at the airport – they are much cheaper there.

Achieve IELTS: negative words

In the reading and listening passages, the answer may be the opposite or negative to words in the question. Recognising negative prefixes and suffixes will help you answer these questions.

Now read the questions in activity 4 and find two questions that have negative words in the answer.

---

8 Work in pairs. Discuss the advantages and disadvantages of a cash-free society.

Listening

1 Match the currencies in **D** with the pictures.

2 Match the words in **E** with the definitions.

1 a number that identifies a bank
2 to move something from one place to another, especially money
3 to change something from one form or system to another
4 a price asked for products or services
5 the amount of money you can get selling and buying money from different countries

①12 **3** Listen to a conversation and complete the notes.

①12 Now listen again and answer the questions.

1 What personal information does the advisor ask for?
2 What happens if Alice sends dollars?
3 What happens if she sends sterling?
4 What is a SWIFT code?
5 Why does she have to give a reason for transferring the money?

4 Work in pairs. Ask each other the questions.

1 Why do international students need to transfer money?
2 Have you ever transferred money abroad?

D	sterling	lira
	dollar	yen
	HK dollar	

E	transfer	exchange rate
	sort code	convert
	charge	

Funds transfer
- cheque (1) _____ weeks
- electronically (2) _____ days
- charges from (3) _____ bank, (4) _____ bank, (5) _____ charges for transferring amount, and additional fee for (6) _____ to local currency.

Bank advisor needs:
- full name of beneficiary and (7) _____ ;
- name of bank and the (8) _____ of the branch; the bank's (9) _____ and SWIFT number.

5 **Work in pairs. Think of three ways students can save money.**

🔊13 **Now listen to a talk and answer the questions.**

1 What is the talk about?
2 How much is the average cost of living in London?
3 How do students help to pay for their studies?
4 How many ways can students save on fuel bills?
5 In which three places can students buy second-hand books?

🔊13 **6** **Listen again and choose A – D.**

1 Most of the cost of living comes from …
   A university fees.
   B accommodation.
   C travel.
   D books.
2 Nearly a quarter of students …
   A work part-time.
   B missed lectures.
   C gave in work late.
   D cover their expenses by working.
3 If you have a bank account with a free overdraft …
   A the interest will be 4.5%.
   B you should withdraw your money and spend it on food.
   C you should take out all the money and put it in a savings account.
   D you should put £1,500 into it.
4 Students can lower their fuel bills by …
   A heating the house properly.
   B using rechargeable batteries.
   C checking the suppliers' prices.
   D buying a student card.
5 Students can save money on shopping by …
   A shopping once a month.
   B shopping with other students.
   C taking out cash twice a week only.
   D leaving their cheque book at home.

7 **Work in pairs. Discuss the questions.**

1 How many ways of saving money can you remember from the lecture?
2 Can you think of other ways of saving money?

Speaking

❶ Work in pairs. Ask each other the quiz questions.

WHAT'S YOUR MONEY PERSONALITY?

Are you a saver or a big spender? Try this quiz and find out.

❶ How do you rate your relationship with money?
   a I never think about it.
   b I get by.
   c I'm in control.
   d People ask me for advice about their finances.

❷ If you see a pair of shoes for 50% off do you …
   a buy them – you're saving 50%.
   b leave them – you don't need another pair.
   c put it on a list for someone to buy for you.
   d make a note and shop around.

❸ When you go shopping do you …
   a buy what you fancy?
   b make a list but don't always use it?
   c make a list and only buy things on the list?
   d only go window shopping?

❹ When you buy clothes do you go …
   a to the most fashionable shops?
   b to a high-street retailer?
   c to the market?
   d to a second-hand shop?

❺ At the end of the month you have …
   a no idea what you spent.
   b added more debt to your credit card.
   c spent as much as you have earned.
   d put aside some money for savings.

Now turn to assignment 2.1 and check your answers.

Express yourself: finances and purchases

Match the phrases with their meanings.

1 get by   a to compare prices in different shops
2 put aside money   b something someone has bought and is selling again
3 window shopping   c looking in shop windows, but not buying anything
4 shop around   d to save money
5 second-hand   e to live on a little money

Now work in pairs. Use the phrases to talk about things you do.

---

❷ Read the introduction to Part 1 and add two more questions. Then read Part 2 and make notes.

Part 1

Let's talk about where, when and why you go shopping.

1 In which part of your town or city do you like to go shopping?
2 _____   3 _____

Part 2

Describe something you bought recently. You should say:
– where you got it from
– why you bought it
– why you like it
and explain why it is important for you.

❸ Work in pairs. Student A, you are the examiner. Ask Student B the questions in parts 1 and 2. Student B, you are the candidate. Answer Student A's questions.

Writing

❶ Answer the questions.

1 How good are you at managing money?
   A very organised   D not very organised at all
   B fairly organised   E don't know
   C not very organised

2 How often do you check your bank accounts?
   A regularly   B not very often

3 When you have spare cash do you try to move it to a savings account or spend it?
   A save it   B spend it

Now ask the other students in the class the questions and make a note of their answers (to use in activity 4).

❷ Compare your answers to question 1, activity 1 with the charts.

Now read the passage and answer the questions.

1 What do the chart and table show?
2 What expressions are used to refer to figures?
3 Which information do you find interesting / surprising?

Managing finances

To what extent would you describe yourself as financially organised?

Not very organised: 20%   Not at all organised: 4%   Very organised: 21%

Fairly organised: 55%

	Very organised
All students	21%
Age up to 22 years	18%
Age 23–25 years	26%
Age over 26 years	35%

Source: UNITE

The two diagrams show students' responses to the question of how good they are at managing their finances. The pie chart shows the ability of UK students to manage their finances at University overall and the table shows the proportion of students by age who think they are very organised at managing their finances.

The majority of students – just over half of the total number – think they are fairly organised financially, while slightly over a fifth of the total believe they are very organised. Exactly a fifth of the students do not think they are very good at organising their finances, while approximately 5% of students are not at all organised.

If we look at the table showing the figures for the very organised section of the pie chart, we can see that older students think they are more organised than younger students, with over a third of students above 26 saying they are very organised, around a quarter of 23–25 year olds saying they are very organised and just under 20% saying they are very organised.

From the information we can conclude that most students in Britain think they are in control of their finances and are managing them at least fairly well or, for roughly a quarter of the students, very well.

Achieve IELTS: describing charts

When you write about a chart or table you will receive marks for organising and describing all the information. You will not receive marks for giving reasons for the information or giving your opinion about the information (but you will not lose marks if you do this). As you have limited time and number of words, write about the information only.

Language study: referring to numbers

3 Study the examples and explanations.

Fractions and percentages

20%	a fifth	50%	a half
25%	a quarter	66%	two thirds
33%	a third	75%	three quarters

We can use percentages or fractions to write about numbers in charts and tables.

The majority of students …

We use *most (of) / the majority (of)* to write about large numbers.

just over half of the total number …

We can use *under, over, at least, up to* to write about numbers up to a limit. We often use *slightly, well, just* to modify these.

approximately 5% of students are not at all organised …

We can use *almost, around, about, approximately, nearly, roughly, in the region of* to write about approximate figures.

Exactly a fifth of the students do not think they are very good at organising their finances …

We can use *precisely* and *exactly* to write about exact figures.

Now write sentences about the charts.

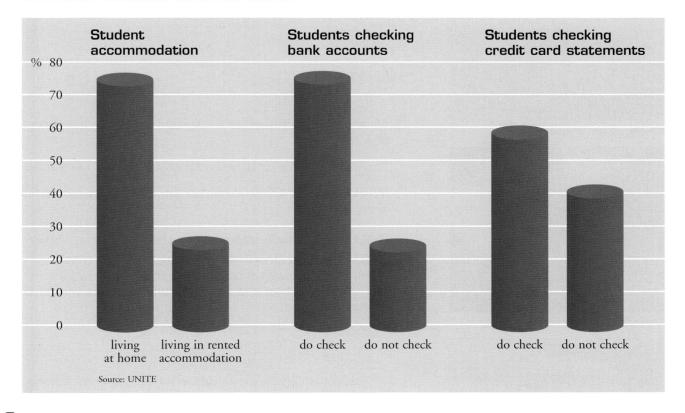

Source: UNITE

4 Write a report on your notes from activity 1. You should write at least 150 words.

Travel

A Holland, Amsterdam ☐
Spain, Madrid ☐
Greece, Athens ☐
Italy, Rome ☐
Switzerland, Bern ☐
France, Paris ☐
Germany, Berlin ☐
the Czech Republic, Prague ☐
Hungary, Budapest ☐

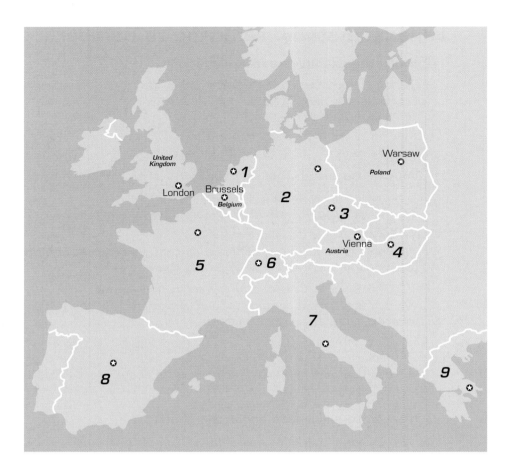

the Acropolis

Buckingham Palace

the Eiffel Tower

the Colosseum

Sightseeing

1 Match the countries and capitals in A with 1 – 9 on the map.

Now match the pictures with the places on the map.

2 Work in pairs. Discuss which countries you would like to visit, and why.

3 Read the passage and answer the questions. Write …

YES if the statement agrees with the information.
NO if the statement contradicts the information.
NOT GIVEN if there is no information about this in the passage.

1   40 million students per year use an ISIC card.
2   An ISIC card will give you discounts on land, sea and air travel.
3   Students can get special deals when they go to the cinema.
4   You can apply for an ISIC card if you are 50 years old.
5   To get an ISIC card, students need a passport.

Discover the world – ISIC

The international student identity card (ISIC) is the only international student ID card. Since 1968, the ISIC has helped over 40 million students to get the most out of their travel experience. As an ISIC card-holder, you can take advantage of the following 35,000 benefits worldwide:

- discounts on entrance to museums and cultural sites
- discounts on flights, buses, trains and ferries
- discounts worldwide at bars, restaurants and on shopping
- *ISIC connect* – a discount communications package including phone, text messaging, e-mail and voice mail.

<< WITH YOU ALL THE WAY

How to apply

If you are a full-time student and at least 12 years old, you are eligible for an ISIC card. You can be in secondary school or in post-secondary studies and there is no upper age limit for the ISIC. To apply for the ISIC, you need to show proof at an ISIC office that you are currently studying full-time. Proof could be a letter from either your college or university or your student ID.

Visit www.ISIC.org for more information.

1.14 **4** **Listen to a conversation, and tick the cities in A that they decide to visit.**

1.14 **Now listen again and answer the questions.**

1 What is the *Eurostar*?
2 What kind of accommodation will they stay in?
3 Why aren't they staying in London?
4 Why will Makiyo enjoy Amsterdam?

5 Why aren't they going to Prague?
6 Why is Budapest wonderful in the spring?
7 Why do they choose Rome, not Bern?
8 What are they going to do next?

5 **Put the questions in the order a ticket agent asks them.**

1 How would you like to pay? _____
2 What is your date of travel? _____
3 Would you like the tickets to be sent by post? _____
4 What is the expiry date of the card? _____
5 Which journey would you like to make? _____

1.15 **Now listen to a conversation and check your answers.**

1.15 **6** **Listen again and complete the notes. Write no more than three words or a number for each answer.**

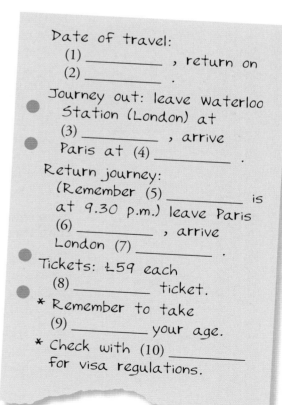

Date of travel:
(1) _____ , return on
(2) _____ .
- Journey out: leave Waterloo Station (London) at
(3) _____ , arrive
- Paris at (4) _____ .
Return journey:
(Remember (5) _____ is at 9.30 p.m.) leave Paris
(6) _____ , arrive
London (7) _____ .
- Tickets: £59 each
(8) _____ ticket.
- * Remember to take
(9) _____ your age.
- * Check with (10) _____ for visa regulations.

Express yourself: asking for repetition

1.16 **Listen and notice how the voice rises and falls.**

Pardon?   Could you repeat that, please?
Could you run that by me again, please?
Sorry, what time was that?
I'm afraid I didn't quite catch that.
Can I repeat that back to you?

1.16 **Now listen again and practise.**

7 **Work in pairs. Plan a rail journey around your country or a country you would like to visit.**

B aerodynamic
double-decker
levitate
alternate
attraction
repulsion
accelerate
maintenance

Reading

1 **Look at the picture. Discuss what kind of train it is and how it works.**

2 **Match the words in B with the definitions.**

1 a vehicle, usually a bus or train, with two floors
2 to change between two things and repeat the change frequently
3 to rise or lift something into the air
4 designed so that it moves quickly and easily through the air
5 keeping something in good working condition
6 to move quickly away from something and keep going faster
7 a force that pulls or keeps things together
8 a force that pushes or keeps things away from each other

3 **Read the passage and choose A – D.**

1 The Shinkansen has …
   A more than one engine.
   B motors in the carriages.
   C an engine at the back.
   D a special type of track.
2 In comparison with the Shinkansen, the Maglev has …
   A a higher average speed.
   B more carriages.
   C a faster maximum speed.
   D lower ticket prices.
3 One advantage of the Maglev over the Shinkansen is that …
   A it can run on a normal track.
   B it is powered by magnets.
   C it is cheaper to build.
   D it can go faster more quickly.
4 One disadvantage of the Maglev is that …
   A it has no wheels.
   B it disturbs the air.
   C it cannot make a profit in Shanghai.
   D it needs a special track.

Now read the passage again and complete the summary with no more than three words or a number for each answer.

The Shinkansen currently runs between the (1) _____ in Japan and achieves average top speeds of (2) _____ . This is made possible by its aerodynamic design and a (3) _____ along the train. It was introduced because of a dramatic increase in the amount of (4) _____ in the capital city. It does not need a special (5) _____ . Even faster is the Maglev, which is powered by (6) _____ . This may be more economical to (7) _____ than the Shinkansen, but it is (8) _____ to build and can only link (9) _____ cities.

4 **Work in pairs. Describe a train journey you have been on or would like to go on.**

HIGH-SPEED TRAINS

The Shinkansen, or bullet train, is a high-speed train which operates throughout Japan, connecting major cities. Services began in 1964, and at 210 kilometres per hour it was then the fastest train in the world. Now, trains operating on the Sanyo line, which connects Shin-Osaka and Hakarta, regularly achieve speeds of 300 kilometres per hour. These speeds are
5 made possible by the aerodynamic design of the Shinkansen and the system of motors it uses. Instead of having an engine which pulls the carriages along, the train is powered by a series of powerful electric motors which run along the length of the train. The zero series train, for example, uses a total of 64 sets of motors with a combined output of 11,840 kilowatts.

In Tokyo, between 1986 and 1996, the number of commuters increased sixteenfold, and it
10 became clear that the motor car was not a sensible solution. Trains are faster and cause less pollution than cars, and most Shinkansens can carry at least 1,200 passengers, as the carriages are double-deckers. The train runs on a normal train track, but it can only reach top speed on the straighter parts of the line.

Another type of high-speed train is the Maglev, which is short for magnetically-levitated train.
15 The first of these to operate commercially was built in Shanghai, connecting the city centre to the Pudong International Airport. The Maglev's top speed is 430 kilometres per hour. This is 130 kilometres per hour faster than the Shinkansen. It can cover the distance between Shanghai and the airport, which is 31 kilometres, in eight minutes, an average speed of 268 kilometres per hour – not quite as fast as the top average speed for the Shinkansen.

20 There are three basic components to the Maglev: firstly, a large electrical power source, secondly, metal coils along a guideway or track, and thirdly, large guidance magnets underneath the train. Magnets in the propulsion coil move the train forward. These magnets rapidly alternate between north and south, so the train is pulled forward by the forces of attraction and repulsion as it moves between them. Similarly, magnets beneath the train and
25 below the track cause it to levitate, or float. As soon as the train is levitated, power is supplied to a second set of coils, the propulsion coils at the side of the track. The Maglev has no wheels and does not make any contact with the ground.

Compared with the Shinkansen, the Maglev has both advantages and disadvantages. The biggest advantage is that because the Maglev makes no contact with the track and has no
30 moving parts, it should in theory need no maintenance, which would make it much cheaper to run. Another bonus is that Maglev trains are almost silent. The only sound is that of the air rushing by. The Shinkansen is quiet, but not as quiet as the Maglev. The Maglev can also accelerate more quickly, and is more efficient when going uphill. It also uses slightly less energy than the Shinkansen, and is less damaging to the environment.

35 The main disadvantage is that the Maglev track is very expensive to build. The Shanghai track cost US $1.2 billion to build, just for 31 kilometres. This makes it the most expensive train track in the world. Also, because it cannot run on a normal railway, it is limited in where it can go. It is only really able to connect two very large areas to be commercially profitable. Nevertheless, Maglevs are currently being considered in Japan, Germany and the United States,
40 and may become the land transport of the future.

Language study: comparatives and superlatives

5 Study the examples and explanations and complete the sentences below.

Comparatives

*Trains are **faster** and cause **less pollution** than cars.   it is **more efficient** when going uphill …*
*The Maglev can also accelerate **more quickly**.*

> We use comparative forms when comparing one thing with another. For shorter adjectives, we add -er to the word. Longer adjectives, nouns and most adverbs (*quickly, badly, carefully*) take *more* or *less*. Some common adjectives are irregular: *good, better*; *bad, worse*.

1 Travelling by air can be _____ (cheap) than trains these days.
2 Airports are often _____ (far) from a city than train stations.
3 Of course, travelling by car is _____ (comfortable) than the train and you have _____ (flexibility) with timing your journey.
4 Despite this, when the traffic is bad you may have to drive _____ (slowly) which means you may arrive _____ (late) than you expect.

C a (little) bit
a great deal
somewhat
(quite) a lot
hardly any
considerably
scarcely
only just
far

> *It uses **slightly less** energy than the Shinkansen.*
> *It needs no maintenance, which would make it **much cheaper** to run.*
>
> We can show small or big differences with the words and phrases in C.

6 Decide which of the expressions in C are for large or small differences.

> *This is **not quite as fast as** the top average speed for the Shinkansen.*
>
> We use *as … as* to show that two or more things are the same or similar and *not as … as* to show the differences between two or more things.

D bicycle
car
train
plane
motorbike
ferry

7 Write three more sentences using *(not) as … as* for the words in D.

8 Study the examples and explanation and write sentences about the table.

Superlatives

*Services began in 1964, and at 210 km/h it was then **the fastest train** in the world.*
*This makes it **the most expensive** train track.*

> When we compare more than two things we use -est for short adjectives, and *the most* or *the least* for longer adjectives, nouns and most adverbs. Some adjectives are irregular: *the best, the farthest*.

	Aston Martin DB9	Toyota Avensis	Citroen C1
cost	$179,220	$29,841	$11,910
speed	299 km/h	209 km/h	148 km/h
economy	6 km/litre	12 km/litre	22 km/litre
comfort	***	***	**
safety	****	*****	***
engine size	5.9 litre	2 litre	1 litre
boot size	172 litres	1320 litres	139 litres

9 Work in pairs. Discuss how you prefer to travel and why.

Listening

1 **Work in pairs. Ask each other the questions.**

1 What is the aircraft in the picture?
2 What do you know about it?

Now label the picture. Use the words in E.

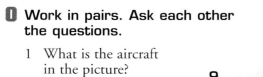

1.17 2 **Listen to an interview and answer the questions.**

1 How many passengers can the plane carry?
2 How high and heavy is the A380?
3 How many countries were involved in building it?
4 How much did it cost?

1.17 **Now listen again and choose A – D.**

1 Airbus started to build the plane in …
   A 2000.   B 2001.
   C 2002.   D 2003.
2 The maximum distance it can fly without stopping for fuel is …
   A 40,801 km.   B 4,210 km.
   C 18,000 km.   D 14,800 km.
3 The function of *stringers* is to …
   A supply data for the computers.
   B keep the plane cool.
   C strengthen the wing panels.
   D fasten the wings to the fuselage.
4 Machines for building the wings required …
   A lots of time to make the wings.
   B great strength.
   C programs to control them.
   D a lot of people to make them work.

5 Which form of transport is not used in the factory?
   A trucks   B bicycles
   C motorbikes   D vans
6 During testing, the engineers …
   A used computers to test the wing.
   B moved the wing repeatedly up and down to test for fatigue.
   C checked the amount of fuel the plane consumed.
   D flew the test aircraft.
7 What did James Carr feel at the end?
   A tiredness
   B a kind of sadness
   C a sense of achievement
   D a sense of relief

E galley
   lounge
   cockpit
   tail fin
   luggage
     compartment
   hold
   wing
   fuselage
   cabin

3 **Complete the notes. Use no more than three words for each answer.**

The Airbus A380 is the (1) _____ in the world. It can carry up to 600 passengers, with a range of (2) _____ kilometres. A team of engineers assembled the (3) _____ in North Wales, and performed (4) _____ and fatigue tests on them to check that they performed well during flight conditions. The first test flight took place in (5) _____ .

Language review: past simple and past continuous

4 Study the examples and explanations.

> *Airbus **invested** heavily in automated machinery.*
> *All these setbacks **cost** the company millions of extra dollars.*
>> We use the past tense to talk about single or repeated actions or states which occurred at a finished time in the past. Past tenses can be regular or irregular.
>
> *We **didn't attempt** a project of this size without expecting some problems.*
>> negatives: subject + **did not** (**didn't**) + verb.
>
> *Did you **have** any problems during the construction?*
>> yes / no questions: **did / was, were** + subject + verb
>
> *How **did you test** the wing?*
> *What **was** the factory at West Broughton **like**?*
>> wh- questions: **Wh-** + **did / was, were** + subject
>
> *I **was working** on the wing assembly. They **weren't** all **working** at Broughton.*
>> **was / were** + verb **-ing**
>>
>> We often use the past continuous to talk about longer actions which took place over a period of time in the past.
>
> *While we **were developing** the programs, the robots nearly **put** holes in the wrong place.*
>> We often use the past continuous with the past simple to show that one action was taking place when another action happened.

Now complete the sentences with the correct form of the verb.

1 The engineering team _____ (begin) construction in 2002.
2 While he _____ (work) at Broughton, they _____ (test) a wing to destruction.
3 Where _____ (he / stand) when the plane first _____ (take off)?
4 They _____ (build) the wings for three years.
5 How many planes _____ (Emirates / buy)?
6 The wing panel assembly machines _____ (cost) around $12,000,000 each.

5 Work in pairs. Student A, ask for information about Concorde and complete the table.

Student B, turn to assignment 3.1 and answer the questions.

Concorde: 1975–2003

built by	
capacity	
range	
speed	
weight	
engines	
route	

Speaking

❶ Look at the picture and answer the questions.

1 Where are they?
2 What are they doing?

❷ Put the words in F in the order that they happen on a plane journey.

F	
customs	passport control
security	duty-free shop
gate	take off
check-in	in-flight movie
land	departure hall
board	arrival hall

1.18 ❸ Listen to a candidate and complete the task card.

> **Part 2**
> *Talk about (1) _____*
> *You should say:*
> – *who (2) _____*
> – *where (3) _____*
> – *(4) _____ transport _____*
> – *and talk about your (5) _____ during the journey.*

Express yourself: correcting yourself

Read the sentences and underline the stressed words.

Well, in fact I did go somewhere
I mean my host family
Not Northern Ireland, I meant to say Eire, which is Southern Ireland
That is to say, my host family had a lot of luggage
No, sorry, it was Holyhead

1.19 Now listen and practise.

Achieve IELTS: language repair

Examiners give marks for *language repair*. This means that you are able to correct yourself if you make a mistake, or if you feel that your meaning is unclear. Use the words and phrases in *Express yourself* to do this.

Pronunciation

4 Match the sentences with the meanings.

1	Cong is **flying** to Taiwan next Tuesday.	a	not Hong Kong
2	Cong is flying to **Taiwan** next Tuesday.	b	not the week after
3	**Cong** is flying to Taiwan next Tuesday.	c	not Ahmed
4	Cong is flying to Taiwan next **Tuesday**.	d	not Thursday
5	Cong is flying to Taiwan **next** Tuesday.	e	not sailing

1.20   Now listen and practise.

5 Work in pairs. Student A, read the sentences for Student B to correct. Student B, turn to assignment 3.2.

1 A hippo has a trunk.
2 Brussels is the capital of Holland.
3 Birds have four wings.
4 American motorways are called autoroutes.

Now listen to Student B and correct their sentences. Use these words.

windscreen   liners   Wellington   wheelchair

6 Decide which topics may round off the task card in activity 3.

1 the cost of transport
2 a frightening experience
3 a good book you read recently
4 transport in your country
5 your favourite place to study
6 fear of flying

Now choose two rounding off topics and write two questions for each.

7 Work in pairs. Student A, talk about the topic in the task candidate card in activity 3. Student B, you are the examiner – listen to Student A and ask one or two follow-up questions.

Writing

① Read the sentences and tick the ones you agree with.

WHY TAKE A YEAR OUT?

1 I want a break from academic study after my school leaving exams. ☐

2 I want to spend time travelling and exploring new places. ☐

3 I want to gain some useful skills – a new language, computing qualifications. ☐

4 I want to spend some time working before I start university. ☐

5 I want to do something to help less privileged people or for a good cause. ☐

6 I want to earn some money so I won't be poor at university. ☐

7 I want time to think and make sure I'm on the right track. ☐

Now work in pairs and discuss your answers.

② Read the sentences and put them in order of importance.

WHY CONTINUE STUDYING?

1 I want to graduate in the same year as my high school friends. ☐

2 I will enjoy travelling more if I have more money and a job to return to. ☐

3 I would find it difficult to start studying again. ☐

4 I don't want to forget everything I know about my subject. ☐

5 Travelling abroad is too dangerous for young people. ☐

6 The price of my degree course might increase while I am away. ☐

7 I want to get a good job and salary as soon as possible. ☐

Now work in pairs. Discuss if you would prefer to take a gap year or continue your studies.

3 Read the question and underline the key words.

The tables show the results of a student survey. The first table shows the reasons why students choose to defer their degrees for a gap year. The second table shows why others choose to continue their studies immediately after high school.

Summarise the information by selecting and reporting the main features, and make comparisons where relevant. Write at least 150 words.

Reasons for continuing later	%
Break from study	42
Travel	27
Learn new skills	11
Earn money	7
Help underprivileged people	7
Other reasons	6

Reasons for continuing immediately	%
Difficult to start studying again	28
Forget knowledge of subject	26
Increased cost of study	16
Find good job sooner	12
Graduate in same year as friends	10
Other reasons	8

Achieve IELTS: comparing data

Part 1 writing task 1 requires you to compare and contrast information. We can contrast each reason in order of importance, or we can contrast all the information in the first table with all the information in the second.

Now read the essay and say which approach the writer takes.

The tables compare the results of a survey which asked why students decided to take a gap year or continue their studies straight after high school. The first table shows why some chose to defer or postpone their studies. In contrast to this, the second shows why others decided to continue. In this report I will look at each reason in turn.

The majority of students who chose to defer said that they wanted to take a break from study. 42% of them stated this reason. By contrast, the main reason given for continuing was that it would be difficult to start studying again. A smaller percentage, 28%, said this. A much lower percentage of those who deferred their degrees in order to take a break, said that they wanted to travel. Conversely, 26% of continuing students felt that they would forget the knowledge they had of their subject if they took a break from their studies.

The third most popular reason for taking a gap year is that students wanted to learn new skills. In comparison with the third most popular reason among continuing students we can see that this group felt the cost of their degree courses might increase while they were away. 16% of continuing students gave this reason.

Two more reasons for deferring the start of higher education, with an equal 7% each, were to earn money and to help underprivileged people. 6% gave other reasons. On the other hand, 12% of continuing students wanted to continue because they hoped to find a good job more quickly, and 10% wanted to graduate in the same year as their friends. 8% of these students gave another reason.

Language study: comparing and contrasting

4 Study the examples and explanation.

> *The tables **compare** the results of a survey.*
> ***In contrast to this**, the second shows why others decided to continue.*
>
> **We can use words and phrases like *compare*, *in contrast to / with this* to talk about similarities and differences between groups of information and data.**

Now read the passage again and complete the table.

comparing	contrasting
compare	in contrast to this
(1) _____	(2) _____
the same ... as ...	conversely
in the same way ...	(on the one hand) ... (3) _____
at the same time ...	on the contrary

5 Read the question and underline the key words.

> *The tables show the results of a survey of students who defer their degrees. The first table shows reasons why some students prefer to stay at home in their own country. The second table shows why others choose to travel overseas.*
>
> *Summarise the information by selecting and reporting the main features, and make comparisons where relevant.*

Reasons for staying at home	%
Easier to find paid work	26
Already speak the language	25
Cheaper to stay with family	18
Dangers of travel	12
Lack of money	12
Other reasons	7

Reasons for travelling overseas	%
Learning about a new culture	25
Adventure and excitement	24
Help people in poorer countries	15
Get away from parents	14
Make new friends	12
Other reasons	10

Now write a report using the information in the tables. You should write at least 150 words.

Quiz night

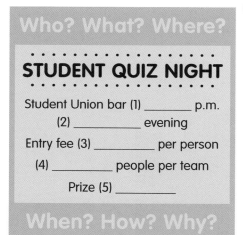

Who? What? Where?

· · · · · · · · · · · · · · · · · ·
STUDENT QUIZ NIGHT
· · · · · · · · · · · · · · · · · ·

Student Union bar (1) _____ p.m.
  (2) _____ evening
Entry fee (3) _____ per person
  (4) _____ people per team
  Prize (5) _____

When? How? Why?

❶ Work in pairs and ask each other the questions.

1 Do you like taking part in quizzes and competitions? Why or why not?

2 Have you ever taken part in a team quiz? When was it?

1.21 ❷ Listen to a conversation and complete the text. Use no more than three words or a number for each answer.

Now choose A – C.

1 At quiz nights people …
 A watch a quiz.
 B take part in a quiz.
 C ask questions.

2 People usually do quiz nights …
 A individually.   B in pairs.   C in teams.

3 During the quiz people answer questions about …
 A trivia.   B technical topics.   C law.

4 At the end of the quiz the teams show their answers to …
 A the other teams.   B the quizmaster.   C the barman.

Express yourself: encouraging someone

1.22 Listen and mark the stressed words.

Come on, just have a go.   You can do it.   Give it a go.   At least have a try.

1.22 Now listen again and practise.

---

❸ Work in pairs. Student A, ask and encourage Student B to join your (a) quiz team, (b) football team or (c) theatre group. Student B, say why you do not want to join and give reasons.

4 Complete the titles for the questions. Choose from the subjects in A.

Now work in teams and do the quiz.

A sports
geography
biology
science and technology
art and literature

		your answer	team answer	correct answer
A _____	1 Who painted *Guernica*? a Charles Monet b Pablo Picasso c Wassily Kandinsky 2 Who wrote *War and Peace*? a William Shakespeare b Emile Zola c Leo Tolstoy 3 When was *The Great Wave* by Hokusai produced? a the sixteenth century b the seventeenth century c the eighteenth century			
B _____	1 Who created the World Wide Web? a Albert Einstein b Stephen Hawking c Tim Berners-Lee 2 What is the science of engineering small things called? a miniaturisation b nanotechnology c minimalism 3 Where was the world's largest particle accelerator built? a Houston, USA b Kyoto, Japan c Geneva, Switzerland			
C _____	1 Which country has won the football world cup the most times? a Germany b Italy c Brazil 2 Where were the 2000 Olympics held? a Greece b Australia c China 3 How many events are included in a heptathlon? a 5 b 7 c 10			

1.23 **5** Listen to the quiz and write the team's answers.

1.24 Now listen to the end of the quiz and check the answers.

Language review: passive sentences (1)

6 Study the examples and explanation.

Present tense
*We think it **is called** miniaturisation.*   *We think five events **are included** in a heptathlon.*
*it's **not called** minimalism*
   is / are (not) + past participle

Past tense
*it **was produced** in the eighteenth century*   *they **were held** in Sydney*
   was / were (not) + past participle

Wh- questions
***What is** the science of engineering small things **called**?*   ***Who was** the World Wide Web **invented by**?*
   Wh- + to be + past participle

We use the passive when we are more interested in the thing or action than the person or thing doing the action. This may be because (a) the person or thing is obvious, (b) not important or (c) not known.

Now work in groups. Write three quiz questions for the other groups.

Hold a team quiz and ask the other groups your questions.

IELTS tasks:
matching
headings with
paragraphs;
true / false / not
given

Reading

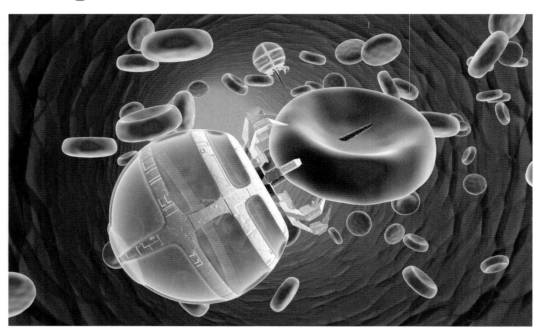

❶ Look at the picture and answer the questions.

1 What is happening?
2 Do you think this will be possible in the near future?
3 What advantages do you think this could have?
4 What other areas of life would this technology benefit?

❷ Work in pairs. Read the title of the passage and decide which topics it will contain.

1 Methods of production
2 The Internet
3 How this technology works
4 The inventor of nanotechnology
5 Advances in medical science
6 Dangers of new technology

Now read the passage and check your answers.

❸ Read the passage again and choose the most suitable headings for paragraphs A – F from the list of headings.

i From theory to practice
ii Recycling with nanotechnology
iii Difficulties facing the development of nanotechnology
iv Advantages and dangers of nanotechnology
v Nanostructures and their uses
vi An alternative method of production
vii Computing and nanostructures
viii Types of nanobots

Now answer the questions.

1 What is *bottom-up* building?
2 What do AFMs and STMs do?
3 What can be used to form computer circuits?
4 What are the problems facing nanotechnology?
5 Why is the creation of nanobots a slow process?
6 Why are environmentalists worried?

NANOTECHNOLOGY: A REVOLUTION IN PRODUCTION

A We make nearly everything by tearing things apart. To make paper, trees are planted, chopped down and sent through our mills. This is often called a top-down method of production. But what if we could work from the bottom up? What if paper was constructed atom by atom, the smallest building blocks of life and matter? It is thought
5 that nanotechnology is the way to do this. Nanotechnology is the science of creating objects on a level smaller than 100 nanometres, a scale 50,000 times smaller than a human hair. The aim of nanotechnology is the bottom-up production of virtually any material or object by assembling it one atom at a time.

a fullerine / buckyball

B
10 Nanotechnology moved from idea to reality when tools such as the Atomic Force Microscope (AFM) and the Scanning Tunnelling Microscope (STM) were developed by IBM in Zurich. These microscopes do more than just let people see small things, they also allow atoms to be manipulated in a vacuum, liquid or gas. Individual atoms and molecules are probed by the AFM to create three-dimensional images at the nanoscale level as the microscope is moved across the surface of an object. STMs can etch
15 surfaces and move individual particles. Even more advanced tools for nanoscale growth and nanoparticle assembly are under development.

C There are two ways to produce nanostructures: they can be grown or assembled atom by atom. At present most nanotechnology applications begin with the growth of basic nanostructures rather than the assembly of materials and objects one atom at a time.

a nanowire

20 By bonding a molecule with a particle, or single atom, scientists are able to create objects such as fullerenes: molecules of carbon atoms that when put together form tubular fibres, called nanotubes. These nanostructures include nanotubes, nanohexagons and nanowires. Such nanostructures are used to create high-strength, low-weight materials – when these fibres are threaded together and crystallised they can act like metal, but are 100 times stronger and four times lighter than steel. Nanostructures can also form super small electronic circuits – it is hoped
25 that these structures will be used in computing and reduce the size of a computer to the size of a full stop. Other nanostructures are circular and include nanoshells, nanospheres and nanocircles. Circular nanostructures are used for energy wave reflection and can be found today in products like sun cream and self-cleaning glass. So far, most of these nanostructures have been relatively expensive to manufacture. However, production costs are dropping with the invention of more efficient manufacturing methods and nanomaterials are being used in a wider and wider range
30 of products.

D The field of nanotechnology has two major problems. The first is learning how to successfully manipulate material at the molecular and atomic level, using both chemical and mechanical tools. This is being developed by researchers and there are successes in the lab and practical applications. The second is to develop self-replicating nanomachines or nanobots. Nanobots are miniature robots that work on the scale of atoms and molecules. One of the most
35 anticipated uses of nanotechnology is the creation of medical nanobots, made up of a few molecules and controlled by a nanocomputer or ultrasound. These nanobots will be used to manipulate other molecules, destroy cancer cells or construct nerve tissue atom by atom in order to end paralysis. Although they are made and function on the scale of atoms and molecules, nanobots will be able to work together to produce macroscale results. Precursor devices to nanobots have already been created, some can even walk. However, true nanobots have not yet been created.

E
40 To produce objects from the bottom up at the level of atoms will need armies of advanced nanobots. These are classified into two types: assembly nanobots and a special class of assembly nanobots: self-replicators. Advanced nanobots will be able to sense and adapt to the environment, perform complex calculations, move, communicate, and work together; conduct molecular assembly; and, to some extent, repair or even reproduce themselves. Yet creating these nanobots is a slow and precise process due to the microscopic size of these tiny machines. Therefore
45 the key to this technology becoming a reality is to make the nanobot replicate itself. It is the discovery of how to create this process, as well as the means to control it, which is key to fulfilling the potential of nanotechnology.

F Some environmentalists are concerned that nanobots may go wrong, leading to unlimited and uncontrolled self-replication. If this takes place, nanobots may destroy our ecosystem. While mankind must be careful to ensure that this does not occur, there is also the possibility that nanobots could form the ultimate environmentally-friendly
50 recycling system. Nanobots may one day convert our mountains of trash and hazardous waste into useful products and beneficial materials.

Achieve IELTS: matching headings with paragraphs / topic sentences

When you are asked to match headings with paragraphs …

1 read the title and look at any diagrams, graphs or pictures that will help you to predict what the passage is about.

2 read the passage quickly to understand the general theme of the passage.

3 use the headings to form questions, for example *What went from theory to practice?*, *How can nanotechnology be used for recycling?* If you can answer these questions you will be closer to the answer.

4 look for topic sentences. Ask yourself
   • What is the main point of the passage?
   • Which sentences in the passage carry the main points?
   • Which sentences give supporting information like examples, definitions and supporting points?

Now read the passage quickly and underline the topic sentences.

4 **Find words in the passage for the definitions.**

1 to examine something with a piece of equipment to find out the truth about it (paragraph B)

2 to make marks on a surface using chemicals or equipment (paragraph B)

3 to put something together piece by piece (paragraph C)

4 to make something change into crystals (paragraph C)

5 to control or make something move in a clever or planned way (paragraph D)

6 to make a copy of something (paragraph E × 2)

5 **Read the passage again. Do the statements agree with the information given in the Reading Passage? Write …**

TRUE if the statement is true according to the passage.
FALSE if the statement is false according to the passage.
NOT GIVEN if the statement is not given in the passage.

1 *Bottom-up production* is the science of small objects.

2 An STM takes pictures of atoms and molecules.

3 Nanostructures are costly to make.

4 Researchers have been successful in making simple nanobots.

5 Nanobots will need to communicate with the scientists who control them.

6 Nanobots could help us with the problems of pollution.

Language review: describing processes

6 Study the examples and explanations.

> *Individual atoms and molecules **are probed** by the AFM to create three-dimensional ...*
> *... the microscope **is moved** across the surface of an object.*
>> We often use passive sentences to describe a process.
>
> *To make paper, trees **are planted**, **chopped down** and **sent** through our mills.*
>> When we describe the stages of a process we do not need to repeat the auxiliary verb when we refer to the same noun.
>
> *If this **takes place** ... mankind must be careful to ensure that this does not **occur** ...*
>> Some verbs do not take an object (intransitive verbs). We cannot make passive sentences with intransitive verbs, we can only make passive sentences with verbs that take an object (transitive verbs).

Now look at the picture and complete the passage with the correct form of the verb in brackets.

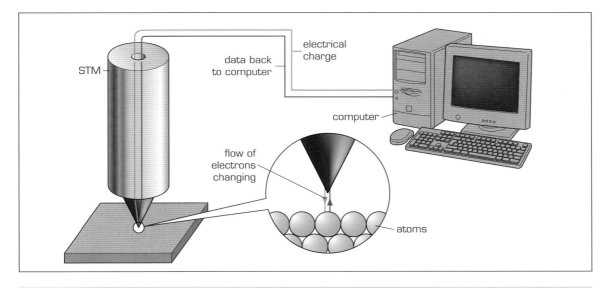

Scanning Tunnelling Microscopes (STM)

We cannot (1) _____ (see) an atom with a normal microscope. However, in 1981, a type of microscope called a Scanning Tunnelling Microscope (2) _____ (develop). The STM works like this: an electric current (3) _____ (supply) to the end of the STM while the scanner (4) _____ (move) rapidly across the surface of the object. When the tip (5) _____ (find) an atom, the flow of electrons between the atom and the tip (6) _____ (change). The change (7) _____ (register) by the computer. The computer (8) _____ (collect) the data and (9) _____ (make) a map using the electrical current of the surface of the atom.

7 Work in groups. Discuss the questions.

1 What did you find interesting or disturbing in the passage?
2 Do you think nanotechnology will be of benefit or a danger to society? Why?
3 Do you think we should control this research, and if so how?

B copyright
monopoly
compensation
patent

Listening

❶ Look at the picture and discuss the questions.

1 What do you think it is?
2 How does it work?
3 Why didn't it become popular?

Now match the definitions with the words in B.

1 to legally control the work of a writer, artist or musician
2 an official document that gives the inventor of something the control over the production of his invention for a period of time
3 money someone receives when something bad has happened to them
4 when one company or person has complete ownership of a product and there is only one of this product in the market

1.25 ❷ Listen to a talk and choose A – C.

1 The original reason for copyrighting inventions was …
  A to give rules that all nations could follow.
  B to encourage manufacturers to produce the same item.
  C to encourage people to give information about their invention.

2 In the nineteenth century, the United States did not protect new inventions because it argued that …
  A new inventions were a way of educating people.
  B it was not appropriate.
  C it believed in freedom.

3 Companies like medical companies spend a lot of time and money on …
  A importing products.
  B researching and developing new products.
  C encouraging inventors.

4 Developing nations began to …
  A patent local products.
  B make less expensive versions of western drugs.
  C enforce copyright protection.

5 Western companies are …
  A compensating people for using their traditional knowledge.
  B producing databases of traditional knowledge.
  C patenting ancient medicines.

3 **Read the notes and decide what information is missing.**

The original purpose of copyright is to give inventors profits from (1) _____ of a product for a limited time. In the nineteenth century countries could introduce (2) _____ for inventors when they thought it was appropriate, in this way some countries in Europe built their economy by (3) _____ other people's inventions.

As part of a trade deal with the World Trade Organisation, countries agreed to (4) _____ for the protection of inventions. This led to a battle between developed and developing nations. Many developing nations ask which comes first: (5) _____ or private profit? On the other hand, Western companies have patented traditional medicines without the (6) _____ of, or compensating, local people.

1.25 **Now listen to the talk again and complete the notes. Use no more than three words for each answer.**

Language study: purpose

4 **Study the examples and explanation.**

*The original **purpose of** patents **was to encourage** innovation.*
We use (for) the purpose of, so that, in order to, so as to to talk about the reason for or purpose of doing something.

The	original main immediate	purpose aim idea function use	of patents	is was has been	to encourage innovation.
Countries could go their own way on copyright	so	that			they could introduce legal protection.
Developing countries are trying to produce databases of traditional knowledge		as to			protect patent rights.
It needed the freedom to copy	in order to				educate the new nation.

Now complete the sentences.

1 Developed countries should give research grants to developing nations _____ encourage inventors from poorer countries.
2 Developing countries want cheap medicines _____ they can afford better health care.
3 The _____ the monopoly commission is to encourage competition in the market.
4 Inventors are given protection _____ make a profit from their new product.

5 **Work in groups. Discuss the questions.**

1 Should developing countries follow the copyright laws of developed countries?
2 Should developing countries be allowed to copy expensive medicines for their own people?
3 Should companies from developed countries be able to patent traditional knowledge from developing countries?

Speaking

1 Match the words in A with the pictures.

 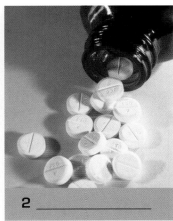  

1 _____

2 _____

3 _____

4 _____

A light bulb
penicillin
cat's eye
internal
   combustion
   engine

2 Work in pairs. Decide which is the greatest invention of the last 250 years.

cat's eye   penicillin   internal combustion engine   radio   the Internet
bicycle   computer   light bulb   telephone   television

Now decide which is the worst invention of the last 250 years.

atomic / nuclear weapon   landmine   internal combustion engine   plastic bag
speed camera   mobile phone   car alarm   television

3 Turn to assignment 4.1 and compare your answers with a UK survey.

1.26 **4** Listen to a conversation and tick which inventions in activity 2 they talk about.

Pronunciation

5 Read the phrases and decide which words are linked.

such a waste of time   he's got a point   all in all   it's certainly an important invention

1.27 Now listen and practise.

6 Read the task card and rounding off questions and make notes.

Part 2

Describe what you think is the most important invention of the last century.
You should say:
1   when it was invented.   2   who invented it.   3   what it does.
and explain why it is important.

Rounding off questions
1   Does your country have any famous inventors?
2   Do you think all inventions have been beneficial?
3   Which, if any, inventions would you like to ban?

Now work in pairs. Student A, you are the examiner – interview Student B. Student B, you are the candidate – answer the questions.

Writing

IELTS tasks:
task 1 – describing
a process; stages and
sequencing

1 Do the questionnaire.

Now work in pairs and compare your answers.

2 Work in pairs. Describe how the Internet works.

Now read the passage and check your answers.

> **How often do you use the Internet to ...**
> 1 chat with friends?
> 2 send e-mails?
> 3 video chat?
> 4 get information (like train times and flights)?
> 5 buy things?

THE INTERNET

In general terms, the Internet is a way of accessing information from many different sources via a computer at home or connected to a local network. At its simplest, the Internet consists of individual computers linked via a network. The network is made up of four basic items: backbones (fibre optic wires), Internet Service Providers (ISPs) and routers connected to servers that store and send data to and from people.

When a person wants to access the data, the information goes through four stages. In the first stage, their computer is connected to an Internet Service Provider (ISP) via a modem or a local area network (LAN). A modem is a piece of equipment for people using a computer at home which converts the signal of the telephone line to a digital signal. A local area network is a network of computers linked together with a digital line.

Following this the request for data is broken into pieces of information about 1 kilobit in size called *packets*. The next step is for these packets to be broken up into three parts: head, data and footer. The head contains the sender's and receiver's addresses, the data contains the information and the footer is constituted of data which shows the end of the packet and an error check. Errors are checked by giving the total of the number of 1s and 0s in the original binary message, so that when the data is received it should still have the same number of 1s and 0s as when it was sent.

The packets are subsequently transferred to a *router* – a specialised computer that sends information to its destination along thousands of pathways. Networks are connected through routers which do two things: firstly they make sure the packet is sent to the correct place, secondly they determine which way is the best way for the packet to go. One router communicates with the next router to make sure the next part of the network is clear. If a network path or part of a network is busy, a different route may be chosen. Thus, information that is sent over the Internet travels in separate packets through several possible different routes.

3 Read the passage again and label the diagram.

Now answer the questions.

1 What is another name for *cables*?
2 What is a *LAN*?
3 How are errors checked?
4 What do routers do?

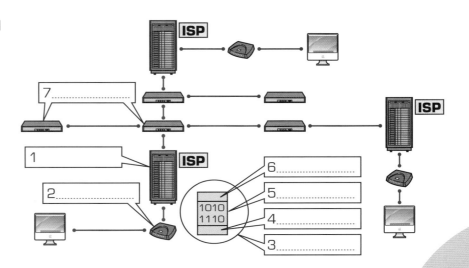

Achieve IELTS: describing a process

In task 1 you may be asked to describe a diagram or flowchart showing a process. To do this …

1 give a general statement of what happens in the process. If the diagram has a title, try to put it in your own words.
2 describe what the process consists of; write how many parts or stages there are and describe these briefly.
3 describe the process in detail using phrases for purpose, staging and sequencing and passive structures.

4 **Work in pairs and answer the questions.**

1 Which information in the passage did you know already? Which information was new?
2 Which information did you find interesting?

Now read the passage and underline phrases for …

1 introducing an overview of the process.   3 describing the sequence.
2 giving components or stages of the process.

Language study: stages and sequences

5 **Study the examples and explanations.**

Components and stages

*The network **is made up of** four basic items …*

We use these words and phrases for parts or components of a system or process …

It is	constituted of made up of	(four)		stages parts things	pieces components items
There are					

*the information goes through **four stages***

We use these words and phrases for stages in a system or process …

The	first second final	step stage part	of the	process procedure	is …

Sequencing

*The packets are **subsequently** transferred to a router*

We use these words for …

adding a new stage	an earlier stage	things happening at the same time	the end of a process
after that then next subsequently later following this having done that	prior to this previously earlier before this	while during at the same time (as)	finally lastly eventually

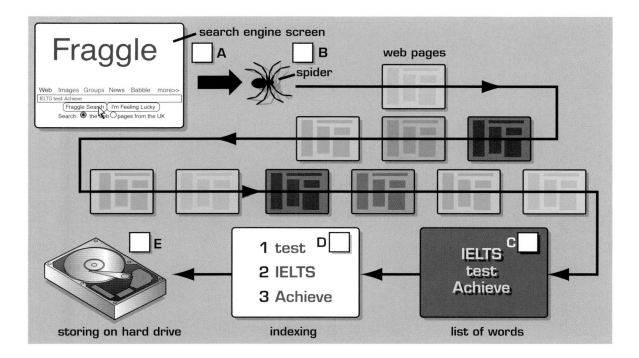

Now label the diagram with 1 – 5.

1 The user tells the search engine what to look for.
2 The search engine saves the data for us to access later.
3 The search engine builds a list of words and notes where they are found.
4 It orders and presents the information in a way we can use – we are given links to the pages according to how often the word appears on a webpage.
5 To find the information, search engines use programs called *spiders*. Spiders start their search at the most popular websites and most heavily used servers. They record the information on these sites. They follow the links to other sites so that the search spreads over the most popular parts of the web.

6 Read the question and underline the important words.

> *The diagram shows how an Internet search engine works. Summarise the information by selecting and reporting the main features, and make comparisons where relevant. You should write at least 150 words.*

Now complete the passage. Remember to include words and phrases for staging and sequencing.

Search engines
When we do an Internet search, we use a web browser or search engine.
Search engines are programs that help us find information from hundreds of
thousands of web pages. There are five stages in the process of finding
information on the Internet ...

City life

New York City

Do the quiz.

Now read the passage and check your answers.

NYC – THE BIG APPLE

What do you know about New York City? Try this quiz and find out.

1. The city was originally called … by Europeans.
   a New York
   b Manna-Hata
   c New Amsterdam

2. New York City was founded in …
   a 1898.
   b 1626.
   c 1783.

3. New York City is made up of … areas, or boroughs.
   a 1   b 3   c 5

4. The city is situated on … river(s).
   a 1   b 2   c 3

5. New York's biggest park is called …
   a Morningside Park.
   b Prospect Park.
   c Central Park.

New York City Guide

New York City is the largest city in the United States of America, with a population of over eight million in New York City itself, and a metropolitan area population of approximately 22 million people. Founded in 1626 and originally named New Amsterdam by European settlers, the city comprises the central island of Manhattan and four outer boroughs: the Bronx is located to the north of Manhattan, Queens is to the east, Brooklyn to the south-east and Staten Island is situated to the south of Manhattan on the Atlantic coast. However, to most people, Manhattan is New York. Manhattan is surrounded by water: the Hudson River to the west, the East River on the other side and New York Bay lies to the south. The island of Manhattan is thirteen miles long from north to south and just two miles wide at its widest point.

Manhattan is made up of different neighbourhoods, each very different from the others. The Financial District is in the south of the island, and north of this is Chinatown. Next door to Chinatown is Little Italy. The Lower East Side to the east of Little Italy is traditionally the gateway to new immigrants. In the middle of Manhattan is New York's biggest park, Central Park, surrounded by the Upper West Side and the wealthy Upper East Side. Immediately north of Central Park is Harlem, historically an African-American community.

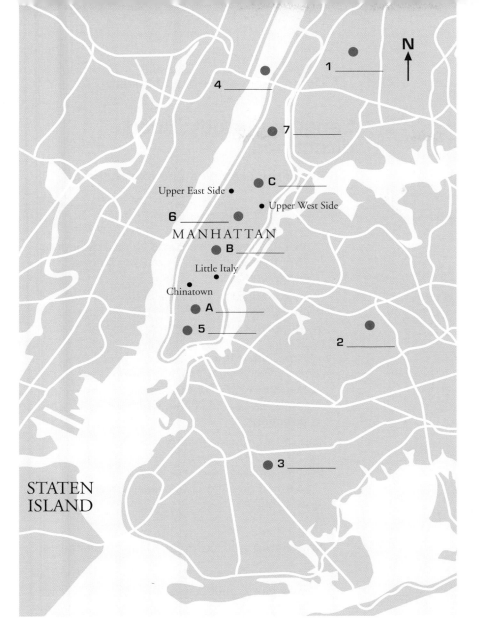

Map labels:
N

1 _____

4 _____

7 _____

C _____

Upper East Side •   • Upper West Side

6 _____

MANHATTAN

B _____

Little Italy •

Chinatown •

A _____

5 _____

2 _____

3 _____

STATEN
ISLAND

1 _____

2 _____

3 _____

4 _____

5 _____

6 _____

2 Read the passage again and label 1 – 7 on the map.

3 Label the pictures with the words in A.

2.1 **4** Listen to a conversation and choose A – C.

1 The person is going to …
  A a meeting.   B a conference.   C the city centre.

2 Roads that go from north to south are called …
  A avenues.   B streets.   C boulevards.

3 Directions downtown and uptown depend upon …
  A if you are in the north or south of the city.
  B where you are standing.
  C if you are travelling towards the east or west side of the city.

4 It is about … to the University.
  A an hour   B 40 minutes   C 20 minutes

Now label A – C on the map with the words in B.

A statue
  junction
  square
  traffic lights
  park
  block

B lower Manhattan
  upper Manhattan
  midtown

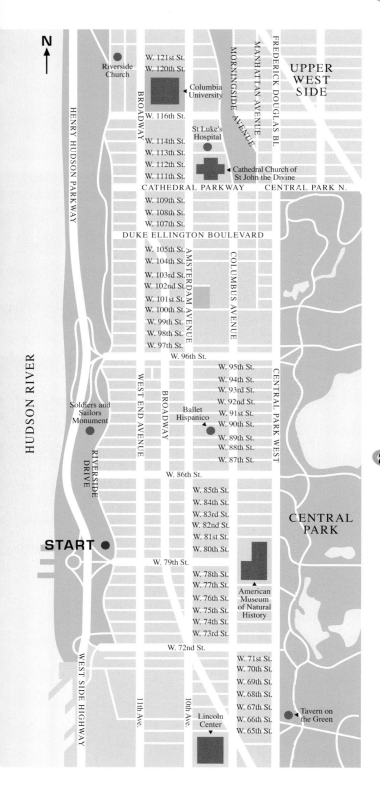

2.1 **5** Listen again and mark the route.

Language study: road directions

6 Study the examples and explanations.

> ***cross*** *Riverside Drive and **head** east*
> ***keep following*** *it north*
> > **We use imperative verbs to give directions. We often use *keep* + verb *-ing* to give directions.**
>
> *go down West 80th Street one block east till you get to **the lights***
> ***at the corner** of West 80th and West End Avenue*
> *turn north*
> *over **the junction** with Cathedral Parkway*
> *through Morningside Heights*
> > **We often refer to landmarks, features on roads and buildings when we give directions.**
>
> *keep going for about **twenty minutes** till you reach the intersection*
> *keep going for about **a mile and a half***
> > **We can give directions with distance or time.**

2.2 **Now listen and complete the conversation.**

B: We're here on the (1) _____ of Central Park North and Central Park West. Go north six (2) _____ to West 116th Street and turn left. Go past Manhattan Avenue onto Morningside Avenue … then you'll see Morningside Park. (3) _____ the park, past the statue and back on to West 116th Street. The University is (4) _____ of you.

A: I see.

B: Keep going down 116th and (5) _____ Amsterdam Avenue, on your left is Hamilton Hall and Kent Hall is on your right. Go past Kent Hall and you'll see Low Plaza on your right, with the Alma Mater statue and the entrance to the Library (6) _____ of you.

7 Work in pairs. Student A, turn to assignment 5.1 and give directions to Student B. Student B, mark the directions on the map.

Listening

IELTS tasks:
table completion;
multiple-choice
questions;
summarising

1 **Work in pairs. Discuss the questions.**

1 What advantages and disadvantages are there to living away from home during university?

2 Do students share rooms or have their own room in your country?

3 Do people prefer to rent or buy places to live? Why?

2 **Match the words in C with the meanings.**

1 a legal contract to rent a place to live

2 a person who watches the main entrance to a building

3 facilities like an elevator or a gym which make a place more comfortable to live in

4 a small apartment where the bed is in the same room as the living room

5 a person who makes financial arrangements for other people

6 someone who rents a place to live

7 to tell the owner of a place you are renting that you will leave

8 an extra amount of money people earn when they sell something

C tenant
give notice
lease
commission
amenities
studio apartment
broker
doorman

2.3 **3** **Listen to a conversation and choose the answer.**

1 The student speaks to a (a) University Housing Supervisor (b) Property company.

2 The apartments in Manhattan are (a) $1,300 (b) $850 a month.

3 The student doesn't want (a) a doorman (b) an elevator.

4 He decides to look (a) by himself (b) with a broker for an apartment.

5 He needs to pay (a) $25 (b) $200 for a credit report.

Express yourself: asking for more information

Underline the stressed words.

Can you tell me a bit more about that?
Can you explain that a bit more?
What's the best way of finding a place?
How do I do that?
What's the other option?

2.4 **Now listen and practise.**

---

4 Listen again and complete the notes.

University of Columbia Finding an apartment

Location

Manhattan is the (1) _____ area in New York. Studio apartments are $1,300 – $1,400, but within (2) _____ distance prices are $850 – $1,000. Prices are lower for smaller apartments with (3) _____ or little or no natural light. Another way to cut costs is to rent (4) _____ and share. The more (5) _____ an apartment has, the higher the price. When you are looking, be ready to take quick decisions and be (6) _____ with your plans.

Finding a place

There are brokers who ask for (7) _____ to find a place for you or you could look in (8) _____ , call landlord companies or do an online search.

What you need

You will be asked to complete (9) _____ form, to provide a credit report and provide evidence of (10) _____ and good credit. You will need someone to be your guarantor and you will need to pay (11) _____ rent and a (12) _____ when you sign the lease.

Now list the ways of saving money on renting an apartment.

5 Work in pairs. Ask each other the questions.

1 What kind of accommodation do you live in?
2 What are the advantages and disadvantages of living in an apartment block?
3 Which building in the pictures do you like and why?

Swiss Re building	Trellick Tower	Flatiron building	Unité d'habitation	Lawn Road flats

1 _____	2 _____	3 _____	4 _____	5 _____

D 1902 1972
1934 2004
1952

2.5 **6** Listen to a lecture and match the buildings with the dates in D.

Achieve IELTS: listening to lectures

In the listening test the questions are in the same order as the information in the listening passage. If you miss the answer to a question, move on to the next question. Read the questions ahead of the listening passage and try to keep the next question in mind.

2.5 **Now listen again and choose A – C.**

1 For modernists architecture was about …
   A buildings only.
   B a new way of living.
   C the age of machines.

2 Modernist architects started with the idea of …
   A beautiful design.
   B effective buildings.
   C social housing.

3 In the 1960s modernists were blamed for …
   A changing society.
   B breaking up communities.
   C international architecture.

4 In the early 21st century, modernism …
   A was just a collection of buildings.
   B changed dramatically.
   C was developed into the Hi Tech style.

7 Complete the summary. Use no more than three words for each answer.

Modernism was a new style of architecture about a new
(1) _____ . They wanted to construct a better life for everyone and believed that nothing was too good for
(2) _____ . Buildings like the *Unité d'habitation* were vertical villages with nurseries for children, a recreation ground and a (3) _____ half way up. By the 1960s modernism was the (4) _____ style of architecture, but by the 1990s the (5) _____ and the dream of an international architecture was over.

Le Corbusier

8 Decide what the words in E mean.

Now decide what a word means when we add *re-*.

E redefine
  re-house
  rebuild

9 Work in groups. Discuss the questions.

1 Do you like the modernist style? Why or why not?
2 Do you agree that architecture can change the way we live? Why or why not?

Reading

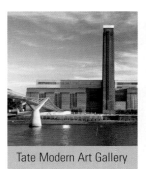
Tate Modern Art Gallery

Oriental Pearl Tower

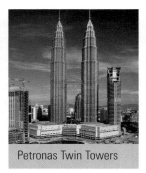
Petronas Twin Towers

Burj al Arab Hotel

F Shanghai
Dubai
Kuala Lumpur
London

1 Match the buildings with the cities in F.

Now work in pairs. Discuss what you know about the cities.

2 Work in pairs. Read the title of the passage and decide what it is about.

Now read the passage and label the map.

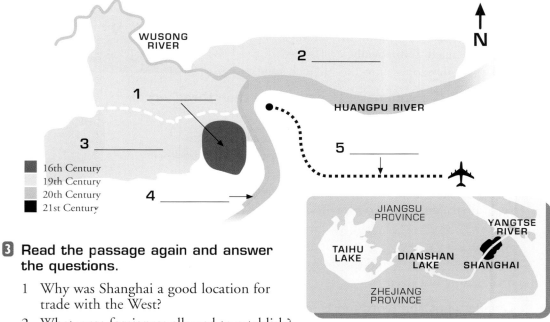

3 Read the passage again and answer the questions.

1 Why was Shanghai a good location for trade with the West?
2 What were foreigners allowed to establish?
3 Why did the international community grow quickly?
4 Why did the city play a smaller role in the world after World War Two?
5 Why did Shanghai begin to expand again?
6 Why has the Pudong area recently developed?

4 Find words in the passage which mean ...

1 an area of land under the control of a country or ruler (paragraph B)
2 one side of a river (paragraph C)
3 an area of land that is next to a river, lake or sea (paragraph C)
4 a district or part of a town or city (paragraph D)
5 the outline of buildings and trees seen against the sky. (paragraph D)

SHANGHAI: BACK TO THE FUTURE

A Today Shanghai is ranked as one of the four most rapidly developing cities in the world. It is the financial and trade centre of China, it is the Chinese city with the biggest population (nearly seventeen million in 2000 in the metropolitan region), it contributes almost 7% of the total industrial production of China and 30% of the country's cargo goes though Shanghai's port. However, Shanghai is a much newer city than many in China and its history and development is a surprising history of international conflict and cooperation. Located on the east coast of China, Shanghai occupies the southern part of the river Yangtse delta. Shanghai is bordered by Jiangsu province to the north-west and Zhejiang province to the south-west and comprises the mainland city and about 30 islands in the Yangtse River. The

Huangpu River cuts through Shanghai to Dianshan lake in the west, the oldest part of the city is situated where the Huangpu River and Wusong River meet. It began as a fishing village 1,000 years ago and continued as a small- to medium-sized settlement. In 1544 a wall was built around Shanghai and this area is generally known as the Old Town and is regarded as the beginning of Shanghai city. By the time of the Qing dynasty (from 1644 to 1911) it became a centre for cotton manufacturing and busy sea port. The position of Shanghai on the Yangtse delta made it an ideal location for trade with the West. However, it was not until the nineteenth century that the city expanded rapidly.

B In 1842 the Treaty of Nanjing ended the Opium Wars between Britain and China and foreigners were allowed to establish residences and trade from Shanghai. Following this, other countries were allowed territories north of the walled city. British, American and French citizens came to live in the city – territorial zones were established to the north for the British and Americans (later they were merged and became the International concession) and a French territory was established to the west. The foreign community was small until the late nineteenth century when China allowed direct foreign investment. As a result, the population of Shanghai's international community grew significantly and by 1927, under the Nanjing National Government, Shanghai was designated as a special city.

C By the 1930s the world's commercial and financial businesses had arrived in Shanghai. In the late nineteenth and early twentieth centuries, many European-style buildings were built along the left bank of the Huangpu River – on the waterfront area known as the Bund. Banks, customhouses, hotels and offices lined the Zhong Shan Road which runs through the area. The population of the city exploded along with its commercial and economic activity. After 80 years of development, Shanghai became the world's fourth biggest city behind New York, London and Paris. Its population rose from between 250,000 and 500,000 in 1843 to almost four million by 1935. However, after World War Two, Shanghai played less of a role in the world as the central government took away 87% of the local revenue generated by the city between 1949 and 1984. However, with economic reforms in the late 1970s and the designation in 1984 of Shanghai as an economic development zone, it began to expand again.

D Once again this has led to rapid industrial and economic expansion. The old two- and three-storey buildings in the French quarter are being replaced by high-rise structures and in the old British / American concession more than 1,000 high-rise apartments have been built. In order to take pressure off Shanghai's centre, an old industrial area east of the River Huangpu has been redeveloped – the Pudong region – giving Shanghai one of the most futuristic skylines in the world. From the mid-1980s a great deal of attention has been given to the infrastructure of the city. Three new underground lines have been built, and eleven more are being planned, elevated roads have been constructed east–west across the city and a new airport has been built in Pudong with a Maglev rail link from the airport to the city. A new exhibition hall has been built, and in the future green corridors will be developed to run into the heart of the city. A new deep-water port will be built at the mouth of the Changjiang delta in order to keep Shanghai's position as the world's third-busiest port.

Language study: passive sentences (2)

5 Study the examples and explanation.

> **present passive**
> *Shanghai **is ranked** as one of the four most rapidly developing cities ...*
>
> **present continuous passive**
> *... buildings in the French quarter **are being replaced** ...*
>
> **past passive**
> *In 1544 a wall **was built** around Shanghai ...*
> *... foreigners **were allowed** to establish residences ...*
>
> **present perfect passive**
> *an old industrial area east of the River Huangpu **has been redeveloped** ...*
> *1,000 high-rise apartments **have been built** ...*
>
> **future passive**
> *A new exhibition hall **will be built**.*
>
> We often use passive sentences when we write about changes and processes when we do not know the people making the changes, they are not important, or it is obvious.

G welcome
begin
win
build
make

6 Complete the sentences. Use the words in G.

1 The competition to host 2012 Olympics _____ by London.
2 The announcement _____ by everyone in the city.
3 Building work in the east of the city _____ already.
4 Several new sports facilities for the future games _____ , including a new Olympic stadium.
5 At the moment plans _____ to construct a new underground line to the Olympic site.

Now write these sentences in the passive.

1 A firm of architects have designed the new underground stations.
2 The government demolished the old housing estates at the edge of the city.
3 The water company built the water management centre on the left bank of the river.
4 A government minister ordered the construction of 10,000 new homes.
5 The city will build a new swimming pool for the international sports competition.

7 Work in groups. Make a five-year plan for your city. Think about ...

how the city was developed   parks and green spaces
what needs changing   housing
road, rail, air and other transport   industry.

Speaking

1 Work in pairs. Discuss the good and bad things about your town or city. Choose from these things.

transport   entertainment   work   parks   sports facilities   shopping

2.6 Now listen to three students and order the pictures.

Language study: location

2 Study the examples and explanations.

> *It **is comprised of** two main parts ...*
> **We use *to be + made up of, comprised of, composed of / comprises* to talk about the composition of a city.**
>
> *It's a relatively modern city **located in the south-east** of Australia.*
> *It is **situated between** the Jura uplands and the Tatra Mountains.*
> **We use *to be + located, situated* to talk about location. We often use points of the compass with these.**
>
> *in the **immediate** south ...*
> **We can use *immediate(ly)* and *directly*, with points of the compass to talk about distance.**
>
> *UNESCO has made **the old quarter** a World Heritage site ...*
> **We use *borough, area, quarter* and *district* to talk about areas of a city.**
>
> *It's **on the coast** ...   **on the banks** of the River Vistula ...*
> **We often use geographical features to describe the location of a city.**

Melbourne ☐

Now complete the description.

Krakow (1) _____ in the south-east of Poland. It (2) _____ between the Jura uplands and the Tatra Mountains, and is (3) _____ of the River Vistula. It (4) _____ two main parts: the old town and the new town.

Krakow ☐

Pronunciation

3 Decide which words are linked with /w/ and which are linked with /j/.

state of the art   developed into a major centre   capital of the UAE
so it has lots of students   about the city are   recently including a new exhibition centre

2.7 Now listen and practise.

4 Read the task card and underline the key words.

Dubai ☐

> **Part 2**
> *Describe a city in which you have lived.*
> *You should say:*
> *– where it is*
> *– how it has changed*
> *– how you hope it will change in the future*
> *and explain what you like or dislike about it.*

Now work in pairs. Student A, you are the examiner – turn to assignment 5.2. Student B, you are the candidate.

Writing

1 Look at the map and find ...

1 the capital city
2 the second city
3 state / regional capitals
4 ports
5 coastal cities.

2 Read the passage and label the places.

A GARDEN CAPITAL

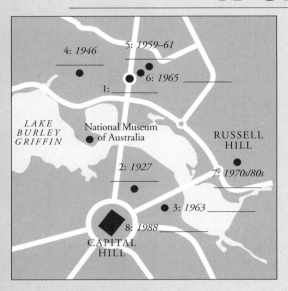

Australia's capital, Canberra, is one of only two planned capital cities in the world. When the Australian territories formed a single country in 1901 a new capital was needed. In order to avoid choosing between Sydney or Melbourne, it was decided to build a new city. Chicago architect

Walter Burley Griffin, influenced by the Chicago school of architecture and the idea of garden cities, won the international prize to design the new capital. Following the competition, land was chosen to build on and a railway to the new site was constructed. Burley Griffin's design was based on three main areas linked together to form a triangle: Capital Hill, the focus of government, City Hill with the commercial and civic centre, and Russell Hill. To begin with, progress was slow. By 1927 only a few government buildings including Parliament (set slightly north-east of the original plan) and the prime minister's residence had been built, together with hotels and houses for civil servants. Later, in 1931, a highway to the new capital was constructed. In 1946 the Australian National University campus was founded to the west of the city centre.

However, it wasn't until the 1960s that work really got underway in Canberra. Civic Square and Civic Offices were built between August 1959 and February 1961, in 1963 the National Library was constructed and in 1965 the Canberra Theatre Centre was built. Meanwhile, in 1964, the Molonglo River had been dammed to form Lake Burley Griffin in the centre of the city. Building continued throughout the 1970s and 1980s and a Defence office complex was begun in 1959 at Russell Hill. From 1927 to 1987 Parliament was held in the provisional parliament house. However, by 1980 it was decided that the building was too small and a competition was held to design a new building. The new parliament building was constructed on Capital Hill and was completed in 1988 on the area Burley Griffin had originally planned.

Now answer the questions.

1 Why did the government decide to build a new city?
2 How did they form Lake Burley Griffin?
3 Why did they construct a new parliament building?

3 Work in pairs. Ask each other the questions.

1 Would you like to plan a town or city? Why or why not?
2 Which things would you include? Which things would you leave out?

Language study: describing changes in a city

4 Study the example and explanation.

> ***To begin with***, *progress was slow.*
> **We use these words when we describe changes over time.**

sequencing	referring to points of time	referring to periods of time	referring to areas
to begin with when later following (the competition) …	by … it wasn't until not until in	between … and … meanwhile … / while … throughout the 60s and 1970s from … to … during	in the centre of the city to the west of the city centre on the southern bank of the lake slightly north-east of

Now look at the map and complete the passage.

LONDON

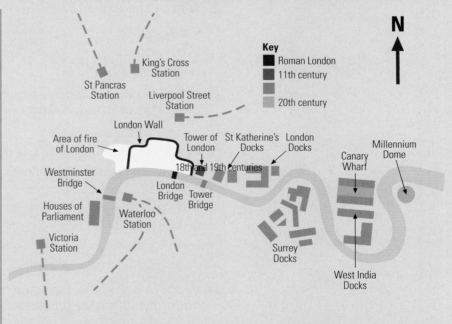

The development of London really began with the Romans. In the year 46 they built London bridge and (1) _____ , in the second century a wall was built around the city. (2) _____ the invasion of Britain by William the Conqueror the Tower of London was built slightly to (3) _____ of London bridge at the (4) _____ end of the Roman wall. London expanded steadily through the middle ages, but was built mainly out of wood. In 1666 the centre of the capital was burnt down in the Great Fire. (5) _____ the second half of the seventeenth century, the centre of London was rebuilt. During the eighteenth and nineteenth centuries, London became the administrative and commercial capital of the British Empire. In 1840 work began on a new Parliament building to the (6) _____ of the river, (7) _____ the second half of the nineteenth century London's

major railway stations were constructed. London became an important port and (8) _____ 1827 _____ 1828 new docks were built in the (9) _____ end of the city. The docks were in use until 1970 when they were no longer needed, but it

(10) _____ 1988 that a new use was found for the area as a commercial and financial centre called Canary Wharf or Docklands. On derelict land to (11) _____ of the river, in 2000 the Millennium Dome was built to celebrate the new century.

5 Write 150 words describing the development of your city.

UNIT 6 Language

Street language

A Urdu
French
German
Spanish
Italian
Swahili

1 Match the words with the languages in A.

1 **Bonjour**   3 **Hola**   5 **Adaab**
2 **Hallo**   4 **Jambo**   6 **Ciao**

2 Work in pairs. Discuss which are the most and least useful ways of improving understanding of native speakers.

1 Join a local sports club. _____
2 Go to courses at a local school or college. _____
3 Have conversations with native speakers, for example in cafés and shops. _____
4 Get a part-time job which involves using English. _____
5 Watch English films. _____
6 Listen to the radio and CDs in English. _____
7 Join an Internet chat room. _____

3 Work in pairs. Decide what things make it difficult to understand native speakers.

1 Accent – how people from a region pronounce words. ☐
2 Dialect – people using a local form of language containing different grammar and words. ☐
3 Speed – how quickly people speak. ☐
4 References – people talk about cities, events, places that speakers from other countries may not know. ☐
5 Other … ☐

2.8   Now listen to a conversation. Tick the difficulties you hear.

4 Work in pairs. Say what ideas to improve their English the students talk about.

2.8 **5** Listen again. Choose A – C.

1 How does Ivan feel?
   A depressed   B bored   C angry
2 He went to the café in the…
   A morning.   B afternoon.   C evening.
3 What does *Hooroo* mean?
   A How do you do?   B Hello.   C See you later.
4 Where does the conversation take place?
   A Sydney   B Canberra   C Adelaide
5 Monica suggests that they go to the…
   A cinema.   B library.   C café.

6 Complete the table.

British English	Australian English
1 _____	chook
2 _____	vegies
3 _____	Oz
4 _____	Aussie
5 _____	ta
6 _____	sanger

Now put the words in B into groups.

B	ta ta	mate	g'day
	sport	hooroo	cobber
	ripper	grouse	bonzer

1 ways of saying something is very good: _____
2 ways of saying *friend*: _____
3 ways of greeting and saying goodbye to people: _____

Express yourself: consoling someone

2.9 Listen and notice how the voice rises and falls.

*Never mind.   Don't worry.   Don't let it get to you.   It's just a matter of time.
You'll be all right.   You'll get used to it.*

2.9 Now listen again and practise.

7 Work in pairs. Student A, turn to assignment 6.1 and ask Student B questions to complete the table. Student B, turn to assignment 6.2 and ask Student A questions to complete the table.

Use these questions.

How do you say		
What's the word for	…	*in Australian English?*
Is there a word for		

8 Work in groups. Discuss the questions.

1 How many accents are there in your country?
2 Is there a standard accent?

Reading

1 Look at the picture and discuss what it is about.

Now answer the quiz. Choose A – C.

WORLD ENGLISH

More people are learning English every year, but do you know the facts behind the boom?

1 How many people will learn English over the next ten years?

A 2 billion   B 3 billion   C 5 billion

2 What percentage of the world's population will speak English within the next ten years?

A 25%   B 50%   C 75%

3 Non-native speakers of English exceed native speakers of English by ...

A 3 to 1.   B 5 to 1.   C 10 to 1.

4 What percentage of electronically stored information is in English?

A 30%   B 50%   C 80%

5 What percentage of scientists read in English?

A 40% to 50%   B 60% to 70%   C 80% to 90%

2 Read the passage and check your answers.

3 Read the passage again and complete the statements with the words in C.

C China (x 2)
Germany
India
Malaysia
Mexico
the Philippines

1 *Englog* is a variety of English spoken in _____ .
2 *Hinglish* is a variety of English spoken in _____ .
3 English is taught in schools from the third grade in _____ .
4 There is demand for pre-school English in _____ .
5 Core subjects are taught in English in _____ .
6 *Spanglish* is a variety of English spoken in _____ .
7 Demand for beginner English courses is declining in _____ .

4 Answer the questions.

1 Which three things encourage the development of globalisation?
2 What is a *tri-English world*?
3 Which new technologies are helping people to learn English?

NOT THE QUEEN'S ENGLISH

A From Caracas to Karachi, parents are paying for lessons for their children at English language schools. China's enthusiasm for English even has its own Mandarin term, Yingwen re, and governments from Tunisia to Turkey recognise that along with information technology and travel, English is an engine of globalisation. In the next decade, two billion people will learn English and about half the world, three billion people, will speak English,
5 according to a recent report from the British Council.

B Non-native speakers of English now outnumber native speakers three to one, according to English language expert David Crystal. 'There's never before been a language that has been spoken by more people as a second than a first', he says. In Asia alone, the number of English users has topped 350 million and there are more Chinese children studying English than there are Britons. But the new English speakers are not just passive learners of the language,
10 they are shaping it. New Englishes are appearing all over the globe, ranging from Englog, spoken in the Philippines to Hinglish, the mix of Hindi and English that now crops up everywhere in India from fast food adverts to college campuses. Indeed, English has become a common language. Whether you are a Korean executive on business in Shanghai, a German bureaucrat making laws in Brussels or a Brazilian biochemist at a conference in Sweden, you are probably already speaking or are going to speak English. And as the world adopts an international brand of English,
15 it's native speakers who will lose most. British graduates who insist on speaking the Queen's English could be met with blank stares. British or American businessmen who do not understand how English is used by non-native speakers might lose out on business deals.

C All languages are works in progress but the globalisation of English is set to revolutionise the language in ways we can only begin to imagine. In the future, suggests Crystal, there could be a tri-English world, one in which you speak
20 a local English-based dialect at home, a national variety at work or school, and international standard English to talk to foreigners. With native speakers becoming a shrinking minority of the world's anglophones, there's a growing sense that students will stop trying to copy the Queen's English and develop their very own versions. Researchers are starting to study non-native speakers 'mistakes' – *She look very sad*, for example – as structured grammars.

D To achieve fluency, non-native speakers are taking up English at an ever younger age. Last year, primary schools in
25 major Chinese cities began offering English in the third grade, rather than in middle school. A growing number of parents are enrolling their small children in a growing number of local pre-school English courses. Why such enthusiasm? In a word, jobs. More and more organisations are recognising the importance of English in the workplace. At the Toyota and Peugeot plant in the Czech Republic, English is the working language of the Japanese, French and Czech staff. Says Jitka Prikylova, director of a Prague English Language School, 'The world is opening up
30 for us and English is its language'. Governments are beginning to agree. From this year in Malaysia core school subjects such as maths and science are to be taught in English.

E Technology also plays a huge role in English's global success. Eighty per cent of the electronically stored information in the world is in English. Sixty-six per cent of scientists read in English, according to the British Council. New technologies are helping people pick up the language too. Chinese students can get English help on their mobile
35 phones. English language teachers point to the rise of Microsoft English, where computers help people to prepare letters. English and its teaching are becoming more complex. Ilan Stavans, a college professor, has finished a translation of Cervante's Don Quixote into Spanglish, the English–Spanish spoken in the United States and Mexico. In China, Hu Xiaoogiong wants to see a revision of the English curriculum toward Chinese English incorporating Chinese phrases as standard English in future. In countries like Germany, where most children begin English as early
40 as the second grade, the market for English studies is already decreasing. German language schools no longer target English beginners but those interested in business English, or English for presentations.

5 **Find words and phrases in the passage which mean …**

1 accepting what happens without trying to control things or take an active part (paragraph B)
2 people who speak the English language as a usual method of official communication (paragraph C)
3 the ability to use language in a clear and confident way (paragraph D)
4 the form of communication used at work (paragraph D)
5 the collection of subjects students study at school or college. (paragraph E)

Language study: *will, going to, be (about) to* + verb, modal verbs

6 **Study the examples and explanations.**

> *more people **are going** to need more English …*
> **We use *going to* to talk about something that will happen in the near future because we see signs that it is going to happen.**
>
> *the globalisation of English **will** revolutionise the language in ways we can only begin to imagine.*
> *This year, Malaysia **will** start teaching school level maths and science in English.*
> **We use *will* when we believe that something will happen. We can also use it with timetabled events in the future.**
>
> *subjects such as maths and science **are to be taught** in English*
> *globalisation of English **is about to revolutionise** the language*
> **We use *to be* + (*about*) + verb to talk about formal events that are scheduled to happen. We can use this in a passive way if we do not know who will do it or it is obvious.**
>
> *graduates who insist on speaking the Queen's English **could** be met with blank stares*
> *non-native speakers **might** lose out on business deals*
> **We use modal verbs like *could*, *might* and *may* to say what we think is possible in the future.**

Now complete the sentences with the word in brackets.

1 Within a decade, about half the world _____ English. (speak)
2 Just think, you _____ management at Harvard University if you pass this exam. (study)
3 My company wants everyone to speak German so I _____ a course. (do)
4 When everyone has their own version of English we _____ to understand each other. (not be able)
5 I really want to get a good score at the end of this course. I _____ really hard. (work)

7 **Work in pairs. Ask each other the questions.**

1 Did any of the information in the passage surprise or interest you?
2 Do you know any other versions of English like *Spanglish*?
3 Do you think it is important to learn a second language early in life? Why or why not?
4 How are you going to use English in the future?

Listening

1 **Work in pairs. Discuss the questions.**

1 How many languages are there in the world?
   A 600   B 1,600   C 6,000

2 How many of the world's languages will die over the next century?
   A a quarter   B a third   C half

3 How quickly are languages currently dying?
   A One a week   B One a fortnight   C One a month

4 How many languages have only one speaker left?
   A 15   B 50   C 150

5 Where are most of the most endangered languages of the world?
   A Australia   B Africa   C Asia

6 Where does the language *Kasabe* come from?
   A Africa   B Australia   C Asia

7 How many people speak *Welsh*?
   A a quarter of a million   B half a million   C a million

2.10 Now listen to Part 1 of an interview and check your answers.

2 **Match the languages in D with the statements.**

Which language …
1 is now extinct?
2 has been successfully revived after a previous decline?
3 comes from the Isle of Man?
4 has suffered a considerable decline in recent years?

D Breton
Kasabe
Manx
Welsh

2.10 **3** **Listen again and complete the sentences. Use no more than two words for each answer.**

1 The language of Kasabe was discovered by a _____.
2 It is not _____ for languages to become extinct.
3 Languages are disappearing at a more increasing _____ now than in the past.
4 Cornish and Welsh can be classified as _____ languages.

4 **Complete the chart. Use no more than two words for each answer.**

Stages of cultural assimilation		
Stage 1	Stress:	people feel (1) _____ to use the new, dominant language.
Stage 2	(2) _____:	people develop competency in the new language but retain their skills in the old language
Stage 3	Monolingualism:	the old language increasingly becomes less (3)_____ to the speaker.

Now work in pairs. Discuss the questions.

1 Do you have many foreign words in your language?
2 Is this a sign of *cultural assimilation* or your language adapting?

2.11 **5** **Listen to Part 2 of the interview and answer the questions.**

1 Can we save all endangered languages?
2 How many languages have fewer than 100,000 speakers?
3 Which two professions can help to save a dying language?
4 Which two types of publication can help in the process of saving a language?
5 In which three areas of the world have languages been successfully saved?
6 Why should we care about language extinction?
7 Which three types of knowledge can be gained by learning languages?

Language study: phrasal verbs (1)

6 **Study the examples and explanations.**

> *minority languages are **taken over** by dominant languages …*
> **Phrasal verbs have two or three words. Phrasal verbs sometimes can be replaced by single verbs: *take over / replace*.**
>
> *he **went back** only to find that Bogon had died …*
> **We can use phrasal verbs in a real, or literal sense.**
>
> *the linguist had no time on that visit to **find out** much about the language …*
> **We can also use phrasal verbs in a metaphorical sense.**

Now match the phrasal verbs with the meanings.

1	come across	A	become extinct
2	die out	B	decrease
3	go down	C	discover (something)
4	hold on	D	destroy
5	get over	E	maintain
6	wipe out	F	recover

The last native speaker of the Catawba tribe language.

7 **Complete the sentences with the correct form of the phrasal verbs from activity 6.**

1 About half of the world's languages are going to _____ within the next hundred years.
2 A linguist _____ a language called Kasabe which had never been studied before.
3 As a result of the earthquake, the number of speakers of these languages has _____ dramatically.
4 Bilingualism means that people learn the new language and at the same time _____ to their old language.
5 Entire villages were _____ and around one third of the population were killed.
6 Welsh is an example of a language which has successfully _____ a decline.

8 **Decide which statements you agree with or disagree with.**

1 If we replaced all languages with just one language, there would be less war.
2 Everyone should be bilingual.
3 Business people do not need to learn languages, they need to learn about business.

Now work in pairs. Discuss your answers and give reasons why.

Speaking

IELTS tasks: individual long turn; rounding off questions; discussion

1 Work in pairs. Read the quotations, decide what they mean and if you agree.

Learn a new language and get a new soul. Czech proverb

He who does not know a foreign language, does not know anything about his own language. Goethe

The limits of my world are the limits of my language. Wittgenstein

2 Decide which is more important for people learning a language.

accuracy _____   pronunciation _____
vocabulary _____   fluency _____

2.12 **3** Listen to a conversation and put the words in activity 2 in the order you hear them.

Achieve IELTS: buying time

If you need time to think during the speaking test, you can use these phrases:

Just a second / (1) _____ / moment.
Let me think / (2) _____ .
Give me a second / (3) _____ .
That's a good question / (4) _____ .

2.12 Now listen to the conversation in activity 3 again and complete the phrases.

Pronunciation

4 Read the phrases and underline words linked with /r/.

I've never really thought about it
For example, you need words to do simple things
I couldn't even order a meal
grammatical rules and speaking accurately are also important
a word or a sentence

2.13 Now listen and check.

2.13 **5** Listen again and practise.

6 Work in pairs. Ask each other the questions for Part 1.

Part 1

Let's talk about languages and learning.

1 When did you start learning English?
2 Do you find it easy or difficult? Why?
3 Which other languages would you like to speak and why?

Goethe

Wittgenstein

Now read the candidate task card, underline the key words and make notes.

Part 2

Describe a language you would like to learn in future.

You should say:

- *which languages interest you*
- *how easy you think it would be to learn*
- *where you would like to study it*

and explain why you would like to learn it.

Rounding off questions

What are the best things about the language you would like to learn?

What are the difficult things about it?

7 Work in pairs. Student A, you are the examiner – time Student B and stop them at the end of two minutes and ask the rounding off questions. Student B, you are the candidate – answer the questions.

Achieve IELTS: discussion

During the discussion the examiner may help you with questions but you should do most of the talking. The examiner will not give any opinion about the topic and you should not ask the examiner for their opinion about the topic.

Now read the questions and underline the key words.

Part 3

Let's consider, first of all, learning languages in your country.

1 *How important is it for people to have knowledge of other languages nowadays?*

2 *Which jobs require knowledge of other languages?*

3 *Do you think there is an 'ideal' way to learn a language?*

8 Work in pairs. Student A, you are the examiner; interview Student B. Student B, you are the candidate; answer the questions.

Now change roles.

Writing

1 **Work in pairs. Ask each other the questions.**

Do you use the Internet to …
- send e-mail?
- buy things?
- download music?
- play games?
- study (distance learning)?
- watch videos?
- look for job and educational opportunities?
- bank online?
- look up facts?
- make travel arrangements?
- get news?
- chat?

2 **Read the essay and decide which title it answers.**

1 **Write about the following topic:**
Modern technology is changing our world. This has advantages such as bringing people closer together through communication. It also has disadvantages such as destroying the differences between cultures. To what extent do you agree or disagree with this statement?

Give reasons for your answer and include any relevant examples from your own knowledge or experience.

2 **Write about the following topic:**
The Internet has transformed our lives. While it has brought many benefits it has also led to deterioration in our ability to communicate with our family and friends. To what extent do you agree or disagree with this statement?

Give reasons for your answer and include any relevant examples from your own knowledge or experience.

A In recent years new technology, especially the Internet, has revolutionised our lives. It affects the ways in which we work, think and behave both inside and outside the family. In this essay I will look at how new technology, and particularly the Internet, has affected our lives. I will begin with the benefits it has brought and look briefly at the disadvantages.

B The Internet has opened up the whole world for us, helping us to learn about anything we want as well as communicate with whoever we want. There are two main points here. Firstly, for many families, the Internet is an important social hub or meeting place. It is an important communication tool which can bring family members together. For example, they can listen to Internet radio, do crosswords and plan holidays together online. So, far from damaging family life, the Internet can play a valuable role in maintaining it. Surfing the net has become a leisure activity for families. They can log on to relax after a day's work or school in the same way as they used to switch on the television. My second main point is that people who go online also tend to develop a greater range of friendships. For example, chat rooms allow us to communicate with people from all over the world.

C It is also true that the Internet can cause problems within family life. An average person spends around one hour a day online and this may, have an effect on the amount of time spent with family and friends. This particularly affects those families where not all family members choose to go online. Therefore, some people may feel left out and this may lead to problems of communication.

D In conclusion, I feel that people who are connected can communicate effectively both with friends and family. In general I disagree with the statement as the Internet as a source of information can give all of us something to talk about to some extent and more reasons to share things with both family and friends.

3 Decide what the student's main point is. Choose A – C.

A The Internet has generally enabled us to communicate more effectively.

B The Internet has led to a decline in communication skills.

C The Internet has replaced the role of television in our lives.

4 Match the sentences with paragraphs A – D.

1 The student gives the argument for the statement and gives the other point of view.

2 The student develops the argument and gives examples disagreeing with the statement.

3 The student gives their own opinion and concludes.

4 The student refers to the question and gives an outline of the essay.

Language study: introductions, main points and conclusions

5 Study the examples and explanations.

*In this essay **I will look at** how new technology … has affected our lives.*
We use words and phrases like *I will look at*, to introduce the subject of an essay.
An introduction often contains …
– a general statement saying why the subject is important.
– some background to the subject saying why it is important.
– definitions of key words, if necessary.
– a brief outline of the essay structure.

My second main point is …
We can use phrases like *my second main point is* to make our main points clear. Main points should be followed by supporting points and examples.

In conclusion, I feel …   *In general, I disagree with the statement*
We use phrases like *in conclusion* to conclude an essay. In the conclusion we can summarise our main points.
In essays that ask for the extent you agree with the statement, we can say this with phrases such as *in general*.

introduction	main point		to what extent	summarising	concluding
To begin with	There are two main points …		in general	In short	To conclude
To start with	The most important main significant major	issues developments are benefits	to some / a large extent	Basically	In conclusion
I will look at	The second point is		I quite agree with	To sum up	(All) In all
I will start by looking at	Another relevant issue is		In broad terms	To summarise	On balance
			I wholly (dis)agree with	In sum	On the whole

6 Look at the essay plan for the other title in activity 2 and complete the introduction. Use the phrases in E.

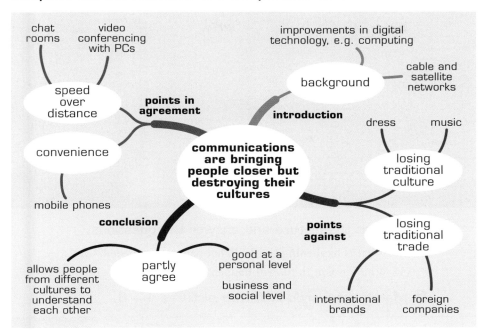

(1) _____ in recent years is the improvement in communications. (2) _____ the background to these developments (3) _____ which points I agree with and which points I disagree with. In my view (4) _____ which led to improvements in communications, firstly digital technology, in particular faster microchips which can be found in mobile phones, laptops and PCs, and secondly cable and satellite networks linking many places around the world. These mean that people in distant countries can communicate with each other in seconds instead of weeks. On the other hand it also means that companies can do business more easily between nations and this has advantages as well as disadvantages. (5) _____ the advantages of changes brought about by modern technology.

E now I would like to look at
I will start by looking briefly at
there were two major developments
then go on to say
one of the most significant developments

7 Complete the conclusion. Use the word and phrases in F.

To summarise, I think modern technology has given us some major (1) _____ : quicker communication over great distances and greater convenience. This has (2) _____ , for individuals it brings us much closer together; but it also brings societies together too. This has the (3) _____ of helping us understand each other better, but when one culture begins to dominate another and traditions and local trade are threatened, (4) _____ this is a negative thing. On the whole, I think that the benefits (5) _____ the disadvantages, but we must also be careful to keep our individual culture and identity.

F outweigh
advantages and disadvantages
benefits
positive effect
in my opinion

Now add your own ideas to the plan and write the essay.

UNIT 7
Crime

Streetwise

1 Look at the picture and answer the questions.

1 What is happening?   2 What has just happened?

3 What do you think will happen next?

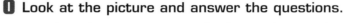

A spitting   mugging
burglary   speeding
dropping litter shoplifting

2 Match the words in A with pictures 1 – 6.

Now work in pairs and discuss the questions.

1 Which of these are crimes in your country?

2 Which crimes are most and least serious?

B Never walk alone   Mark it up
Careful with cash   Close call
Be sure – insure!   Lock it up
Auto-matic safety

3 Read the passage and match the paragraphs with the headings in B.

PERSONAL SAFETY

The UK is a safe place to live. Nevertheless, there can be problems in certain areas, so you should take some simple, sensible precautions. Here are ten tips for a safe stay.

1 Half of all burglaries happen because a door or window has been left open. If you are in a private home or flat, lock up whenever you go out. If you live in a hall of residence, be careful who you let in – or who follows you into the building. Lock your bedroom door even if you are only going down the corridor.

2 Robbers like an easy target. Walk in groups at night, travel by taxi or stay over with a friend. Your safety is worth more than the fare home.

3 Don't flash your cash. Note down all your credit card details at home so you can cancel them quickly. Use cash machines wisely, in groups, and during the day if possible. Put your card and cash away quickly and be aware of who is around you. Never write down your cash card number. Keep your purse or wallet in a secure place – don't make life easy for pickpockets.

4 Follow basic rules and protect your car. Always lock it up, put valuables out of sight and never leave the keys in the car – even when paying for petrol.

5 Take your mobile everywhere, but do not leave it on display. If you have to make a call, keep an eye on who's around. If someone steals your phone, immobilise it.

6 Protect yourself with good insurance. Keep lists of the make, model and serial numbers of your electronic items to help police if they are stolen.

7 Marking your property is a great defence against crime, and can sometimes help you get it back. Mark your property with the initials of your university (e.g. LMU – Leeds Metropolitan University) and your student ID number.

Now work in pairs. Say which things in the passage you do or do not do.

4 Read the passage again and find words which mean ...

1 something done to protect people or things from danger.
2 to take something from someone without asking them and without returning it.
3 a person who steals money or property from a place or person by force.
4 a person who takes things from people's pockets or handbags.

5 Work in pairs. Discuss three more ways you can keep safe.

6 Describe the pictures.

2.14   Now listen to a conversation and write ...

1 what kind of crime took place. _____
2 three places the student went that day. _____
3 why the student called the porter. _____

2.14 7 Listen again and answer the questions.

1 Which things are missing?
2 What did Ester do in the kitchen?
3 What did she do after she left the kitchen?
4 Why should she call the porter's lodge?
5 Is she upset because the laptop ...
   (a) is not insured?   (b) has all her work on it?   (c) is not security-marked?

Express yourself: (un)certainty

Decide which phrases we use to say we are (a) sure (b) not sure.

I can't be sure   I'm not certain   I'm pretty sure I did   I suppose so
I'm almost certain it is   I'm not 100% positive

2.15   Now listen and practise.

Language study: past perfect

8 Study the examples and explanations.

statements:	*Before I went to the bathroom **I'd been** with Keith in the kitchen.*
negatives:	*I asked Keith before I rang you, he **hadn't seen** my keys.*
yes / no questions:	***Had** you **locked** the door before you went to the kitchen?*
wh- questions:	***What had** you **done** before you took a shower?*

subject + *had* + past participle

We use the past perfect to talk about an event that took place before the time we are referring to.

We often use *before, when, as soon as, after, then, earlier* to make the order of events clear.

Now read the sentences and put the events in order.

1 I couldn't find my keys, I'd left them somewhere in the hall.

She looked for her keys.   _____
She left her keys in the hall of residence.   _____

2 We talked about a few things, like the concert he'd been to the night before and the lecture we'd attended earlier in the afternoon.

We talked.   _____
He went to a concert.   _____
We went to a lecture.   _____

3 As soon as I'd discovered I was locked out, I called the porter.

I discovered I was locked out.   _____
I called the porter.   _____

9 Complete the incident report form with the events in C.

C discovered the laptop was stolen
went back to the room and
    called the porter
went to a lecture
looked for keys
went to the kitchen and spoke
    to Keith
called security
had a shower
the porter opened the door

INCIDENT REPORT FORM

Location: Western Hall

Caller: Ester Toporek

Time of call: 4.50

3.00 p.m.   Student went to lecture

4.00 p.m.

4.15 p.m.

4.30 p.m.

4.35 p.m.

4.40 p.m.

4.45 p.m.

4.50 p.m.

Now complete the summary.

At 4.30 Ester went back to her room. Before she went back to her room she (1) _____ a shower. At 4.00 she (2) _____ and talked to her hallmate about a lecture they (3) _____ earlier. After her shower, when she (4) _____ back to her room, she couldn't find her keys, so she (5) _____ the porter and he (6) _____ the door. When she was back in her room she (7) _____ that someone (8) _____ her laptop.

10 Work in pairs. Student A, turn to assignment 7.1, Student B, turn to assignment 7.2. Make notes on the events.

Now compare your answers.

Reading

1 Match the words in D with the pictures.

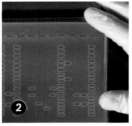

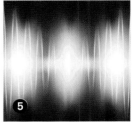

Now work in pairs. Discuss what you know about the things.

D fingerprint
iris scan
voice recognition
DNA profiling
signature

2 Read the passage. Do the statements agree with the information in the passage? Write ...

TRUE if the statement is true according to the passage.
FALSE if the statement is false according to the passage.
NOT GIVEN if the statement is not given in the passage.

1 Biometrics is the analysis of a person's character. _____
2 Biometrics is used to identify criminal behaviour. _____
3 People can be identified by their bodies and the way they do things. _____
4 Measuring how quickly a person types is a biometric method. _____

BIOMETRICS

Finding out who a person is was previously done in different ways: by showing something you have, such as a passport or by saying something you know, such as a password. Nowadays people are using what you are: *biometrics*. Biometrics refers to 5 measuring and analysing a person's unique physical or behavioural characteristics. Biometrics are used in two major ways: *identification* and *verification*. Identification is determining who a person is, verification is determining that a person is who they say they are. There are two types of biometrics: *physical* and *behavioural*. Examples of physical 10 biometrics include fingerprinting (analysing patterns on our fingers); facial recognition (measuring facial characteristics); iris scan (analysing the coloured ring of the eye); and DNA (analysing genetic makeup). Examples of behavioural biometrics include: analysing signatures and analysing 15 keystrokes (measuring the time spacing of typed words).

Achieve IELTS: true / false / not given; yes / no / not given

When you are asked to decide whether information in a statement is in the passage, if the opposite information is in the passage or if the information is not in the passage ...

1 underline the important words in the question.
2 read the passage quickly for general meaning, then read it again and find where the information is in the passage.
3 look for similar words or phrases, e.g. *physical – bodies, behavioural – the way they do things* to find information that matches the statement (true / yes).
4 look for opposite words or meanings, e.g. biometrics measures a person's *physical characteristics*, not *character*, to find information that contradicts the statement (false / no).
5 make sure the information is in the passage – not what you think is in the passage, e.g. one use of biometrics is to identify criminals, but it does not give this in the passage (not given).

3 Look at the diagrams and put them in order.

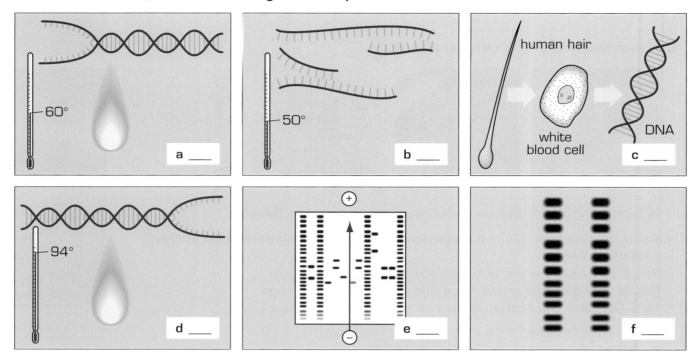

Now read the passage and check your answers.

4 Read the passage again. Do the statements reflect the claims of the writer? Write ...

YES if the statement reflects the claims of the writer.
NO if the statement contradicts the claims of the writer.
NOT GIVEN if it is impossible to say what the writer thinks about this.

1 The differences in DNA between people are small.
2 DNA profiles look like the codes on products in shops.
3 DNA fragments move through the gel because they have a positive charge.
4 By treating DNA fragments with radioactivity we can see them by using X-rays.
5 Information about our health can be found in genes containing features of the face.

Now complete the summary. Use no more than three words.

DNA profiling has completely changed the (1) _____ of forensic analysis and has become an important way of (2) _____ crime. DNA profiling (3) _____ in the 1980s when Dr Alec Jeffreys was looking for (4) _____ between human genes. By separating DNA and processing it, he found a way of (5) _____ individual DNA samples. In Britain (6) _____ have collected genetic material from people for a National DNA database. Discoveries in medical science are being used to (7) _____ crimes, but Sir Alec questions the (8) _____ to have this information.

5 Work in pairs. Discuss the questions.

1 Do you think governments should have records of our DNA? Why or why not?
2 Do you think it is fair for the police to take samples from people before the person has gone to trial? Why or why not?
3 Do you know if DNA profiling is used to solve crime in your country? Can you give more details about any cases?

DNA profiling:
the greatest advance in forensic science since fingerprinting

The analysis of genetic material, to create DNA profiles, has revolutionized forensic science. Since its first application, DNA profiling has taken paternity disputes and forensics by storm. In 2001, American labs alone performed more than 300,000 paternity tests, and many countries have collected large DNA databases. Two decades after its discovery, forensic DNA analysis has become an important crime-fighting tool.

The origins of DNA profiling go back to the early 1980s, when Sir Alec Jeffreys identified places in human DNA that differ from one individual to the next. Since over 99% of the human genome is common to everyone, such variation between people is minimal. Indeed, the differences are in the number of DNA sequences at different locations of the genome. The number of DNA sequences at different genome locations is highly variable between individuals, but are identical within individuals. In each individual 50% of their genes are related to their parents as each parent contributes 50% of their genetic material to their children. These DNA sequences are non-coding, that is, they do not contribute to the genetic blueprint that makes us what we are and so are not responsible for distinguishing our appearance or features. By determining the number of DNA repeats at each genome location for eleven different locations, scientists can establish a DNA profile for an individual, which is almost unique. When this information is presented visually by bars of different thickness for the eleven different locations, it resembles a barcode, which is why DNA profiles have been compared to supermarket barcodes. The DNA codes of two people can then be compared side by side.

In order to obtain a DNA profile, DNA samples need to be collected. When these samples arrive at the laboratory, the DNA has to be chemically extracted from blood (it is present in white blood cells) or another source such as single hair roots. The DNA is heated to 94°C at which temperature the DNA double helix becomes a single strand. It is then cooled to 50°C to allow an enzyme (DNA polymerases) to attach itself to the single DNA strand and copy it. At 60°C, double helixes are formed and the cycle begins again. The process allows a DNA profile to be determined in less than eight hours. As the number of DNA repeats alters the size of the copied DNA, they are separated on the basis of size as they move through a gel under the influence of an applied electric charge (DNA has a slight negative charge). After profiling, the DNA strands look like supermarket barcodes.

In the mid-1990s, as DNA profiling became more powerful, automated and easier to conduct, Britain started to compile a national DNA database. For years, the police have taken genetic tissue from people charged with offences whether or not they are found guilty of the crime with all the resulting DNA profiles held indefinitely. Since 1995, the National DNA Database has collected 2.3 million profiles, representing 5% of the adult population (and 9% of all men). This is more than any other country in the world: in America, by contrast, the FBI's database holds profiles for less than 1% of adults.

While it is difficult to criticise innovations that have uses in fighting crime, such technologies need special public attention, as their abuse could lead to discriminatory practices and invasions of privacy on a massive scale. New advances in biomedical sciences are being looked at for possible use in criminal investigations. However, Sir Alec Jeffreys strongly opposes crossing the boundaries between forensic and medical analysis. 'If you were to look at genes involved in facial features, you can bet your bottom dollar that you'd also access information about serious congenital defects,' he says. 'Police have absolutely no right to that information. I believe forensics and medicine should forever remain separate.' However, the existence of laws that allow the police to collect such genetic information in Britain, the Netherlands and Japan suggests that lawmakers think differently.

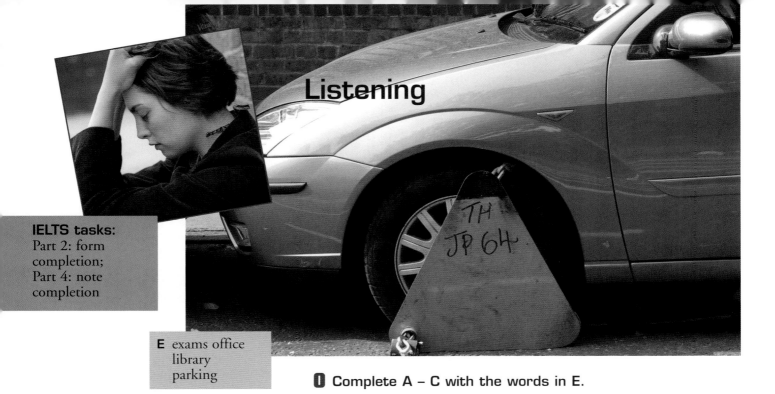

Listening

IELTS tasks:
Part 2: form
completion;
Part 4: note
completion

E exams office
library
parking

1 Complete A – C with the words in E.

A _____ **regulations**

LOAN PERIODS
undergraduate: 10 weeks
postgraduate: 15 weeks
journals, periodicals,
reference books:
(1) _____

reference collection:
not on loan

FINES
(2) _____ on
overdue overnight books
35p per day on other
overdue books

B _____ **guidelines**

Hand in all work
(3) _____

All work must have a
(4) _____

All work must be
word-processed.

Hand in two copies
of all work.

Students may lose marks if
they do not do the above.

C _____ **rules**

For University
(5) _____ only.

Put cars between
white lines.

Park only in places that
are not (6) _____ .

Note:
unregistered vehicles
may be clamped
and fined £60.00

2 Read the forms and match the words in F with the
definitions.

F reference book
overdue
word-processed
clamp
fine

1 to lock a car wheel with a piece of equipment to stop the car
  moving
2 money you pay for breaking a rule or law
3 a book that contains facts
4 work that is written on a computer
5 something that is late or should have been done before now

2.16 Now listen to three conversations and complete the forms.

2.16 **3** Listen again and answer the questions.

1 When is the library open?
2 Why didn't Susan return the overnight loan?
3 How late was Mohammed handing in his work?
4 What were the other problems with his work?
5 What has happened to Sema's car?
6 Why did it happen?

Language study: third conditional sentences

4 Study the examples and explanations.

> statements: *If **I'd known** that, I **would have renewed** it before the due date*
>
> negatives: *If you **had made** arrangements with your tutor to hand in your essay late, we **wouldn't have taken** off any marks.*
>
> *if* + past perfect + subject + *would* (*not* / *n't*) + present perfect
>
> questions: *If I **hadn't parked** here, **where would** we **have parked**?*
>
> We use the third conditional to talk about alternative outcomes for past events.
>
> We often use the third conditional to talk about regrets, wishes and possible results of actions in the past.
>
> When the *if* clause is the first part of the sentence we separate it from the *would* clause with a comma.
>
> *I **wouldn't have** parked here **if** I **didn't have** one.*
>
> We can change the order of the clauses, but we do not use a comma.

Now write the sentences in full.

1 If Mohammed / his work on time, he / any marks. (hand in / lose)
2 If Susan / her books, she / a fine. (renew / pay)
3 If Sema / late, she / in a rush and / her car in a student parking space. (not be × 2 / park)
4 Mohammed / any marks if he / a cover sheet. (not lose / include)
5 Sema / in the Vice Chancellor's place if she / the sign. (not park / see)

Pronunciation

2.17 **5** Listen to the sentences in activity 4 and notice how the voice rises and falls.

2.17   Now listen again and practise.

6 Work in groups. Ask each other the questions.

1 Have you ever broken a rule or a law? Why or why not?
2 What would have happened if you had been caught or punished?

7 Work in pairs. Ask each other the questions.

1 Is crime a big problem in your town, city or country? Why do you think this is?

2 Do you worry about crime? Why or why not?

3 Do you think crime is getting better or worse?

8 Work in pairs. Discuss which statements you agree with.

1 Crime is human nature – anybody would commit a crime if they knew they could get away with it.

2 People commit crimes because of psychological or physical forces they cannot control.

3 Where someone lives in a city influences whether or not they have criminal behaviour.

4 People commit crime because their friends or family think crime is acceptable.

5 People turn to crime because they do not have opportunities for good education and good jobs.

6 People turn to crime because they have poor self-images and weak ties to their families.

7 Treating individuals like criminals can make them become criminals over time.

Now make notes on why you disagree with the other statements.

2.18 **9 Listen to a lecture and tick the statements in activity 8 you hear.**

2.18 **Now listen again and complete the notes. Use no more than three words or a number for each answer.**

CAUSES OF CRIME

Classical theory: developed in (1) _____ . Believes crime is an activity of (2) _____ and individuals balance the result of their actions with the (3) _____ .

Biological determinism: see the cause of crime as (4) _____ factors. Scientists today are still looking for (5) _____ which causes individuals to become criminals.

Social theories:

1 (6) _____ theory: crime is an acceptable form of behaviour and people learn this.

2 Strain theory: crime is a result of a (7) _____ which encourages people to expect things.

3 Control theory: looks at people's relationship with others who (8) _____ society.

10 Work in pairs. Discuss the questions.

1 What solutions to crime are suggested in the listening passage?

2 Which ideas did you agree with?

3 Are there any other causes of crime?

Speaking

IELTS tasks:
Part 2, individual long turn; rounding off questions

1 Label the picture. Choose from the words in **G**.

G verbal abuse
bullying
vandalism
truancy

Now answer the questions.

1 Is this a problem in your country?
2 Who do you think commits this crime most often?

2 Match the words in **H** with the definitions.

H exclusion
community service
tagging
imprisonment
probation

1 a period of time when a criminal reports to an officer instead of going to jail
2 stopping someone entering a place or taking part in an activity
3 putting an electronic device on someone to show where they are
4 unpaid work criminals do instead of going to prison
5 going to prison for committing a crime

3 Work in pairs. Decide which punishment is appropriate for A – C.

A A 40-year-old man was arrested outside a city centre bar. He had been drinking and threatened a passer-by.
B A fifteen-year-old boy was caught after smashing a shop window and spraying graffiti on a nearby wall. It was the third time he had been caught for vandalism.
C A 22-year-old woman was photographed taking clothes from a shop without paying for them. When police questioned her, she said it was the first time she had done anything like this.

2.19 Now listen to a conversation and say which punishments the speakers decide for the people.

A _____   B _____   C _____

Language study: agreeing and disagreeing

4 Study the examples and explanations.

> *(I'm afraid)* **I agree with** *Jan*   *I think you're right*   **I don't agree with** *you*
> We use these phrases to show that we agree or disagree with someone.
>
> | agreeing | disagreeing |
> |---|---|
> | *I'm in complete agreement* | *I'm sorry, I couldn't disagree more* |
> | *I completely agree* | *I don't entirely agree with Jan* |
> | *I agree in part with that* | *I can't agree with you* |
> | *I still don't agree fully with you* | *I totally disagree with that* |
>
> We can show how much we agree or disagree with someone by using words and phrases like *completely, totally, partially, in part, entirely, fully.*
>
> *I'm afraid we have to* **agree to disagree** *on this one*   **let's compromise**
> We use the first phrase when we cannot agree with someone and the second to try to reach agreement.

Now work in pairs. Decide which punishments are appropriate for D and E.

D An eighteen-year-old man was caught after he had driven into someone else's car by accident. He drove away quickly. The car was damaged, but no one was hurt.

E A 30-year-old man grabbed a 75-year-old woman's handbag and ran away.

5 Read the task card and rounding off questions and underline the important words.

> **Part 2**
> *Describe something you have which is important to you.*
> *You should say:*
> *– when and where you got it*
> *– how long you have had it*
> *– how you would feel if you lost it or it was stolen*
> *and explain why it is important.*

Rounding off questions
Have you ever found anything valuable?
What did you do with it?

Now make notes on the task card.

6 Work in pairs. Student A, you are the examiner – interview Student B. Student B, you are the candidate – answer the questions.

Now change roles.

Writing

1 Read the passage and match paragraphs A – G with the summaries.

i   Punishment has become too soft
ii   Materialism and the media
iii   City centre poverty
iv   Ways to deal with the problem
v   Poor discipline in education

vi   Young people should have army training
vii   A breakdown in family values
viii   Youth crime in Britain
ix   Poverty and unemployment

A Youth crime is by far and away the biggest problem facing British society at this time and over half of all crimes are committed by young men under 21. Furthermore, much of it is vandalism - the destruction of property. In this essay I would like to offer some opinions why this happens.

B 5 The first thing many people point to is family life as the cause of this. They say that parents do not discipline their children and they do not teach them right from wrong. Above all, this leads to the young person having no sense of right or wrong. Although this may be true to an extent, there are other social factors we need to take into account.

C 10 In my opinion, a major thing that can be held responsible is the school system. A liberal attitude at school with no real punishment for bad pupils continues the absence of discipline and values at home. Moreover, pupils do not have to concentrate or work properly - they leave school with few educational qualifications and little hope of a satisfactory career.

D 15 After school these teenagers are employed in uninteresting jobs or are unemployed. In addition, young people do not have much money and what is more, are bored and have time on their hands. Consequently, they have few alternatives - crime is one of them.

E 20 Another cause of crime is the media. Some people believe that the media cannot influence people. Nonetheless, it seems to me that television and the cinema make robbery and violence seem part of everyday life. As well as the effect of television we have an advertising industry which promotes a lifestyle that values money and possessions: crime can seem like a short cut to this lifestyle - an easy way of making money.

F 25 Finally, young criminals realise that they have a better chance of getting away with crime than getting caught. Despite increased police numbers, the rate of catching criminals is very low. Additionally, the courts and the police do not have enough powers to deal with these young people. The young offender feels he is above the law but he also has no fear of being punished.

G 30 Just as there are a number of problems that create the situation, there are a number of ways to solve this. First of all, I would like to see people in positions of authority given back the rights to deal with young people who do not behave properly. Secondly, I think we should not accept any amount of bad behaviour in society as this allows worse behaviour to happen. Finally, we need 35 to educate young people better so they can get well-paid jobs. By doing this we should see an improvement in our society.

Achieve IELTS: problem / solution essays

Essays about a problem often have the structure: background – problem(s) – solution / evaluation.

Now read the passage again and find the different parts of the problem / solution essay.

Language study: adding information

2 **Study the example and explanation.**

*In addition, young people do not have much money and **what is more** are bored and have time on their hands.*

> We use words and phrases like *in addition* and *what is more* to add information to a point we are making.

adding information	
(1)	what is more
(2)	(3)
in addition	(4)

Now complete the table with words and phrases from the passage in activity 1.

3 **Work in pairs. Discuss the three most important reasons for youth crime in western countries and suggest some solutions.**

Now read the passage and see if your solutions are included.

ZERO TOLERANCE

Tolerance is the ability to accept a wide range of behaviour; *zero tolerance,* however, does not accept any behaviour outside the law. Zero tolerance is a concept which came from a famous article by two criminologists in 1982. They said that by refusing to tolerate small criminal acts like dropping litter and spray-painting walls, the authorities could create a climate in which more dangerous crime does not take place. The article was called *Broken Windows*. It argued that if one window in a building was broken, all the others would soon be broken. Their answer was to repair the window, quickly.

Many people were critical of the idea, but in spite of this, the underground rail system in Washington, DC, was one of the first places where zero tolerance was tried. This drew public attention, especially when one passenger was arrested for eating a banana on the underground. Although the police seemed to focus on very minor crimes the number of overall crimes dropped. In a better environment, people's behaviour improved. Nevertheless, under zero tolerance people feel that their right to freedom is more limited even if they feel safer.

Language study: concession

4 Study the examples and explanations.

> *zero tolerance **however** does not accept any behaviour outside the law*
> *citizen's behaviour was more closely policed, **nevertheless** the crime rate dropped dramatically*
>
> We use these words and phrases to give information that follows the previous information in an interesting or unexpected way.

concession	
however	(1) _____
nevertheless	(2) _____
yet	(3) _____
in spite of (this)	

> ***Many people*** *were critical of the idea, …*
> We often give an opposing opinion first before giving our own ideas.

Now read the passage in activity 1 again and …

1 complete the table with more words and phrases for concession.
2 find examples of giving opposing opinions.

5 Match the two parts of the sentences.

1 Capital punishment is not used in most countries
2 Some people say humans should not kill each other
3 Supporters say capital punishment stops crime

A it is still used in the United States of America.
B the US has one of the highest rates of crime in the world.
C others say if a person kills another person, they should be killed too.

Now write the sentences in full. Use words and phrases for concession.

6 Work in pairs. Discuss the essay title.

> Write about the following topic:
> *It is often said that crime is one of the main things that makes their quality of life poorer. Crime in developed countries is one of the biggest problems in society.*
> *What are the causes of the problem and what measures can be taken to reduce it?*
> Give reasons for your answer and include any relevant examples from your own knowledge and experience.

Achieve IELTS: task 2 titles

Titles for writing task 2 usually have three parts: background, statement and question.

Now read the writing task title and underline the three parts.

7 Make notes about the causes of crime and measures that can be taken to reduce it.

Now present a written argument or case to an educated reader with no specialist knowledge of the topic. You should write at least 250 words.

Shopping

A shopping mall
supermarket
retail park
market

1 **Label the picture. Choose from the words in A.**

Now answer the questions.

Where can you …

1   window shop?   4   see different individual shops?

2   buy cheap food?   5   visit different shops without going outside?

3   buy furniture, electrical goods and DIY equipment?

B charity shop ☐
chain store ☐
chemist ☐
second-hand shop ☐
milk bar ☐
outdoor shop ☐
delicatessen ☐
newsagent ☐
army store ☐

2.20 **2** **Listen to a conversation. Tick the words in B you hear.**

2.20 **Now listen again and write numbers and / or no more than three words for each answer.**

1   Where can the student buy cheap clothes?

2   What is another name for a charity shop?

3   What is the total price of the books on the book list?

4   What price can students buy books for in a second-hand bookshop?

5   In how many places can the student buy stationery?

Express yourself: talking about shopping

Match the phrases with the meanings.

1   *a discount*   a   it's too expensive

2   *I can't afford that much*   b   to compare prices

3   *You can pick up a real bargain* c   a reduced price, usually in a sale

4   *check out the prices*   d   to go into a place

5   *I'll certainly pop in there*   e   to find something at a cheap price

2.21 **Now listen and practise.**

3 **Work in pairs. Decide if the sentences are true or false.**

In Australia …

1 you will not receive any discount on goods in shops.

2 the shop assistant will pay you a lot of attention.

3 you can take something back to the shop if you decide you do not like it later.

4 you can pay for expensive items in instalments.

Now read the passage and check your answers.

SHOPPING IN AUSTRALIA

When you shop in Australia, keep in mind these guidelines.

▶ Read all tags, labels and signs carefully and make sure you understand the price.

▶ Bargaining is not the custom in Australia. Most shops and even markets have fixed prices and you will not receive a large discount on any item.

▶ If you are purchasing a very expensive item, however, you could ask for a discount, but do so very subtly, *Is it possible to do any better on this price?* You just might receive a 5–10% discount.

▶ The shop assistant will usually wait for you to approach him or her, do not expect to be greeted at the shop door.

▶ Save your receipts in case you want to exchange or return an item. Many stores allow you to return items if you change your mind – providing not too much time has passed and you have not used the item.

▶ *Lay-by* is a good way to buy goods that you cannot afford straight away. You are required to make a small deposit and service fee, make regular payments until the total amount is paid, the shop will keep the item until the cost is paid in full.

▶ Finally, try to shop around as prices can vary from store to store and city to city.

2.22 **4** **Listen to three conversations and match them with A – C.**

1 conversation 1   A a second-hand bookshop

2 conversation 2   B an outdoor shop

3 conversation 3   C a stationery shop

2.22 **5** **Listen again and complete conversation 2. Use no more than four words for each answer.**

A: (1) _____ at all?

B: Oh, sorry I didn't see you there. No, it's okay, I don't need any help, (2) _____.

A: Are you looking for (3) _____?

B: (4) _____ books on management – total quality management.

A: I see, well, the (5) _____ is over there, you should be able to find something.

B: Thanks.

A: If you need any help or if you find anything you like, just (6) _____.

Now work in pairs. Write a similar conversation and practise it.

Reading

❶ Work in pairs. Read the quote and discuss what it means.

> *The Dell Theory says: no two countries that are both part of a major global supply chain, such as Dell's, will ever fight a war against each other as long as they are both part of the same global supply chain.*

Tom Friedman,
The World is Flat: a brief history of the 21st century

❷ Work in pairs. Ask each other the questions.

1 How much do you know about how international trade works?
2 What are the good points about international trade?
3 Are there any bad points?

Now read the title of the passage and decide if it is for or against globalisation.

❸ Match the words in C with the definitions.

1 money or property
2 when prices of products increase so that money becomes less valuable
3 something that can be sold and bought, especially food or fuel
4 the average amount a person from a particular country earns
5 the situation of having plenty of money

C per capita income
prosperity
inflation
commodity
capital

❹ Read the passage and choose A – C.

1 Globalisation is …
  A about financial development only.
  B the international expansion of market forces.
  C a recent phenomenon.
2 Globalisation gives countries the opportunity for development but …
  A world per capita income is dropping.
  B poor countries are not developing at all.
  C African countries became poorer in comparison with developed nations.
3 Outward-looking economic policies include …
  A democratic government.
  B low barriers to international trade.
  C good environmental policies.
4 Foreign investment …
  A reduces a country's debt.
  B leads to better rates of exchange.
  C expands a country's capital and technical knowledge.
5 The international community should help poorer countries by …
  A bringing them into the world economy.
  B strengthening their political system.
  C giving advice.

Why international trade is the key to development

Globalisation is an economic process that increases the integration of economies around the world, particularly through trade and finance. The term also refers to the movement of people (labour) and knowledge (technology) across international borders. It is an extension of the same market forces that have operated for centuries at all levels of human economic activity – village markets, urban industries, or financial centres beyond national borders. Today's global markets offer greater opportunity for people to tap into more and larger markets around the world, which means that they can have access to more capital, technology, cheaper imports, and larger export markets. Globalisation, however is not just a recent phenomenon. Some analysts have argued that the world economy was just as globalised 100 years ago as it is today.

Globalisation offers extensive opportunities for truly worldwide development but it is not progressing evenly. The growing gaps between rich and poor countries, and rich and poor people within countries, are getting bigger. The richest quarter of the world's population saw its per capita income increase nearly six-fold during the last century, whereas the poorest quarter experienced less than a three-fold increase. However, in some countries, especially in Asia, per capita incomes have been moving quickly toward levels in the industrial countries since 1970. Having said this, a larger number of developing countries have made only slow progress or have lost ground. In particular, per capita incomes in Africa have declined relative to the industrial countries and in some countries have declined in absolute terms.

It is clear that some countries are integrating into the global economy more quickly than others. Countries that have been able to integrate are seeing faster growth and lower poverty. Outward-looking policies like low taxes and low trade barriers brought greater prosperity to much of East Asia, transforming it from one of the poorest areas of the world 40 years ago. Due to these policies, living standards have risen, and it has been possible to make progress on democracy and issues such as the environment and work standards. By contrast, in the 1970s and 1980s when many countries in Latin America and Africa pursued inward-looking policies (such as protectionism and state-owned companies), their economies stagnated or declined, poverty increased and high inflation became the norm. In many cases, especially in Africa, there were external developments such as war and natural disasters, which made the problems worse. Encouraging this trend towards outward-looking policies, not reversing it, is the best course for promoting growth, development and poverty reduction.

We see the effect of globalisation in three main areas: trade, movement of people and shared knowledge. First of all, trade. Developing countries as a whole have increased their share of world trade – from 19% in 1971 to 29% in 1999. As mentioned, Asia's newly industrialised economies have done well, while Africa as a whole has done poorly. What countries export is also important. The strongest rise by far has been in the export of manufactured goods. The share of primary commodities in world exports – such as food and raw materials, most of which are often produced by the poorest countries – has declined. Secondly, movement of people. Workers who move from one country to another to find better employment opportunities in advanced economies provide a way for global wages to converge. There is also the potential for skills to be transferred back to the developing countries and for wages in those countries to rise. Thirdly, information exchange is an important, often overlooked, aspect of globalisation. Direct foreign investment, which is private capital from outside the country, brings not only an increase in the amount of a country's capital, but also technical innovation. More generally, knowledge about production methods, management techniques, export markets and economic policies is available at very low cost, and it represents a highly valuable resource for the developing countries.

In conclusion, globalisation is one of the most effective ways of helping developing nations we know. As globalisation has progressed, living conditions have improved significantly in virtually all countries. However, no country, least of all the poorest, can afford to remain isolated from the world economy. The international community should try – by strengthening the international financial system, through trade, and through aid – to help the poorest countries integrate into the world economy, grow more rapidly, and reduce poverty. That is the way to ensure all people in all countries have access to the benefits of globalisation.

5 Read the passage again and answer the questions.

1 What three things does globalisation refer to?
2 What advantages do global markets have?
3 Which policies are inward-looking and which are outward-looking?
4 Which three areas are affected by global trade?
5 Which three ways can the international community help developing nations?

Language study: information clauses

6 Study the examples and explanations.

*Globalisation is an economic process **that** increases the integration of economies*
Defining relative clauses give more information about a person, place or thing. We use them to say which thing exactly we are referring to. For defining and non-defining relative clauses we use: *which* or *that* for objects, *who* for people, *where* for places, and *when* for times.

*Direct foreign investment, **which** is private capital from outside the country, brings not only an increase in the amount of a country's capital*
Non-defining relative clauses give additional information about a subject.

*food and raw materials, **most of which** are often produced by the poorest countries*
We can talk about a number of things with *most, many, all, some, a number + of which.*

***globalisation** is one of the most effective ways of helping developing nations (that) **we** know*
[object]   [subject]

When the relative pronoun is about the object of the sentence, we can leave out *that.*

Now join the pairs of sentences using information clauses.

1 Nigeria has over 60% of its population below the poverty line. It is a country in Africa.

   Nigeria, which is a country in Africa, has over 60% of its population below the poverty line.

2 The concert was given in order to reduce poverty in developing countries. It took place in 2005.
3 The lecture on globalisation was given by the Professor. He wrote the book called *Small World.*
4 Global politics is a subject in business studies. I really don't like it.
5 Japan, China, Germany and the US are countries. All of them are in the G8.

7 Work in pairs. Ask each other the questions.

1 Can you see any effects of globalisation in your country? If so, what?
2 Do you agree with the writer of the reading passage? Why or why not?
3 Is globalisation always good? Give reasons for your answers.

Listening

IELTS tasks: multiple-choice questions; note completion

❶ Match the words in D with the definitions.

1 the results of a study
2 to find information about a subject
3 a list of questions for a large number of people
4 a small example taken from a large amount of information
5 a list of questions to find out peoples' opinions
6 information usually collected from a detailed study

D survey
questionnaire
data
findings
sample
research

Now work in pairs. Ask each other the questions.

1 Have you ever taken part in a survey?
2 Have you ever collected information with a questionnaire?
3 What would you do if someone asked you to take part in a survey?

2.23 ❷ Listen to a conversation and complete the form.

ETHICAL BUYING

How ethical are you in your shopping? Find out with this quiz.

1	What do you look at when you buy food?	A freshness B ingredients C price	☐ ☐ ☐
2	Where do you usually go shopping?	A at the local market B at the local shops C at a supermarket	☐ ☐ ☐
3	When something is getting old do you …	A keep it? B upgrade it? C throw it away?	☐ ☐ ☐
4	When you buy cleaning products, do you buy …	A an environmentally friendly product? B an expensive product? C the cheapest product?	☐ ☐ ☐

2.23 Now listen again and choose A – C.

1 The woman has a short amount of time because …
   A she does not like questions.
   B she is meeting someone.
   C she is late for a train.
2 The woman avoids food if …
   A it goes off quickly.
   B it does not have nice packaging.
   C it has lots of e-numbers in it.

3 The woman does not like to shop in supermarkets because …
   A she is not organised enough.
   B she has to travel there.
   C they are more expensive than local shops.
4 She does not throw things away because …
   A she does not have the time to learn about new products.
   B it harms the environment.
   C they can be upgraded.

❸ Work in pairs. Ask each other the questions in activity 2.

Now turn to assignment 8.1 and check your scores.

4 Work in pairs. Look at the pictures and discuss the connection between them.

Look for this Mark on Fairtrade products

E tariff
subsidy
shareholder
exploitation
sustainable

5 Match the words in E with the definitions.

1 the act of using someone in an unfair way for profit
2 being able to continue something for a long time
3 the money a government pays to help reduce the cost of a product
4 someone who has an investment in a company and receives a regular payment from this
5 a tax that governments charge on products that enter or leave the country

6 Read the sentences and choose A – C.

1 Rich countries spend $1 billion per (a) day (b) week (c) year on subsidising agriculture.
2 The Fairtrade movement started in (a) Brazil. (b) Holland. (c) South Africa.
3 The value of not-for-profit products is (a) $258 million. (b) $28 billion. (c) $500 million.
4 Fairtrade aims to (a) make good coffee. (b) provide trade between poor producers and rich consumers. (c) increase prices for consumers.
5 Fairtrade producers mentioned in the lecture make (a) furniture. (b) coffee and jewellery. (c) pens and stationery.
6 Most Fairtrade shops are run by (a) paid shop assistants. (b) volunteers. (c) shareholders.

2.24 Now listen to a lecture and check your answers.

2.24 **7** Listen again and complete the notes with no more than three words.

FAIRTRADE

This week's lecture: the network of (1) _____ organisations.

Background – aims to build sustainable (2) _____ relationships between producers in the South and (3) _____ in the richer parts of the world. Fairtrade is defined as an (4) _____ to conventional international trade.

There are six main goals: to improve the livelihoods of producers by (5) _____ , paying better prices and providing a continuous trade relationship. Secondly, to promote (6) _____ for

disadvantaged producers; thirdly, to raise (7) _____ consumers; fourthly, to give an example of partnership though dialogue; to get changes in the (8) _____ of international trade; finally, to protect (9) _____ and the environment.

Three kinds of Fairtrade organisations: first, producer organisations: these are at (10) _____ Fairtrade; second, (11) _____ which buy products from producer organisations; third, World shops which also have (12) _____ functions.

Now work in pairs. Answer the questions.

1 What do you think about Fairtrade?   2 Would you buy Fairtrade products?

Achieve IELTS: signposting in lectures

When the listening passage is from part of a lecture, it will contain words and phrases that help the listener follow the stages of the lecture. Listening for these will help you understand the topic and answer the questions.

introduction
> *I'm going to kick off by ...*

moving between sections
– ending a section
> *That's enough about the background and definitions,*
> *So much for the goals of Fairtrade,*
– starting a new section
> *So, let's take a closer look at ...*
> *let's explore these aims in more detail.*
> *I'd like to turn now to look at these three aims individually*
> *I'd like to move on to describe*
> *At this point I'm going to go into more detail about*

listing points
> *Fairtrade has six main goals.*
> *There are at least three types of Fairtrade organisation*
> *The first country I'm going to talk about is*

repeating a point
> *I'll quickly recap on the main points*
> *This goes back to my point about subsidies*
> *this returns to my point about the WTO*
> *I'm going to continue with these themes*

concluding
> *In effect,*
> *To sum up today's lecture*

Now work in pairs. Think of more phrases for introducing and concluding a lecture.

8 Use the information to write a short talk.

The World Trade Organisation (WTO)	points against:	points for:
beginning: GATT (General Agreement on Trade and Tariffs) to lower trade tariffs between industrialised nations; 1995 became WTO	– the WTO is too powerful – it can put pressure on countries to change their laws	– the WTO is democratic – democratic countries wrote the WTO rules and selected its leadership
aim: to increase help economic development with loans and advice	– WTO trade rules do not sufficiently protect workers' rights, the environment, or human health – the WTO is not democratic, rich countries appoint people to run it	– it plays a critical role in helping to expand world trade and raise living standards around the world.

Now work in groups. Give your talk to the group.

F rug
statue
houseplant
painting
good luck charm

1 _____

2 _____

3 _____

4 _____

5 _____

Speaking

❶ Match the words in F with the pictures.

2.25   Now listen to three speakers and tick the things they talk about.

> ## Express yourself: talking about objects
>
> Read the expressions and put them into groups.
>
> *I bought it from a carpet dealer   whenever I look at it, it reminds me of our trip*
> *she gave me this for helping her   I got it as a prize   I remember all the hard work*
> *and fun   it always brings to mind the day we nearly won a football competition*
>
> **1 where they got it   2 remembering**
>
> 2.26   Now listen and practise.

Pronunciation

2.27 **❷** Listen and say which are defining relative clauses and which are
    non-defining relative clauses.

1 *This was a gift from my friend who lives next door*
2 *the day when we nearly won a football competitition*
3 *I bought it in Antakya, which is a very ancient city, when we were on holiday*
4 *a football competition, which we entered for fun, last summer*

2.27   Now listen again and practise.

❸ Read the candidate task card and rounding off questions and make
    notes.

> ## Part 2
> ***Describe an object that is special to you.***
> *You should say:*
> *1 when you got it   2 where you got it   3 why you got it*
> *and explain why it is important to you.*

Rounding off questions
1 Do you like shopping? Is there anything you dislike about shopping?
2 Where do you usually go shopping?

Now work in pairs. Student A, use your notes to talk about the topic.
Student B, time Student A and ask them the rounding off questions.

❹ Work in pairs. Discuss the topics in part 3.

> ## Part 3
> ***Let's consider changes in trade and commerce.***
> *1 Do you like to buy international brands or do you prefer to buy products*
> *from your country?*
> *2 Are people too materialistic nowadays?*
> *3 What are the benefits of international trade and are there any*
> *disadvantages?*

Writing

1 Work in pairs. Student A, find the paragraphs in favour of
international trade. Student B, find the paragraphs against.

A Rather than being a force for development, globalisation promises wealth to everyone but only delivers it to a few. Although global average per capita income rose strongly in the twentieth century, the income gap between rich and poor countries is getting wider.

B **The reason** globalisation has not worked **is** because there has not been enough of it. If countries, including the rich industrialised ones, removed all their protectionist measures everyone would benefit, producing an increase in international trade.

C Low-income countries have not been able to integrate with the global economy, partly **due to** inward-looking economic policies and partly **because of** factors outside their control. No country, especially the poorest, can be isolated from the world economy.

D The International Monetary Fund is an organisation which manages world exchange rates. It also tells developing countries how to manage their economies. However, even though developing nations followed the IMF's advice, they did not see any benefits subsequently. The fact is that no industrialised society developed through free trade policies. American businesses grew **as a consequence** of protection from foreign competition in the 19th century. The same was true of companies in successful countries such as South Korea. Free trade alone does not **create** a successful economy, there has to be some kind of protection too.

E Global financial markets limit the power of governments to make tax policies and their ability to control companies. **The result of this is that** countries are now lowering taxes and decreasing labour and environmental standards to attract and retain investment from multinational corporations. This in turn **leads to** poorer conditions for workers and more pollution in poorer countries.

F Figures shows that governments around the world are collecting slightly more taxes than they were ten years earlier. The argument that workers in poorer countries are being exploited is hard to support. Research shows they are better off as a result of working for multinationals.

G Organisations like the IMF and the WTO are not democratic. **This results in** decisions made in private which affect countries and **produces** a lack of trust in these organisations.

H Less developed countries have a chance to improve their situations **on account of** organisations such as the IMF and World Bank. The IMF helps countries that get into financial difficulties. Therefore, if the IMF and the World Bank were closed, the flow of resources to developing countries would diminish, leaving the developing world worse off.

Now write more points for or against international trade.

2 Work in pairs. Tell your partner about your points.

Language study: formal definitions

3 Study the example and explanation.

> *The International Monetary Fund is an organisation which manages world exchange rates ...*
>
> **We give formal definitions with defined word or thing + classification + definition.**

Now read the definitions and underline the defined word, classification and definition.

1 A charity is an organisation which helps people in need.
2 An economist is a person who studies economic conditions.
3 Aid is food or money which is sent to a region to help it.

4 Complete the formal definitions.

1 The World Bank _____ aims to help economic development with loans and advice.
2 Globalisation _____ integrates the economies of countries around the world.
3 Volunteers _____ work without payment.

Now work in pairs. Student A, turn to assignment 8.2. Student B, try to guess the word.

Language study: reasons and results

5 Study the examples and explanation.

> *The reason globalisation has not worked is because there has not been enough of it.*
> *This in turn leads to poorer conditions for workers*
>
> **We use words and phrases like The reason is, because ... and lead to to show reasons for an event, situation or problem or the result of the event, situation or problem.**

Now complete the table with words and phrases in bold from activity 1.

reason		result
	cause	
	1	
Unfair trade rules	2	world poverty.
	result in	
	3	

reason		result
	Thus,	
	For this reason,	
	Because of this,	
Trade rules favour developed nations.	As a result,	the gap between rich and poor nations is widening.
	4	
	5	
	6	

result		reason
Globalisation is increasing.	7 There are two reasons for this, This is due to	unfair trade rules.

result			reason
World poverty	is	caused by 8 9 a result of 10	unfair trade rules.

6 Complete the passage.

Industrialised nations say that a global economy (1) _____ multinational companies transferring production to developing nations. This (2) _____ loss of industry and (3) _____ unemployment. As (4) _____ of manufacturing goods in developing nations, the price of products is lower. (5) _____ this, advanced nations benefit indirectly from the process and (6) _____ wealth is distributed between rich and poor countries.

7 Read the essay title and underline the key words.

> **Write about the following topic:**
>
> *Giving aid to poorer countries does not work. The richer nations have given billions of dollars to poorer nations, but while some nations have benefited, many more are still poor. What are the causes of the problem and what measures can be taken to reduce it?*
>
> **Give reasons for your answer and include any relevant examples from your own knowledge or experience.**

8 Work in pairs. Write a list of ideas to include in the essay.

Now order your ideas from most to least important.

9 Think of examples and evidence to support your points.

Now write about the topic in activity 7. You should write at least 250 words.

Opportunity

Election

1 Work in pairs. Ask each other the questions.

1 Do you have elections at your school, college or university? If so, what do students vote for?

2 Have you voted in an election? Why or why not?

3 Do you think students should be involved in how a school, college or university is run? Why or why not?

2 Complete the passage with the job titles in A.

A Treasurer
Equal Opportunities Officer
Academic Affairs Officer
Sports and Societies Officer
Communications Officer

STUDENTS' UNION REPRESENTATION

The Students' Union provides support, representation and advice to all students. Student Union officers are paid and take a one-year sabbatical before going back to their studies.

The (1) _____ is responsible for student representation on University committees ranging from academic appeals to teaching quality to counselling and career issues and term dates.

The (2) _____ is responsible for all the internal and external publicity and communication.

The (3) _____ is responsible for the finance, administration and development of all sports clubs and societies.

The (4) _____ controls Union finances, including student finance and dealing with financial and other external consultants.

The (5) _____ promotes equal opportunities, health, safety and welfare of all students. The officer also deals with all non-academic issues such as child care, runs campaigns, looks after disability services and crèche facilities and is the sabbatical officer with responsibility for the university bus.

3 Decide which responsibilities A – G are part of an Equal Opportunities Officer's job.

A Photocopying and addressing envelopes

B Health and safety on campus

C Giving personal advice

D Making sure students with children can take them to the University nursery

E Attending meetings

F Promoting equal opportunities

G Organising entertainment

3.1 Now listen to a conversation and check your answers.

4 Listen again and choose A – D.

1 Joanna is a student of …
  A sociology.
  B chemistry.
  C medicine.
  D biology.

2 She is worried about …
  A graduation.
  B the elections.
  C getting a job.
  D living at home.

3 The Students' Union elections will be held …
  A in June.
  B next month.
  C next year.
  D on Saturday.

4 After taking a sabbatical year, students will …
  A get a real job.
  B do work experience.
  C have a management position.
  D continue their studies.

5 Joanna's friend offers to help her with …
  A starting a website.
  B finding a job.
  C publicity.
  D social services.

6 One part of the job Joanna will not enjoy is …
  A meetings.
  B running the bus service.
  C day-to-day responsibilities.
  D listening to women's problems.

Express yourself: talking about responsibilities

Read the sentences and underline the words for talking about responsibility.

they are responsible for anything which concerns women
they are responsible to the Students' Union executive committee
you would supervise the running of the clinic   you're in charge of a budget
The Equal Opportunities Officer represents all the students

3.2 Now listen and practise.

---

5 Read the manifestos and decide which candidate you would vote for.

Sarah Lee: I intend to make every attempt to make the campus safer. I also have every intention of continuing the work already started to create a night time telephone service for students when they need help.

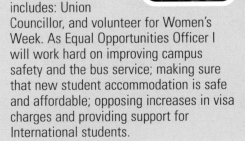

My name is **Heather** and I am in my final year of Peace Studies. I have been an active member in the Union since my first year. My experience includes: Union Councillor, and volunteer for Women's Week. As Equal Opportunities Officer I will work hard on improving campus safety and the bus service; making sure that new student accommodation is safe and affordable; opposing increases in visa charges and providing support for International students.

Joanna: I will continue campaigning for health issues and student fees. I have been on the student magazine as an editor for almost two years, during which time I have had the chance to work with a wide range of students. I feel that after almost three years at the university, I should give something back to the Union, and as Equal Opportunities Officer, I believe I can make a real difference.

---

6 Work in pairs. Ask each other the questions.

1 Do you think it is a good idea to take a sabbatical year? Why or why not?
2 Have you ever had a position of responsibility? What was it?

Speaking

❶ Put the words into groups.

caring   aggressive   bad tempered   loyal   quiet
intelligent   gentle   good humoured   selfish   (dis)organised
generous   bossy   lively   hard working   patient

1   positive characteristics
2   negative characteristics
3   neutral characteristics

Now work in pairs. Decide what characteristics these jobs require.

1   a doctor
2   a civil engineer
3   a teacher

Pronunciation

❷ Put the words in activity 1 into groups.

1   ■■ ■ *caring*   2   ■■ ■■ ■   3   ■■ ■ ■

4   ■ ■■ ■   5   ■ ■■ ■ ■

3.3   Now listen and practise.

3.4   **❸ Listen to a description and answer the questions.**

1   What job does the person do?
2   When did the people meet?
3   How does she describe the person's character?

Express yourself: talking about other people

Read the expressions and decide which are positive, neutral or negative.

on the whole she's got **more good than bad points**

there's never a dull moment *around her*

she can **get on your nerves** *a bit*

she's **always up to something**

She'll **do anything for you**

she's **the most** *disorganised* **person I've ever come across**

3.5   Now listen and practise.

---

4 Match the people with the jobs in B.

Indira Gandhi
_____

Hillary Clinton
_____

Agatha Christie
_____

Marie Curie
_____

B writer
scientist
prime minister
senator

5 Complete the mind map with the phrases in C.

Now use the mind map to talk about the person for two minutes.

C wrote several books
Yale Law School
grew up in Illinois
Senator, New York City
2000 – present

Achieve IELTS: mind maps in task 2

Mind maps are a good way of preparing notes for speaking task 2 as they help you write information quickly in a way that is organised and easy to read.

6 Read the task card, underline the key words and make notes. You have one minute to do this.

Part 2

Talk about a person that you admire.

You should say:
– who he or she is
– what he or she does
– when and where he or she lives or lived
and explain why you admire them.

Achieve IELTS: time limits

During the individual long turn, the examiner will only listen as you speak. He or she will not say anything until you have finished talking, or when two minutes is over. Making notes will help you to keep going.

7 Work in pairs. Take turns to talk about the topic.

8 Work in pairs. Student A, turn to Assignment 9.1, Student B, turn to Assignment 9.2. Choose a question from the list to discuss with your partner.

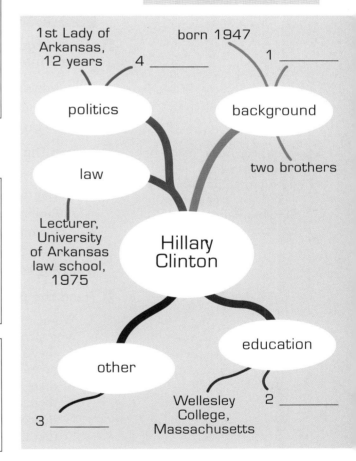

1st Lady of Arkansas, 12 years

born 1947

4 _____

1 _____

politics

background

law

two brothers

Lecturer, University of Arkansas law school, 1975

Hillary Clinton

other

education

3 _____

Wellesley College, Massachusetts

2 _____

Reading

1 Work in groups. Discuss whether it is better to have a male or female manager and why.

Now answer the questions.

1 Can you make any conclusions from the results of your survey?
2 Who gave the best reasons?

D public relations
double standards
deep-rooted prejudice
middle management
human resources
interpersonal skills

2 Match the words in **D** with the definitions.

1 a department within a company which manages the employees
2 a department which deals with the company's image
3 the ability to work well with other people
4 saying one thing but doing something different
5 a strong feeling not based on good reason
6 having some responsibility, but not in the top job

3 Read the passage and choose **A – D**.

1 Women managers are becoming more accepted because …
  A they are more like men nowadays.
  B there are more of them than there used to be.
  C the economy has slowed down.
  D they are starting their own businesses.

2 The areas where women managers are more effective are …
  A giving directions to staff.
  B fighting their way to the top.
  C dealing with their male bosses.
  D talking to people and helping them.

3 Women are often overlooked for the top jobs because …
  A they do not take credit for their own ideas.
  B other women do not like working for them.
  C they cannot make big decisions.
  D they leave to start their own businesses.

4 Many women prefer a male boss because …
  A male bosses work harder.
  B men are more competitive.
  C female bosses are less demanding.
  D it is more usual to work for a man.

Women Manage Better

The days when only men would hold management positions are over. More and more women are moving into top jobs in the USA. Despite a slowing economy, the number of women in management has risen to 16% since 1995, when it used to be less than 9%. This means that out of every 14,000 managers, 2,000 are women. One result of the increasing number of female managers is that women are now more accepted in these roles, and it has also been found that women in management ease tension and gender conflict in the workplace.

Whereas women who wanted promotion used to imitate men in their behaviour, the findings now suggest that men might benefit from being more like women. A comprehensive nation-wide study of executive performance accidentally found that women scored higher in almost all areas of performance evaluation, while compiling a large-scale analysis of 425 high-level managers. When the results were further analysed, it was found that women out-performed men in 42 of the 52 skills rated in the study. Areas where women are particularly effective are in supporting their staff, and sharing information. They tend to work harder behind the scenes, while men prefer the glamorous, more aggressive side of management. The masculine approach is more suited to the traditional style of business, where the boss would work alone and simply dictate orders to his staff. Now, in the global information age, teamwork and partnering are increasingly important, and these are exactly the areas where women excel.

Although the number of women in middle management is on the increase, there are still few women running large companies. Of the 1,000 largest corporations in North America, only six have a female director. It may be that the same qualities that make women more effective as managers are also holding them back. Most women get stuck in jobs which involve human resources or public relations, as their people skills make them highly suitable for this type of work. However, these posts rarely lead to the top. Ambitious women are frustrated by this, and many leave to start their own companies. The number of women-owned businesses in the USA has doubled in the past twelve years. Another reason why women are overlooked for promotion is that men are seen as more dynamic and competitive. Women tend to work for the good of the company as a whole, while men are looking out for themselves. Some bosses may interpret the feminine approach as showing a lack of vision. A woman will often adopt the strategy of making people think something is their idea, so that they will co-operate with her plan. Although this is an effective way of achieving an objective, the result is that she will lose credit for her creativity and innovation.

It is also surprising to learn that the greatest prejudice against female bosses comes from women themselves. In a recent Gallup poll, 70% of men said that they would be prepared to accept a female boss, compared to 66% of women. Although this gap is narrowing, women continue to be more prejudiced against their own sex than the men. One possible reason for this is that of tradition. Since nearly all bosses used to be male, women feel more comfortable being supervised by a man than by another woman. Some women also feel that a male boss is less demanding, and feels more relaxed about being in a position of authority. Since women have to work harder to get to the top, they expect more of their staff when they get there.

In conclusion, although more and more women are rising to higher positions, there are still many deep-rooted prejudices and double standards that keep them from achieving the very top positions. Companies may say that they value interpersonal skills, but they still look for a leader who is decisive and a risk taker. These qualities are perceived as being mainly masculine, and a new study has shown that a woman may be penalised for having the same attributes. Although women have proved that they are capable of leading a company, it seems that they will not get the chance to do so unless their superiors are prepared to enter the 21st century.

Now read the passage again. Write ...
TRUE if the statement is true according to the passage.
FALSE if the statement is not true according to the passage.
NOT GIVEN if the information is not given in the passage.

1   Women managers make the place of work less stressful.
2   Working with other people has become more important in modern business.
3   Businesses owned by women are more successful than businesses owned by men.
4   Women work for their own promotion, not for the good of the company.
5   More men than women work for female bosses.
6   Companies may not tell the truth about the qualities they look for in a manager.

Language study: *would* and *used to*

4 Study the examples and explanation.

> *The days when only men **would hold** management positions are over. Women who wanted promotion **used to imitate** men in their behaviour.*
>
> We use *would* and *used to* for repeated actions in the past when the situation is no longer happening. *Used to* can be used with any verb, but *would* can only be used for actions, not states. For questions and negatives, *used to* takes *did(n't)*.

Now complete the sentences, using *would* where possible.

1   In the 1950s, not many female directors _____ exist.
2   Very few women _____ work outside the home.
3   Women at university _____ (not) study business management.
4   In those days, people _____ think men were better managers.
5   The majority of women _____ live with their parents until they got married.
6   Most women _____ want to get married and have children.
7   Men _____ (not) like their wives to work, but most women work now.

5 Work in pairs. Talk about how women's lives have changed since the 1950s.

Listening

IELTS tasks:
note completion;
multiple-choice
questions

1 **Circle what is true for your country and underline what you think is true in New York.**

1   Family life is more / less important than work.

2   Children are with their parents often / not very often.

3   Fathers do / do not have enough time with their children.

4   People employ / do not employ other people to do jobs in their homes.

2 **Match the jobs in E with the descriptions.**

1   a person who makes food for people

2   a person who takes care of other people's children for a short time

3   a woman who takes care of other people's children and does jobs in the home

4   a person who cleans and tidies other people's houses

Now work in pairs. Say which people help in your home.

E baby-sitter
      cleaner
      cook
      nanny

3 **Tick the things you think a male nanny does.**

shopping ☐   making beds ☐   playing basketball ☐

taking the children to school ☐   reading stories at bedtime ☐

helping with homework ☐   changing nappies ☐

3.6   **Now listen to an interview and check.**

3.6   **4** **Listen again and complete the notes. Use no more than three words or a number for each answer.**

1   Bill gave up a _____ in drama therapy to become a *manny*.

2   Men feel more comfortable with _____ play – essential for young boys.

3   Bill provides all the things a nanny provides and also provides a _____ in the home.

4   In the USA, families employ male nannies to keep children away from _____ and computer.

5   Bill trained in first aid _____ and nappy changing.

6   In Britain only _____ of men are in childcare.

7   The positive points about the job for Bill are that he is free and can see _____ and grow.

5 **Work in pairs. Ask each other the questions.**

1   Do people in your country work long hours? What hours do they work?

2   Would you like to work at home? Why or why not?

3   Would you like a *manny* or other helper? Why or why not?

4   What would you say if your friend became a *manny*?

5   What would your friends say if you became a nanny or a *manny*?

Language study: reporting speech

6 Study the examples and explanations.

> He **said that** he had a good relationship with his children.
> They **told me that** many families wanted a male figure in the home.
>
> **We *say something*, but we *tell someone something*. When we report or talk about what someone said, we make changes because the time, the place and the speaker have changed.**
>
> ### Tense changes
> I **think**, Well, he's a good guy, so I **guess** they'll be OK.
>
> **When we report an opinion we often leave *say* or *tell* in the present tense and the reported speech in the present tense.**
>
> He **said** they **loved** him very much ...
>
> **We generally use past tense verbs to report speech and change the reported speech back one tense.**

present simple: *love*	past simple: *loved*
present continuous: *are working*	past continuous: *were working*
past simple	no change or past perfect
past continuous	no change
present perfect: *has studied*	past perfect: *had studied*
future: *will, is going to*	*would, was going to*

> **'We were sure you wouldn't complete the course'.** They **said that** they **had been** sure that I wouldn't complete the course.
>
> **We use the past perfect to report something further back in the past.**
>
> ### Other changes

this / these	*that / those*	*yesterday*	*the day before*
today	*yesterday*	*my / mine*	*he, she / his, her*

> ### Reported questions
> I **asked** Bill **how he became a male nanny**.
>
> **Wh- questions have the same structure as statements.**
>
> I **asked** him **whether** he really liked his job.
>
> **For *yes / no* questions we use *whether* or *if*.**

Now put the sentences into direct or reported speech.

1 Jake's dad: 'Bill has made our lives better'.
2 Bill told me that he had played football with the children the day before.
3 I questioned him about the worst part of the course.
4 The agency said that they didn't believe *mannies* were worse than female nannies.
5 Jake's mum (Lauren): 'Female nannies were never little boys. They can't understand little boys as well as male nannies.'

7 Work with a different partner. Tell them about your discussion in activity 5.

8 Work in pairs. Look at the picture and discuss what it means.

Now discuss which topics you may hear in a talk about women in work.

1 health and safety
2 pay
3 education
4 women and promotion
5 childcare
6 ethnic minorities
7 the workforce in Britain
8 jobs women do

3.7 **9** Listen to parts 1 and 2 of a seminar and check your answers.

3.7 **10** Listen to part 1 again and complete the information. Write no more than three words or a number for each answer.

Population of Britain: (1) _____ million
64% of working age, 16 – (2) _____ years

	women		men	
	millions	%	*millions*	%
of working age	(3) _____	32	*	32
in employment	12.3	(4) _____	14.6	(5) _____

In full-time (6) _____ : 486,300 (7) _____ , 429,000 (8) _____ .

3.7 **11** Listen to part 2 again, and choose A – D.

1 Women work in low-paid jobs …
   A although their exam results are better.
   B because they choose to do so.
   C if they fail their degree course.
   D because they are doing research.

2 The highest percentage of women in low-paid jobs are …
   A waitresses.   C office workers.
   B care workers.   D hairdressers.

3 The lowest percentage of women in highly-paid jobs are …
   A lawyers.   C marketing managers.
   B doctors.   D Internet technicians.

4 The speaker feels that women are lower-paid because …
   A there are fewer of them in the workforce.
   B they are over-educated.
   C they work in caring or service jobs.
   D men get all the best jobs.

12 Work in pairs. Make notes on the points for and against the statements.

1 Women are more caring than men by nature, because they are mothers.
2 Men have more ambition to make money than women do.

Now work in groups. Discuss the statements.

Writing

1 Use the words in **F** to complete the table.

specific gender	neutral
1 fireman	fire _____
2 wife / husband	_____
3 housewife	_____
4 air hostess	flight _____
5 chairman / chairwoman	chair _____ (or chair)

F spouse
attendant
home-maker
person
fighter

Achieve IELTS: referring to gender

In formal, academic writing we avoid referring to gender where possible. When writing about people in general, do not use *he*. Make the subject plural, and more neutral with *they*.

Now rewrite the paragraph without referring to gender.

A fireman has a dangerous occupation. He must enter burning buildings and rescue frightened women from the flames and smoke. His wife will be worried about him while he is at work. Officer Holmes, chairwoman of the Firemen's Union, said, 'My men are well-trained, but there is always a chance that he may be injured or even killed while doing his job.'

2 Read the essay title and underline the key words.

Write about the following topic:

Since the 1970s many more women have taken management positions, although few women have reached top positions in companies. Is this a positive or negative development?

Give reasons for your answer and include any relevant examples from your own knowledge or experience.

Now read a summary of the essay and underline the main points.

In many societies women have become a major part of the workforce and today many women hold management positions. However, few women have reached the very top, even in careers traditionally seen as female. Women seem to reach middle management positions and go no further.

The culture of working long hours makes it difficult for women to reach senior positions. Women bring the right skills to develop companies in the modern global economy. It is not good for companies to keep women in junior positions and will hurt the economy in the long run.

3 Work in pairs. Think of examples and sub-points to support the main points.

Now read the essay and check if you have similar examples and supporting points.

In many societies women have become a major part of the workforce and today many women hold management positions. Between 1974 and 1998 the number of women company directors in Britain increased by 600%. In my opinion this is a positive development. However, few women have reached the very top, shown by the fact that less than four in every hundred directors are women. This can be demonstrated by careers that are traditionally seen as female such as nursing, where men still hold the top jobs. Women seem to reach middle management positions and go no further. In this essay I will expand upon the reasons for this, then move on to my conclusion.

I think that the culture of working long hours makes it difficult for women to reach senior positions. When women ask for more flexible working hours to keep their job and look after their family, their commitment to the company is questioned. In many workplaces there is a culture of *presenteeism* – that is, you must be seen at work. An illustration of this is the person who does not want to go home on time and stays at work only to prove they are there. However, this is not the case in many European countries where not leaving work on time is seen as a sign of inefficiency. This attitude also hurts men, for instance men with young families who would rather leave work on time and spend time with their children.

Due to this lack of women in top management levels, some companies could be missing important business skills in today's global economy. If we consider that women are better communicators, better at for example, forming relationships and networks of people, these are exactly the skills that a successful company needs in a globalised world.

In conclusion, I believe that it is not good for companies to keep women in junior or middle management positions as they have valuable skills that are not being used for the wrong reasons. Furthermore, this could hurt the country's economy in the long run.

Language study: exemplification

4 Study the examples and explanation.

> ***An illustration of this is*** *the person who does not want to go home on time*
> ***If we consider that*** *women are better communicators*
>
> We can use words and phrases such as *an illustration of this is* and *if we consider that* to introduce examples to support main points in an essay.

Now complete the table with words and phrases from the passage.

for example (1) _____	like (2) _____	(3) _____
An example / (4) _____	of this	is
This can be	illustrated shown (5) _____	by

5 Work in pairs. Read the essay title and make a list of points and supporting examples.

> **Write about the following topic:**
>
> *Despite the fact that many women now have rights to equal pay, there is still a gap between the average earnings of male and female workers. What do you think are the main reasons for this?*
>
> **Give reasons for your answer and include any relevant examples from your own knowledge or experience.**

UNIT 10 Food

Invitation

❶ Match the word in A with the pictures.

A salad niçoise
lasagne
noodles
burger and fries
curry and rice
profiteroles
cheese salad sandwich

a

b

c

d

e

f

g

B spicy   healthy
savoury   nutritious
filling   tasty
sweet   delicious
light   flavourless

Now describe the pictures with the words in B.

❷ Work in pairs. Ask each other the questions.

1 Which countries do you think the food in the pictures come from?
2 Which kind of food do you prefer?
3 What do you usually eat for breakfast / lunch / dinner?

3.8 **3** Listen to a conversation and choose A – C.

1 The students have just come from …
  A a café.
  B a lecture.
  C a seminar.
2 The students want to …
  A have lunch.
  B have lunch and talk about the lecture.
  C go to the library.

3 The students will meet in …
  A the main refectory.
  B the reception.
  C the seminar room.
4 The students decide to go to …
  A the university restaurant.
  B a café.
  C a fast food outlet.

Express yourself: suggesting

Read the expressions and find two ways of saying *go for a meal*.

Why don't we grab lunch?
Let's get together at say ten past one.
How about something light?
What about going to the Fair Trade Café for a bite to eat?
Do you want to go to the main refectory?

3.9 **Now listen and practise.**

---

4 Work in pairs. Student A, your partner will invite you to lunch – decide whether or not to accept. Student B, turn to assignment 10.1.

5 Complete the menu with the words in C.

C vegetable lasagne
grilled fish
roast beef
broccoli
boiled potatoes
garlic bread
mushroom paté
sponge pudding

DAILY MENU
Wednesday May 15

Starters	Main courses	Side dishes	Dessert
1 _____ ☐	2 _____ ☐	5 _____ ☐	8 _____ ☐
soup of the day ☐	3 _____ ☐	6 _____ ☐	profiteroles ☐
	salad niçoise ☐	7 _____ ☐	
	4 _____ ☐		

3.10 Now listen to a conversation and tick what the students order.

3.10 **6** Listen again and complete part of the conversation.

C: Hello, good afternoon. (1) _____ ?
B: (2) _____ the vegetable lasagne, please.
C: Which vegetables would you like with that?
B: Could I have broccoli and boiled potatoes, please?
C: Certainly, sir. Here you are.
A: And (3) _____ salad niçoise, please.
C: (4) _____ ?
A: No, thank you, but I'll take some garlic bread please.
C: Here you are.
A: Lovely, thank you very much. And I'll have some profiteroles, please.
C: Here you are. (5) _____ .

Express yourself: offering to pay

Complete part of the conversation with the phrases.

it's my treat	I'll buy	I'll get this	I insist
Lunch This one It	is	on me.	

Greg: (1) _____ .
Caroline: No, no. We'll pay for our own.
Greg :   No, it's okay, (2) _____ , it's my treat.
Caroline: I couldn't let you pay, no, really.
Greg :   Caroline, (3) _____ – as long as you tell me what your tutor said about total quality management.
Caroline: Well, okay. (4) _____ next time.
Greg :   It's a deal.

3.11 Now listen and practise the phrases.

7 Work in pairs. Practise the conversations above.

Listening

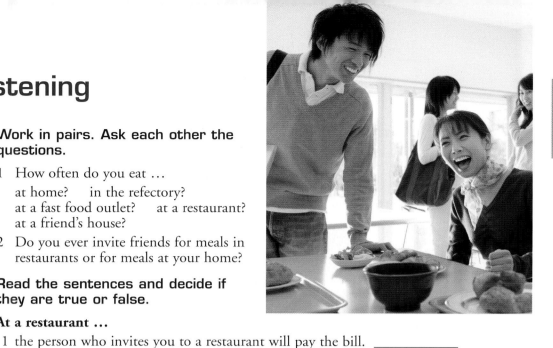

IELTS tasks: summary completion; table completion

1 **Work in pairs. Ask each other the questions.**

1 How often do you eat …

at home?   in the refectory?
at a fast food outlet?   at a restaurant?
at a friend's house?

2 Do you ever invite friends for meals in restaurants or for meals at your home?

2 **Read the sentences and decide if they are true or false.**

At a restaurant …

1 the person who invites you to a restaurant will pay the bill. _____

2 if you are not paying the bill, you can order the most expensive thing on the menu. _____

3 you should not tell the person about any special things you cannot eat. _____

At someone's house …

4 arrive 30 minutes early to dinner at a friend's house. _____

5 take a small gift. _____

6 sit where you like. _____

7 it is polite to refuse food the first time you are offered it. _____

8 if you want some food, you should reach over the table to get it. _____

9 at the dinner table you can burp if you need to. _____

10 if you cannot see an ashtray, you probably should not smoke in the house. _____

3.12 **Now listen to a talk and check your answers.**

3.12 **3** **Listen again and complete the notes.**

DINING ETIQUETTE

At University students are invited to formal meals and meals at (1) _____ occasions. When you get an invitation reply in (2) _____ days. When people go Dutch this means (3) _____ for their own meal.

When you are invited to someone's house for a meal an (4) _____ may be wine or chocolate. When the meal starts (5) _____ people to start eating. Do not reach across the table for food as it is (6) _____ – ask someone to pass the food to you. When you have finished eating say 'What (7) _____' and put your knife and fork (8) _____ your plate.

4 **Work in pairs. Discuss any similarities and differences in dining etiquette between your country and the UK.**

Now write five pieces of advice for a foreigner dining in your country.

D cheese
lentils
lamb
beans
chicken
mushrooms
strawberry
milk
beef
cabbage
cream
rice

5 Put the words in D into groups.

1 beans and pulses   2 dairy   3 meat, fish and poultry   4 fruit and vegetables

Now work in pairs. Discuss which kinds of food contain ...

1 protein   2 fibre   3 carbohydrate   4 vitamins   5 minerals.

3.13 **6 Listen to a talk and match the approach with the aims for each answer.**

1 western approach   a eating foods in the right season
2 oriental approach   b food is medicine
3 naturopathic approach   c a balance of nutrients

3.13 **Now listen again and complete the table. Use no more than three words or a number.**

western approach	oriental approach	naturopathic approach
1 eat _____ portions of fruit and vegetables	6 in summer eat _____ grown above ground	11 eat slowly and _____ thoroughly
2 use _____ and free-range products	7 in winter eat _____ vegetables	12 have meals in a _____ place
3 do not eat so much fast and _____ foods	8 food is classified according to if it is warming or _____ food	13 avoid other _____ like reading
4 limit your intake of tea, coffee and _____	9 boiled, grilled or _____ are thought to be warming	14 cook food _____ possible
5 drink _____ litres of water a day	10 raw, cold and _____ foods are thought to be cooling	15 treat stomach problems with _____ juice

7 Work in pairs. Ask each other the questions.

1 Do you have a balanced diet?
2 What do you eat too much or too little of?
3 Which foods do you like or dislike?
4 Are there any foods you will not eat? Why?
5 Which approach to eating do you prefer: western, oriental or naturopathic?

Reading

1 **Work in pairs. Discuss the questions.**

1 What are the people doing? Why?
2 What is *genetically modified* (GM) food?
3 What are the advantages and disadvantages of GM food?

Now read the passage and check your answers to 2 and 3.

2 **Match the words in E with the definitions.**

1 the variety of living things
2 the ability to endure something without being harmed
3 a chemical that kills insects
4 growing something on the basis of certain desirable qualities
5 a chemical that kills weeds

E pesticide
herbicide
biodiversity
resistance
selective
  breeding

3 **Read the passage again. Do the statements agree with the views of the writer? Write ...**
YES if the statement reflects the views the writer.
NO if the statement contradicts the views of the writer.
NOT GIVEN if it is impossible to know what the writer thinks about this.

1 African nations have made a particular point of rejecting GM food.
2 There is not much evidence showing that GM food is bad for humans.
3 GM crops breeding with wild crops is a real problem.
4 Some crops are changed to be pollution resistant.
5 GM crops can help with the problem of world food shortages.
6 Companies who develop GM crops encourage farmers to be independent.

Achieve IELTS: understanding views and attitudes

Some *yes / no / not given* questions ask you about the views of the writer. When you answer this kind of question ...

1 read the questions carefully and underline the key words.
2 look for words that show attitude such as *believe, agree, oppose* (see Language study).
3 look for phrases like *the truth is, in reality* and *in (actual) fact* that give the writer's opinion.
4 be careful about statements that give the opinions introduced by *Some / Most / A few people say ...* , this may be followed by the writer's real and opposite opinion.

Now read the passage again and follow steps 1 – 4.

GENETICALLY MODIFIED FOODS

A Although GM crops are widely accepted in countries as different as India and the
USA, they are very rare in Europe. Strict labelling laws and regulations are in place
for food and public opinion towards the technology remains largely negative.
Leading consumer organisations have urged their governments for more information
5 about GM crops and public debates. Some African nations have also opposed GM
crops, even to the point of rejecting international food aid containing them. So
what exactly are GM crops and why are people in these countries opposed to
them?

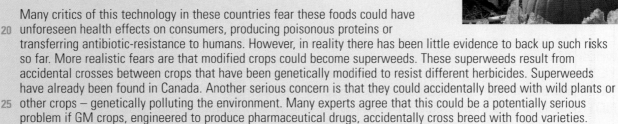

B Put simply, GM crops are plants that have been altered genetically for a specific
10 reason. This is hardly new however. The truth is that the human race has improved
crop plants through selective breeding for many thousands of years, but genetic
engineering allows that time-consuming process to be accelerated and genes from
unrelated species to be introduced. The root of genetic engineering in crops lies in
the 1977 discovery of a soil bug that can be used as a tool to inject useful foreign
15 genes into plants. Scientists were able to transplant genes from unrelated species
into crops to produce a multitude of new crop types for four basic reasons: to be
pest free and disease resistant, to be able to withstand extreme temperatures, to
be more nutritious and to produce medicines.

C Many critics of this technology in these countries fear these foods could have
20 unforeseen health effects on consumers, producing poisonous proteins or
transferring antibiotic-resistance to humans. However, in reality there has been little evidence to back up such risks
so far. More realistic fears are that modified crops could become superweeds. These superweeds result from
accidental crosses between crops that have been genetically modified to resist different herbicides. Superweeds
have already been found in Canada. Another serious concern is that they could accidentally breed with wild plants or
25 other crops – genetically polluting the environment. Many experts agree that this could be a potentially serious
problem if GM crops, engineered to produce pharmaceutical drugs, accidentally cross breed with food varieties.

D However, as Kiran Sharma (International Crops Research Institute for the Semi-Arid Tropics in Hyderabad) stresses,
'Rich Europeans can afford to reject the technology, here we don't have a choice.' He believes passionately that GM
crops can go a long way towards tackling hunger in the developing world. 'GM succeeds where conventional
30 breeding cannot,' states Sharma, 'because it can produce traits, such as disease resistance and drought tolerance,
that do not exist in its wild relatives.' Most crops are modified to be pest-, disease- or herbicide-resistant, and
include: soya, wheat, corn (maize), cotton, potatoes, peanuts, tomatoes, tobacco, peas, lettuce and onions among
others. In actual fact, the bacterial gene *Bt* is one of the most commonly inserted genes. It produces a poison that is
harmless to people, but kills insects. Some scientists insist that these insect-repelling crops reduce the biodiversity
35 of the environment by killing the insects that feed on these crops. Alternatively, advocates of GM crops say it helps
the environment as farmers need to use less pesticide – typically one or two sprays per harvest as opposed to three
or four sprays for conventional varieties. Moreover, they argue this makes GM crops not only cheaper but safer as it
reduces risks to farmers who need to have less contact with pesticides. Scientists have also found ways of improving
the nutritional value of crops by supplementing them with vitamins. Supporters of GM technology argue that
40 engineered crops – such as vitamin A-boosted golden rice or protein-enhanced potatoes – can keep people with poor
diets healthier. Furthermore, drought- or salt-resistant varieties can grow in poor conditions and fight world hunger.

E More general criticisms surrounding GM crops are about the balance of power between developed and developing
nations. On one hand, genetic modification of crops may offer the largest potential benefits to developing nations,
but on the other hand multinational companies control the use of these crops. Farmers worry that the agricultural
45 industry is creating monopolies. These agricultural companies have investigated technology protection systems. One
type, called *the Terminator system*, is a genetic trick that means GM crops do not produce fertile seeds. This prevents
the traditional practice of putting seeds aside from the crop to replant the following year and forces farmers to buy
new seed every year. Suman Sahai is the organiser of the anti-GM group Gene Campaign in New Delhi. She objects
to GM foods as she believes it will hand over control of India's food supply to multinational companies that are
50 motivated by profit rather than the best interests of farmers and consumers. 'Why gamble on a potentially dangerous
technology with economic risks', she questions 'when old-fashioned selective breeding has served so well?'

4 Read the passage again and complete the table. Use no more than three words.

Advantages of GM crops	Disadvantages of GM crops
1 can help _____ hunger	5 may have unpredicted _____ on people who eat GM food
2 it has characteristics like _____ and drought tolerance not found in the wild	6 modified plants could become _____ – already found in Canada
3 helps farmers reduce their _____ pesticides	7 they could accidentally breed with wild plants and _____ the environment
4 it can help people with _____ stay healthy	8 multinational companies _____ the crops

Language study: reporting verbs

5 Study the examples and explanation.

*Some scientists **insist** that these insect-repelling crops reduce the biodiversity of the environment*

We use reporting verbs to show different attitudes and ways of saying something.

urge – to say something strongly, *propose* – to put forward an idea, *claim* – to say something without proof

Common reporting verbs are ...

agree   argue   assert   believe   claim   concede   conclude   explain
maintain   point out   recommend   suggest   summarise

Now find words in the passage that mean ...

1 to give an opposite opinion to something (x2, paragraphs A and E)
2 to be afraid that something bad will happen (paragraph C)
3 to emphasise something (paragraph D)
4 to say something in a factual way (paragraph D)
5 to ask about the truth about something. (paragraph E)

6 Rewrite the sentences using the verbs in brackets.

1 The Consumer Council: 'We would like the government to listen to our proposals.' (recommend)
   The Consumer Council recommended that the government listened to their proposals.
2 The government: 'We are trying to have an independent assessment of food safety.' (claim)
3 The National Consumer Council: 'The government is not releasing important information.' (believe)
4 Dr Sahai: 'We could learn more about the effect of GM food with a longer medical trial.' (suggest)
5 The government: 'Dr Sahai is right.' (concede)

7 Work in pairs. Ask each other the questions.

1 Do you think GM foods are a positive or negative development? Why or why not?
2 Would you eat GM food? Why or why not?

8 Work in groups. Two students prepare arguments and examples for growing GM crops and food in developing countries. Two students prepare arguments and examples against growing GM crops and food in developing countries.

Now discuss the advantages and disadvantages of GM crops and food.

Speaking

❶ Tick the things we talk about when we describe a place to eat.

1 location ☐
2 prices ☐
3 menu ☐
4 heating ☐

5 type of food (vegetarian, French, Spanish, Chinese …) ☐
6 service ☐
7 the owner ☐

Now read the reviews and decide which place …

1 has the best discount
2 gives you as much food as you want
3 has good cakes
4 you would like to go to.

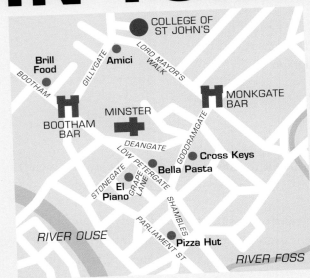

CHEAP EATING IN YORK

Bella Pasta
89 Low Petergate, 01904 611221

Italian food and a massive 50% student discount on food bills on Mondays for groups of 8 and over. Every day and night except Saturdays, 20% discount on food bill. This discount is only on food, not drinks.

Brill Food
3 Bootham, 01904 638822

Cheap and cheerful – this is the place to get a cheap sandwich or baked potato. All sandwiches and baked potatoes are 99p. Fillings include beans and cheese.

Cross Keys
34 Goodramgate, 01904 686941

In a great location for York St John students, Cross Keys has some fabulous cheap food. Get a burger and a drink for £4.75.

Pizza Hut
35 Parliament Street, 01904 644523

Pizza Hut deserve a mention for their All-You-Can-Eat lunchtime buffet with lots of different salads. At £4.95 it's a definite stomach-filler between 12 and 2.30 p.m.

Amici Espresso Bar
81 Gillygate

A great selection of sandwiches which are huge and very tasty. Gorgeous cakes too, but coffee is what this place is about. Really, really good coffee at amazingly low prices. Staff are great, really friendly and make you feel welcome. Great music, great people, great coffee.

El Piano
5 Grape Lane, 01904 610676

Imagine you had a Latin American mum – this is the food she would cook! Home-made, wholesome, tasty and filling, a good choice of food on the menu and not too expensive.

3.14 **❷ Listen to three conversations and decide which places are recommended.**

Pronunciation

3.15 **3** Listen and decide where the final sound is missing.

just past the gate   most things are under a pound
you don't need to go hungry   just around the corner
Friday and Saturday

3.15   Now listen again and practise.

4 Read the speaking test and underline the key words.

> **Part 1**
>
> *1 Who does the cooking at home?*
>
> *2 Can you cook? / Do you enjoy cooking?*
>
> *3 What's your favourite food / meal?*

Read the candidate task card. You have one minute to think about what you are going to say. You can make some notes to help you.

> **Part 2**
>
> **Describe a place to eat. You should say:**
>
> *– where it is and what it's like*
>
> *– what kind of food it serves*
>
> *– when was the last time you went there*
>
> *and explain why it is special for you.*

Rounding off questions
1 Would you recommend this place to your friends?
2 Do you think you will go there again?

Now work in pairs. Student A, you are the examiner; interview Student B with parts 1, 2 and 3. Student B, you are the candidate; answer the questions.

> **Part 3**
>
> **Let's consider food in the modern world.**
>
> *1 Do you think we worry too much about what we eat?*
>
> *2 Do you think meals still have an important social function?*
>
> **Finally, let's talk about food production.**
>
> *Do you think we should change crops genetically to feed the world?*

5 Change roles. Student B, you are the examiner; interview Student A. Student A, you are the candidate; answer the questions.

Writing

❶ Work in pairs. Ask each other the questions.

1 How often do you eat …
    meat and poultry?   fish?   dairy products?   vegetables only?

2 Are there any advantages of eating only vegetables?

3 Are many people vegetarian in your country?

❷ Put the sentences into groups.

A For vegetarianism   B Against vegetarianism

1 If it is wrong to eat animals, it is wrong to wear products from animals. _____ ☐

2 Killing animals for pleasure is wrong. _____ ☐

3 We do not need to eat animals. _____ ☐

4 People are free to choose to eat animals or not. _____ ☐

5 Keeping animals for food is an inefficient use of land. _____ ☐

6 Farm animals have a better life than wild animals. _____ ☐

7 Eating only vegetables is not healthy. _____ ☐

8 Plants are living things too. _____ ☐

9 Because we eat animals, we look after them. _____ ☐

10 Eating animals is natural. _____ ☐

11 Eating animals is not healthy. _____ ☐

12 Eating vegetables only is cheap. _____ ☐

Now read the essay and tick the points it includes.

Today many people are vegetarian of some sort of description, from people who eat mainly vegetables, along with dairy products such as milk, cheese and eggs, to vegans who do not eat animals or any animal products at all. In this essay I am briefly going to look at the arguments for and against eating meat. There are many reasons for and against eating animals and in this essay I am going to look at moral, health and environmental issues.

The first and foremost reason is that eating meat is murder. Some people think it is wrong to take the life of another creature for pleasure and as we can get the same proteins and nutrients from other food sources that we can get from eating meat, the only reason to eat meat is for pleasure. Alternatively, it could be argued that what we eat is a matter of personal choice according to how we feel and what suits our bodies best. Some people enjoy life more and feel healthier when they eat meat.

This brings me on to the second point: health issues. It is said that we can get all the nutrients from plants that we can get from meat. In other words, we can obtain the same proteins and nutrients from other food sources that we can get from eating meat: proteins from pulses like lentils and beans; calcium, protein and other vitamins from dairy products; vitamins, minerals and fibres from vegetables. However, plants on the whole are very poor sources of protein, especially protein containing amino acids. These are available in some plants, but not in great quantities. Conversely, there are plenty of proteins containing amino acids in milk, eggs and fish which is why many vegetarians still eat animal products.

Now let's look at the environmental issues. Perhaps the most serious reason for becoming vegetarian is ethical. People go hungry because a lot of land is used to grow food for animals rather than people.

For example, in the US, 157 million tons of food per year – all suitable for human consumption – is fed to animals. This produces just 28 million tons of animal protein in the form of meat. Then again, if we look at this more closely it is clear that millions of animals on farms are bred for food. To put it simply, if people became vegetarian there would be no need for these animals and we would have to kill them all. Rather than saving these animals, it would result in killing them instead of looking after them responsibly and killing them for a good purpose at the end of their natural life-cycle.

In conclusion, I believe that it is everyone's right to eat what they want. However, cutting down on the amount of meat we eat has benefits for our health and our environment and is fairer to other animals.

3 Choose the title of the essay.

1	**Write about the following topic:** *Worrying about diets and farming methods is a luxury that people in rich nations have. Developing nations have different but equally important priorities. To what extent do you agree or disagree with this opinion?* **Give reasons for your answer and include any relevant examples from your own knowledge or experience.**
2	**Write about the following topic:** *Many people go on diets in order to control their weight. However, people on diets only put on weight again as soon as they have finished. Do you think the benefits of diets outweigh the disadvantages?* **Give reasons for your answer and include any relevant examples from your own knowledge or experience.**
3	**Write about the following topic:** *The decision to eat vegetables, instead of meat, is morally and ethically correct. Do you think the benefits of vegetarianism outweigh the disadvantages?* **Give reasons for your answer and include any relevant examples from your own knowledge or experience.**

Language study: rephrasing and giving alternatives

4 Study the examples and explanations.

> *In other words, we can obtain the same proteins and nutrients from other food sources*
> **We use these words and phrases to express the same idea in a different way.**
>
> *Again, if we look at this more closely …*   *Alternatively, it could be argued that …*
> **We use these words and phrases to express another point of view.**

rephrasing	*in other words*	
	to put it differently	
	to look at it from another	*angle / perspective / point of view*
giving alternatives	*alternatively* *(then) again* *rather (than)*	

Now read the passage again and find one more way of repeating an idea and two more ways of giving an alternative idea.

5 Work in pairs. Ask each other the questions.

1 Which point of view do you agree with?
2 Would you like to be vegetarian?
3 Are there any difficulties being vegetarian in your country?

Now choose a title from activity 3 and present a written argument or case to an educated reader with no specialist knowledge of the topic (minimum 250 words).

Our earth

Changing climate

❶ Work in pairs. Describe the picture and discuss how it happened.

Now look at pictures A – C and discuss the relationship between them.

3.16 ❷ Listen to the news reports and match them with the pictures.

3.17 ❸ Listen to a conversation and choose A – C.

1 Karl has a …
   A high temperature.   B sore head.   C heavy cold.
2 This summer may become the _____ summer on record.
   A hottest   B second hottest   C third hottest
3 Firefighters been attempting to control forest fires for _____ days.
   A three   B five   C seven
4 Some glaciers have been melting _____ times faster than usual.
   A five   B ten   C fifteen
5 Ocean temperatures have been increasing over the last _____ decades.
   A two   B three   C four
6 Monica thinks that global warming is a result of _____
   A nature.   B human activities.   C both nature and human activities.
7 She saw the poster in the _____
   A refectory.   B student union.   C sports hall.

Express yourself: talking about the weather

3.18   Listen and mark the stress in the sentences.

This heat is really getting to me.   It's almost too much.
Just look at the weather!   It's absolutely boiling!   I can't stand it.
It's a real scorcher.

3.18   Now listen again and practise.

3.17 Now listen again. Match the words in A with the statements. You may use each word more than once.

1 Fields have been turning yellow in _____ .
2 Fire fighters have been tackling forest fires in _____ .
3 Rivers have been drying up in _____ .
4 Many heat-related deaths have occurred in _____ .
5 Glaciers have been retreating in _____ , _____ and _____ .
6 Serious droughts have been happening in _____ and _____ .

A China
France
India
Italy
Switzerland

4 Complete the summary. Choose from the words in B.

Studies of the world's oceans indicate that our planet is heating up. Climate models based on the temperatures of the world's oceans are thought to be more reliable compared with those based on (1) _____ temperatures. Some scientists claim global warming can be explained by natural phenomena such as changes in (2) _____ activity, (3) _____ eruptions and variable changes in the (4) _____ . However, many others disagree, claiming that the only possible explanation is the increase in (5) _____ emissions caused by human activity.

B volcanic
solar
heat
greenhouse
earthquake
climate
atmospheric

Language study: phrasal verbs (2)

5 Study the examples and the explanation.

> *it may **turn out** to be the third hottest summer*   *trying to **put** all those fires **out***
> We can put an object between the two parts of some phrasal verbs (transitive phrasal verbs), especially when the object is a pronoun. Other phrasal verbs are intransitive and cannot take an object between the two parts.

Now put the phrasal verbs in C into groups.

1 transitive   2 intransitive

C bring down
cut down
dry up
go up
use up
turn out
come down

6 Correct the incorrect sentences.

1 We can all take steps to stop climate change by cutting on the amount of energy down we use.
2 The 1990s is turning to be one of the hottest decades out in the twentieth century.
3 Scientists say that flooding will increase. It will go during the next few decades up.
4 The Kyoto agreement aims to bring greenhouse gases down within the next few years.
5 We can save water by taking a shower because it less uses water up.
6 During one recent heat wave in Europe, fields turned yellow and dried up completely.
7 It was several months before temperatures came it down again.

7 Work in pairs. Discuss the questions.

1 Do you think climate change is a real thing? Why or why not?
2 What could be the causes of climate change?
3 Have you noticed any effects of the changing climate in your country? If so, what are they?

Reading

1 Work in pairs. Look at the cartoon and discuss what it means.

2 Label the pictures with the words in D.

D savannah
coral reef
wetlands
estuary

1 _____

2 _____

3 _____

4 _____

E living on
borrowed time
take something
for granted
living beyond
their means

Now match the expressions in E with the meanings.

1 someone who does this is spending more than they can afford

2 a person who has a limited amount of time is said to be …

3 if you do this, you are not thankful for what you have been given

3 Read the title of the passage and the expressions in activity 2 and think of three points the passage may contain.

Now read the passage and check your answers.

4 Read the passage again and answer the questions.

1 Which five habitats under threat are mentioned?

2 Which two diseases are linked to cutting down forests?

3 Which three business services are supplied by nature?

4 Which three rivers are dried out for part of each year?

5 What is responsible for the reduction of fish in the Black Sea?

6 Which two actions to help save the environment does the report call for?

Now complete the summary. Use no more than three words from the passage for each answer.

Over the last half a century, people have used too much of the world's resources. Natural environments like forests that (1) _____ air and water are being damaged. Due to human demand for food and fuel, more land is used for (2) _____ now than in previous centuries. A team of (3) _____ valued natures free services at $33 trillion. Changes in the ecosystem led to a quarter of animals and nearly a third of amphibians coming under the threat of (4) _____ . A scientific report has put forward a suggestions for protecting ecosystems by asking governments to treat them like (5) _____ systems.

USING UP THE WORLD'S RESOURCES

Humans have destroyed two thirds of nature's machinery that supports life

A The human race is living beyond its means. A report backed up by 1,360 scientists from 95 countries – some of them world leaders in their fields – has warned that almost two-thirds of the natural machinery that supports life on earth is being destroyed by human pressure. Over the past fifty years, it reports, the human race has drawn down heavily on the Earth's natural resources – so much so, in fact, that our planet is in danger of becoming
5 'overdrawn', leaving future generations to pay an environmental debt that will reverse all the best efforts to lift the poor out of poverty. The report contains what its authors call a *stark warning* for the entire world. The wetlands, forests, savannahs, estuaries and other habitats that recycle air, water and nutrients for living creatures are being irretrievably damaged. In effect, one species is now a hazard to the other 10 million on the planet, and to itself.

B 10 'Human activity is putting such a strain on the natural functions of Earth that the ability of the planet's ecosystems to sustain and keep up with the demands of future generations can no longer be taken for granted', it says. The report, prepared in Washington, issues a series of bleak warnings in respect of land and water resources. Due to human demand for food, fresh water, timber and fuel, more land has been claimed for agriculture in the past 60 years than in the eighteenth and nineteenth centuries combined. An estimated 24% of
15 the Earth's land surface is now farmed. Furthermore, the amount of water drawn out of lakes and rivers has doubled in the past 40 years. Humans now use between 40% and 50% of all available fresh water running off the land. At least a quarter of all fish stocks are over-harvested. In some areas the catch is now less than one hundredth of that before industrial fishing. Since 1980 about 20% of the world's coral reefs have been destroyed and another 20% badly damaged. Deforestation and other changes could increase the risks of malaria and
20 cholera and open the way for new and so far unknown disease to emerge.

C A few years ago, a team of biologists and economists tried to put a value on the *business services* given away by nature – the free pollination of crops, the air conditioning provided by wild plants and recycling by the oceans. What would the cost be if these services were put up for sale? The team came up with an estimate of $33 trillion, almost twice the global gross national product for that year. But after what the new report, Millennium
25 Ecosystem Assessment, calls an *unprecedented period of running down Earth's natural resources*, it was time to check the accounts. The scientists warn, 'In many cases it is literally a matter of living on borrowed time.'

D Flow from rivers has fallen back dramatically. For parts of the year, the Yellow River in China, the Nile in Africa, and the Colorado in North America dry up before they reach the ocean. An estimated 90% of the total weight of the ocean's large predators – tuna, swordfish and sharks – has been wiped out in recent years. An estimated
30 12% of bird species, 25% of mammals and more than 30% of all amphibians are threatened with extinction and may die out within the next century. Some of them are threatened by invaders. The Baltic Sea is now home to 100 creatures from other parts of the world, a third of them native to the Great Lakes of America. Conversely, a third of the 170 alien species in the Great Lakes are originally from the Baltic. Invaders can make dramatic changes: the arrival of the American comb jellyfish in the Black Sea led to the destruction of 26 commercially
35 important stocks of fish. Global warming and climate change could make it increasingly difficult for the surviving species to adapt.

E However, nature, the scientists warn, is not something to be enjoyed at the weekend. Conservation of natural spaces is not just a luxury. 'These are dangerous illusions that ignore the vast benefits of nature to the lives of six billion people on the planet. We may have distanced ourselves from nature, but we rely completely on the
40 services it delivers'. So the question remains as to what is to be done. The report puts forward some suggestions for protecting the remaining ecosystems. For example, it calls on governments to include environmental indicators in a country's national accounts, treating ecosystems as vital as education or health infrastructures. However, perhaps most importantly, it calls for the need for global action to at least preserve what we have now. Technology and voluntary life change will not be enough to make up for what the Earth has already lost.

5 Find words in the passage which mean ...

1 something dangerous and likely to cause damage (paragraph A)
2 the plants, animals and people living in an area together with their surroundings, such as earth and weather (paragraph B)
3 the cutting down of trees in large areas and the destruction of forests (paragraph B)
4 never having happened or existed in the past (paragraph C)
5 to change in order to cope with different conditions (paragraph D)
6 to not think about something or pretend that you have not noticed someone or something. (paragraph E)

Language study: phrasal verbs (3) – multi-word verbs

6 Study the examples and explanations.

> They **came up with** an estimate of $33 trillion ...
> Multi-word verbs are made up of verb + adverb + preposition. These verbs take an object. We cannot put the object between the parts of the verb.
>
> the human race has **drawn down** heavily **on** the Earth's natural resources
> With some multi-word verbs, we can put an adverb between the adverb and preposition, but not between the preposition and object.

Now choose one of the verbs in brackets. Complete the sentences using the correct form of the verb.

A few years ago a group of scientists attempted to estimate the value of this contribution by nature. They (1) _____ (draw out of / come up with) a figure of 33 trillion dollars. Their report explained that we have been (2) _____ (draw down on / put up with) Earth's resources to such an extent that our planet may not be able to (3) _____ (keep up with / come up with) the demands placed on it by generations in future. It also warns that it may be too late to (4) _____ (keep up with / make up for) the harm already done to our ecosystems.

7 Work in pairs. Discuss the questions.

1 How would including the ecosystem in a country's accounts help?
2 What global action needs to be taken to help the environment?

Listening

IELTS tasks:
multiple-choice questions;
note completion

The roof of the world – the Himalayan mountains

How much do you know about the highest region in the world? Try this quiz and find out.

1 How many countries does the Himalaya mountain range cross?   A 3   B 5   C 7

2 Siachen, Gangotri, Yamunotri are all …   A glaciers.   B mountains.   C rivers.

3 The Himalayan range contains _____ out of the ten highest mountains in the world.
A five   B seven   C nine

4 The three highest mountains in the world are …
A Everest, K2, Kanchenjunga.   B Everest, Mount Blanc, Kanchenjunga.   C Everest, Kilimanjaro, Kanchenjunga.

5 The _____ rivers begin in the Himalayan mountains.
A Ganges, Yellow and Indus   B Ganges, Mekong and Indus   C Ganges, Euphrates and Indus

❶ Answer the quiz.

Now turn to assignment 11.1 and check your answers.

❷ Listen to a talk and match 1 – 7 with A – G.

3.19

1	rivers from the Himalayas	A 0.06°C
2	glacier melt rate	B 1.4 – 5.8°C
3	average temperature rise of Nepal	C 13%
4	rivers experiencing loss of water flow	D seven
5	Earth's average temperature increase in 2100	E three
6	number of extinct animal and plant species	F 10 – 15 metres per year
7	reduction in CO_2 by making less car journeys	G 1 million

3.19   Now listen again and complete the notes.

The Himalayas feeds several great Asian (1) _____ , including the *Mekong*. Two extreme weather conditions caused by glacier melt include (2) _____ and (3) _____ . People who inhabit flood (4) _____ are most at risk from rising water levels. Farmers in the Himalayas depend on (5) _____ from these rivers in order to successfully cultivate their crops. Some snow-fed rivers have been experiencing decreases in water (6) _____ . Rising water levels in Qinghai have affected habitats such as rivers, (7) _____ and (8) _____ . The *Gangotri* glacier has been (9) _____ by 23 metres every year. Animal species at risk of extinction include the polar bear, (10) _____ and (11) _____ . The role of government should include promoting cleaner (12) _____ and following the requirements of (13) _____ . Individuals can save energy by avoiding unnecessary car journeys, (14) _____ and ensuring the safe disposal of (15) _____ in the home.

Pronunciation

3.20 **3** Listen and notice how we say the symbol and numbers.

1.4 – 5.8°C   0.06°C   13%   10 – 15 metres per year   2050   1 in 10   2100 CO_2

3.20   Now listen again and practise.

Language study: future continuous and future perfect

4 Study the examples and explanations.

> *two thirds of the world's people **will be living** in areas of acute water stress by 2025.*
> **We use the future continuous to talk about a period of time in the future and to refer to an action or event that is the result of an earlier action or event – in this case global warming.**
>
> *scientists have predicted that 1 in 10 animals and plants **will have become** extinct by 2050.*
> **We use the future perfect to talk about an action or event in the future that we believe will be finished at a point in the future.**

Now complete the sentences. Use the correct form of the words in brackets.

1   Scientists estimate that more than one million species _____ (die out) by 2050.

2   As the problem of global warming gets worse, two billion people_____ (live) in water scarce countries within the next few decades.

3   Climatologists predict that by 2100, the Earth's average temperature _____ (rise) by six degrees.

4   By 2015 we _____ clean ways of generating electricity. (invent)

5   After the geography lecture tomorrow, I _____ Prof Thomson between 10 and 11 about my essay. (see)

6   If we look at this chart, we can see that by 2050 we still _____ enough to prevent the desert expanding southwards. (not do)

5 Work in pairs. Ask each other the questions.

1   What did you find interesting or surprising about the talk?

2   Do you think the world will have found answers to global warming by 2050?

3   What will you be doing this time next year?

4   What will you have achieved in the next two years?

Writing

IELTS tasks: discursive essay – cohesion

❶ Read the essay titles and underline the key words.

1 | **Write about the following topic:**
Climate change is entirely caused by human activity. It is therefore the responsibility of all individuals to take action to save the planet from complete destruction. To what extent do you agree or disagree with this statement?
Give reasons for your answer and include any relevant examples from your own knowledge or experience.

2 | **Write about the following topic:**
Climate change has damaged the planet beyond repair. It is too late to save it from complete destruction. To what extent do you agree or disagree with this statement?
Give reasons for your answer and include any relevant examples from your own knowledge or experience.

Now read the essay and decide which title it answers.

A There is certainly a great deal of evidence to support the view that global warming is a result of the build-up of greenhouse gases caused by human activities. In this essay I will look briefly at the scientific debate surrounding **its** causes and, perhaps more importantly, consider what action we can take to slow the process down.

B Climate change has been happening since the late 19th century, but has increased significantly since **then**. The world's oceans are steadily warming up and ice is melting at the north and south poles and mountain glaciers. Furthermore, scientists have demonstrated a clear link between man-made greenhouse gases and global warming. **This** finding clearly has serious implications for both human beings and animals alike. One outcome for humans will presumably be drought in areas where major water sources are fed by snow or glacial melt. For example, **those** who depend on river water are likely to be left without adequate water supplies during the summer. For animal and plant species **such** consequences are undoubtedly even more serious. Animals like polar bears face extinction if **their** natural habitats continue to disappear. Some scientists, however, dispute the view that global warming is man-made. **They** claim that it can probably be explained by natural phenomena, such as changes in solar activity or variable changes in our climate.

C I personally believe that the problem has largely been caused by human activity. Frankly, it is our responsibility to reduce greenhouse gas emissions, such as switching to technologies that produce little or none of **them**. We can obviously also make lifestyle changes such as reducing the number of car journeys and recycling our household rubbish. **These** small changes, surprisingly enough, can slow down the pace of global warming if we make the effort to do **them**. They can also increase the pace of global warming if we **do not**.

D In conclusion, I agree with the statement that global warming is caused by human activity. It will change our way of life for the worse in future if we do not make changes in the way we live now. If we continue to ignore the threat, we will surely regret it.

❷ Match the paragraphs with the sentences.

1 The student gives the argument for the statement then gives the other point of view.
2 The student develops the argument giving examples agreeing with statement.
3 The student provides a short concluding paragraph.
4 The student refers to the question and generally agrees with the statement.

Language study: adverbs of certainty and attitude

3 Study the examples and explanations.

> *There is **certainly** a great deal of evidence to support the view ...*
> We use words like *certainly, evidently, probably, obviously, likely, clearly, undoubtedly, perhaps* and *presumably* to talk about how certain we are about something.
>
> *I **personally** believe that the problem has largely been caused by human activity.*
> We use words like *personally, honestly, in truth* and *frankly* to introduce our personal opinion or attitude to a situation or topic.

Now write the sentences again using an adverb of certainty.

1 Increasing world temperatures are linked to pollution from CO_2.
2 Less developed countries will feel the effects of climate change more than developed countries.
3 There will be more extreme weather as the world gets warmer.
4 Volcanoes are responsible in part for climate change.

4 Write the sentences in activity 3 again with a personal opinion and an adverb of attitude.

Language study: cohesion

5 Study the examples and explanations.

> ***They** claim that **it** can probably be explained by natural phenomena,*
> We use words for cohesion to refer back to information in a piece of writing in order not to repeat information and to guide the reader through our argument. We use words like *he, she, it, they, this, that, these* to refer back to people and things.
>
> *has increased significantly since **then***
> We use *then* for time and *there* for places.
>
> *They can also increase the pace of global warming if we **do not**.*
> We refer back to verbs using auxiliary verbs like *are, do, can* and *have*.

Now match the words in bold in activity 2 with 1 – 11.

1 small changes to fight global warming   _____

2 global warming   _____

3 greenhouse gases   _____

4 effects of global warming   _____

5 practical ways to tackle global warming   _____

6 scientists   _____

7 human beings   _____

8 ignoring the problem   _____

9 animals   _____

10 the 19th century   _____

11 make the effort to make small changes   _____

6 **Delete the underlined information or replace it. Use these words.**

this   these   it   us   they (x2)

Researchers have claimed that global warming is due as much to cosmic rays as CO_2 emissions from man. CO_2 emissions come from burning fossil fuels. Cosmic rays are rays which are emitted from explosions deep in space.

5 Cosmic rays are thought to have an effect on cloud formation – when cosmic rays hit the atmosphere, clouds are formed. Clouds are important in keeping the earth cools as clouds reflect the sun's energy back into space. Clouds reflecting the sun's energy keeps the earth cool. The number of cosmic

10 rays hitting the earth depends upon the sun's magnetic field. When the sun's magnetic field is weak, at this time more cosmic rays hit the earth and we get more cloud. When the sun's magnetic field is strong, fewer cosmic rays hit the earth and less cloud is formed above the earth. Fewer clouds

15 mean that more of the sun's energy hits the earth and temperatures on the earth increase.

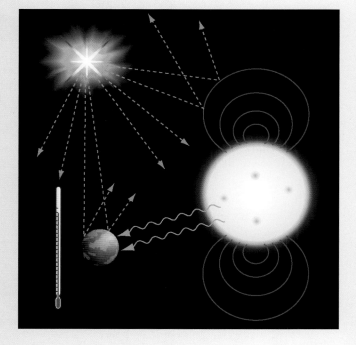

Achieve IELTS: timed writing

Practise for the writing test by giving yourself time limits and practising test questions. For writing test task 1 you should spend about 20 minutes, for writing test task 2 you should spend about 40 minutes. Make sure you timetable your timed writing sessions, are not disturbed and have no distractions during this period.

7 **Write about the topic for the other essay title in activity 1. You have 40 minutes.**

Speaking

1 Match 1 – 5 with pictures A – E.

1 buy second-hand goods
2 cycle or walk whenever possible
3 use radiator panels to reduce heat loss
4 reuse plastic bags
5 put a *hippo* bag in the cistern to save water

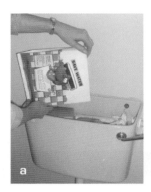
a

b

c

d

e

3.21 **2** Listen to the conversation and complete the table for Monica and Karl.

	You	Monica	Karl	Your partner
1 What things in activity 1 do you already do to help the environment?				
2 What things in activity 1 would you like to try in future?				
3 Is there a link between our health and the environment?				

Now answer the questions for yourself.

Express yourself: interrupting and continuing

Read the expressions and put them into groups.

Anyway, as I was saying …   Can I just stop you there for a second?
Can I butt in here?   Could I interrupt you there?
I was just about to explain what that is …   I was just about to talk about that …
Now, where was I?

1 interrupting someone
2 continuing

3.22 Now listen and practise.

Achieve IELTS: interrupting

At the end of part 2, the examiner may interrupt and stop you at the end of two minutes. This is a normal part of the test and does not mean that you have done badly. You should not interrupt the examiner, however.

3 Work in pairs. Ask each other the questions in 2 and complete the table for your partner.

4 Read parts 1, 2 and 3. Decide what the topic is about.

Part 1: Introduction

1 *What kind of place do you live in?*
2 *What do you like most and least about it?*
3 *What is the weather like there in summer?*
4 *When is the best time of year to visit it?*

Part 2

Talk about an environmental issue you have read about or heard about.

You should say:
– *what happened*
– *where it happened*
– *how you felt about it*
and explain why you think the issue is important.

Rounding off questions

1 What do you do to help the environment?
2 Which environmental issues are young people most interested in?
3 What is the most serious environmental issue in the world at the moment?

Part 3

Let's consider how attitudes towards the environment have changed.

1 *What do young people learn about the environment at school in your country?*
2 *Why is it important for people to become more aware of environmental issues nowadays?*
3 *Do you think that it is the responsibility of governments to tackle environmental problems? If so, how?*
4 *What can be done to encourage more people to take an interest in the environment?*

Finally, let's talk about how people might live in future.

1 *Do you think there is an ideal environment for people to live in? What is it?*
2 *Do you think that green living will become more common in future? Why or why not?*
3 *Do you think that green living may help people live longer in future?*

Now make notes on part 2.

5 Work in pairs. Student A, you are the examiner; interview Student B. Student B you are the candidate; answer the questions.

Now change roles. Student B, you are the examiner; interview Student A. Student A, you are the candidate; answer the questions.

Graduate

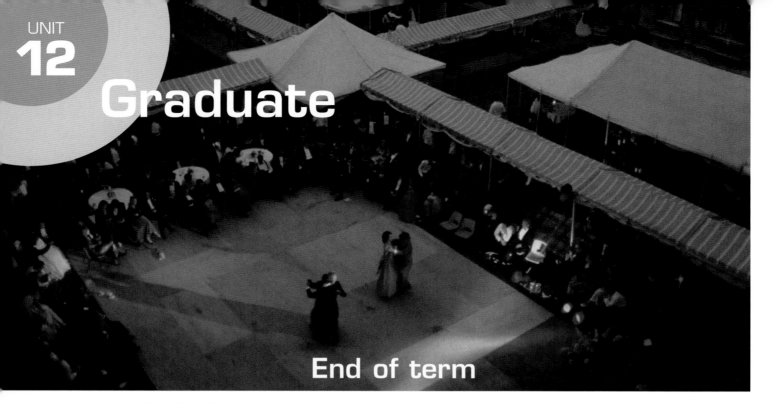

End of term

A a get-together
a fancy dress /
   costume party
a dinner party
a ball
a cocktail party
a garden party

**MODERN LANGUAGES
END OF TERM PARTY**

❖ ❖ ❖

in Harrington's Bar
Kick off at 8pm – till late
byob
snacks provided

❖ ❖ ❖

RSVP

1 **Label the picture. Choose from the words in A.**

Now work in pairs. Ask each other the questions.

1 Which of the items in A (a) are formal, (b) are informal, (c) can be formal or informal?
2 Do you like parties? Why or why not?
3 Have you ever been to a fancy dress / cocktail / dinner party?
4 When was the last party you went to? What happened?

2 **Read the invitation and match the words and abbreviations with the meanings.**

1 Please reply   4 Finishing late
2 Bring your own drink   5 Small things to eat
3 Start

3.23 **3** **Listen to a conversation and tick the topics the students talk about.**

1 What they did after the tests.   ☐
2 How they felt before the tests.   ☐
3 The music at the party.   ☐
4 How they prepared for the exams.   ☐
5 What they plan to do after the course. ☐
6 The graduation ceremony.   ☐

B attitude
cram
distinction
exception
panic

Now match the words in B with the meanings.

1 someone or something that is different from other people or things and cannot be included in a general statement
2 a very high mark in an examination
3 try to learn as much as possible in a short time
4 a strong feeling of nervousness that stops people thinking clearly
5 how you think and feel about something

Express yourself: talking about studying

Match the phrases with the meanings.

it really cleared my mind   I really knew it inside out   I didn't lift a finger.
if you don't know it by now, you never will   stay on top of things

1 to know a subject very well
2 it helped me think
3 to not do any work
4 if you do not understand a subject after a period of time, you will not be able to understand it at all
5 to keep up with your studies, work or be in control of a difficult situation

3.24 **Now listen and practise.**

4 **Match the people with the exam techniques.**

1 Tomas   a did relaxation activities
2 Michie   b revised and practised alone and with friends
3 Marta   c crammed for the exam
4 other students d studied throughout the year

3.23 **Now listen again and write true (T) or false (F).**

1 Michie thought the tests were not fair. _____
2 Marta was a bit frightened when she saw the exam timetable. _____
3 Michie studied better after doing breathing activities. _____
4 Tomas thinks students can cram three years into three weeks. _____
5 Tomas believes that the examiner is trying to get the best from the candidates.
_____

5 **Work in pairs. Decide which test preparation activities are most and least helpful.**

 1 write test questions yourself
 2 form groups to practise speaking and listening
 3 stop any part-time jobs
 4 do relaxation activities
 5 do practice exam papers
 6 practise speaking by talking to yourself
 7 cram
 8 watch / listen to programmes in English
 9 read magazines and newspapers in English
10 translate articles from your language to English
11 read the dictionary and memorise as many words as possible

Now ask each other the questions.

1 What was the last test or exam you took?
2 How do you feel about taking exams?
3 How do you prepare for exams?

Reading

C loyalty to company
smart dress
independence
free-agent
creative
separate hours for
home and office
experience is important
opportunity is better
than money

❶ Put the words and phrases in C into groups.

1 old work style
2 new work style

Now work in pairs. Say which work style suits you.

❷ Read the passage. Do the statements reflect the claims of the writer? Write ...
YES if the statement reflects the claims of the writer.
NO if the statement contradicts the claims of the writer.
NOT GIVEN if it is impossible to say what the writer thinks about this.

1 The number of older workers in companies will decline.
2 The Internet is the most important development since the industrial revolution.
3 Company structures are now based on ability, not length of employment.
4 Older people are behaving more like young people.
5 At *Microsoft*, managers watch their workers carefully.
6 Older workers are better at social skills than younger workers.
7 Managers at *Microsoft* become managers because they did not want to work long hours anymore.

Now read the passage again and complete the summary. Use no more than three words or a number.

In today's workplace (1) _____ and work are becoming mixed and older workers are losing power in their companies. The most important reason for this is (2) _____ which has allowed (3) _____ to enter the workplace and make changes. A second reason was the changes made to company (4) _____ in the 80s and 90s which emphasised (5) _____ over seniority. The final reason is that values have changed. Today's workers want opportunity more than (6) _____ . Another effect is that older people are behaving like younger people with society's average age between (7) _____ in some US cities. At *Microsoft* the manager's role is not to give workers orders but to (8) _____ from their way and help them discover (9) _____ to business problems.

YOUTH WORKS

As the pace of today's working life blurs the line between personal time and work time, so it increasingly mixes personal lifestyle and work style. And as companies concentrate on attracting and keeping a younger workforce for its technical skills and enthusiasm for change, office culture is becoming an extension of youth culture. This may be no bad thing. Along with the company games room come things that matter deeply to
5 young people: opportunity, responsibility, respect. For most of human history the middle-aged have ruled. With years came wisdom, experience, connections and influence. Rarely did they change jobs, years of loyal service counted most. However, in the future, older workers will not disappear, or even reduce in numbers, but they will have to share power with fresh-faced youths.

There have been a number of reasons for this change; the most dramatic of these is technology. Children have
10 always been more expert than their parents at something, but usually a game or a fashion, not the century's most important business tool. The Internet has triggered the first industrial revolution in history to be led by the young. This is the age group that created *Netscape*, the first commercial web browser; *Napster*, the music-sharing technology that shocked the music industry; *Yahoo!* and many of the other web giants. Though there have been youth revolutions before, none of them made the leap from teen bedroom to boardroom the way
15 the Internet has. Throughout the twentieth century, had a young person wanted to enter corporate America they needed to leave their youth behind. They got a haircut, and probably a suit or at least a tie. Now the same hair, same clothes, even nearly the same hours apply to office and home.

Had it not been for the Internet, this change could not have happened. However, it did not happen because of the Internet only, the corporate restructurings of the 1980s and 90s broke down traditional hierarchies. In
20 many companies, rigid seniority-based hierarchies have given way to hierarchies based on merit. No longer are the abilities to navigate internal bureaucracies and please your superiors the most valued skills. Today's employees are free agents who stay with companies only as long as they feel challenged and rewarded; moving from job to job is now a sign of ambition and initiative. Today's young people are valued as workers for different reasons than their predecessors: they welcome change; they think differently; they are
25 independent; they are entrepreneurial; they want opportunity more than money and security and finally, they demand respect.

This revolution is not just about the young. Youth itself is being redefined. Increasingly, 35-year-olds listen to the same music as 20-year-olds, dress like them and even look almost like them. Never before has there been a time when there was so little difference between age groups. Imagine a society converging on an age
30 somewhere between 20 and 30, and you have a fair picture of New York or San Francisco now, with other American cities not far behind.

The rise of the young is a good thing, not least because it gives people at their most creative stage in life more opportunity to put their ideas and energy into practice. But will there be a takeover by the young? A good place to look for an answer is *Microsoft*. *Microsoft's* most important employees are not its managers,
35 but individual programmers. They have great independence in choosing how to do their job. By and large, the managers' task is not to tell the programmers what to do, but to clear obstacles from the path they choose. *Microsoft* workers are valued most for their ability to think for themselves, they are trusted to find their own solutions to business problems. Managers hold back, knowing that the more specific their order, the more it is likely to undermine their employees' ability to find creative solutions. So they concentrate on the diplomatic
40 tasks that most of the independent young programmers are not much good at: co-ordinating with other teams, resolving conflicts, motivating people and ensuring that everybody is happy. *Microsoft* starts to look like a model for the workplace of the future: programmers tend to be in their twenties and early thirties, whereas the managers are about a decade older. Many of the managers are former programmers who reached a point where they no longer wanted to sleep under their desk. The effect of all this is that youth and youth
45 qualities apparently dominate, but the experience and maturity of older employees is put to good use too.

D boardroom
hierarchy
initiative
restructuring
seniority

3 Read the passage again and match the words in D with the meanings.

1 a way of organising things according to position and status
2 a place where company directors have meetings
3 to organise something in a different way so that it works better
4 the ability to take decisions independently
5 a social position or position in a company that is more important than others

Language study: inversion

4 Study the examples and explanations.

technology **is** *the most dramatic of these* ➤ *the most dramatic of these* **is technology**

    subject verb   verb subject

> When we put the verb before the subject we call this *inversion*. We use inversion in formal academic writing to focus on the important information in a sentence.

Rarely did *they change jobs …*   ***No longer are*** *the abilities to navigate internal bureaucracies and please your superiors the most valued skills.*

> We often use inversion after negative adverbs and with expressions with *no.*

Rarely Seldom Never before	**did** they change jobs.
Never … Hardly …	**has** there been a time (**when**) …
No longer Under no circumstances At no time	**are** students allowed to eat in lectures.

If it had not been for the Internet, this change could not have happened. ➤
Had it not been *for the Internet, this change could not have happened.*

> We can use inversion with conditional sentences. With negatives we use the full form, not contractions.

Now write the sentences again beginning the sentence with the word(s) in brackets.

1 Businessmen in Britain do not wear shorts and T-shirts at work very often. (rarely)
2 I don't see my manager very often. (seldom)
3 If William hadn't left university, he wouldn't have founded his software company. (had)
4 Employees are not allowed to use the Internet at work. (at no time)
5 As soon as Miki joined the company, she asked for a pay rise. (hardly … when)

5 Work in pairs. Discuss the questions.

1 Which companies in your country work like Microsoft?
2 Which kinds of jobs can this work style apply to?
3 What are the disadvantages in letting young people run companies?
4 Are people 'becoming younger' in your country? In what ways?

Listening

1 Match the words in E with the picture.

2 Complete the form with the words in F.

E cap _____
gown _____
hood _____
degree _____

F procession
announcements
address
assembly

ORDER OF PROCEEDINGS
- (1) _____ outside Main Hall
- members of the congregation stand as soon as candidates enter the Hall
- procession
- (2) _____
- degree ceremony
- (3) _____ by Vice-Chancellor
- (4) _____ out of Hall

3.25 **3** Listen to a conversation and complete the table.

	Marta	Michie	Tomas
was nervous before the ceremony			
imagined falling over	✓		
thought graduation was enjoyable			✓
saw his / her parents during the procession			
kept looking at the person in front			
was relieved when it finished		✓	

4 Put the words in G in groups.

1 positive feelings:
_____ ☐, _____ ☐, _____ ☐, _____ ☐

2 negative feelings:
_____ ☐, _____ ☐, _____ ☐, _____ ☐

G relaxed
frustrated
panicky
wound up
excited
interested
petrified
delighted

3.25 Now listen again and tick the words you hear.

3.25 **5** Listen again and choose A – C.

1 Before the ceremony, during the assembly Marta …
A couldn't walk through the Main Hall.
B couldn't speak to anybody.
C thought about her friends at home.

2 Michie thought Andras looked …
A cool.   B stressed and tense.   C relaxed and happy.

3 The Vice-Chancellor …
A wanted to finish quickly.
B liked the speeches.
C spoke for a long time.

4 Michie … when she got to the stage.
A nearly cried   B smiled at her tutor   C felt panicky

Express yourself: talking about feelings

Read the expressions and decide which are positive, negative or neutral.

*I nearly burst into tears   it was such a relief   I had butterflies in my stomach
I was shaking like a leaf   I was so wound up ... I couldn't speak
they were smiling from ear to ear   I had mixed feelings*

3.26   **Now listen and practise.**

Language study: adjectives for people and things

6 **Study the examples and explanations.**

*I **enjoyed** it   I thought it was just very **enjoyable***
*I got a bit **bored**   it was **boring***
*I was **petrified**.   standing up in front of all those people was **petrifying***

We use adjective –*ed* for people's feelings and adjective –*ing*, –*able* and –*ful*
for things.

*I was **so** wound up ... I **couldn't** speak*

We use *so* adjective + (*that*) + verb to talk about the effect of our feelings.

Now correct the sentences.

1 I'm pleasing that's over, it was the most uninterested speech I ever heard.
2 Oh dear, Maria looks exhausting after that test.
3 Thanks for the great party, it was really excited to meet all those new and
   interested people.
4 Jonathon was that angry he was late so he nearly kicked the taxi.
5 The graduation ceremony was delighted, it was wonderful to be invited.

7 **Work in pairs. Talk about an important occasion you went to, when it took
place, what happened and how you felt.**

8 **Work in pairs. Decide which things are good job interview techniques and
which are bad.**

1 have a positive attitude
2 ask the interviewer to repeat a question if you do not understand it
3 criticise previous employers
4 do research about the job and company
5 repeat phrases like *you know*
6 tell the interviewer what you think they want to hear
7 talk as much as you can to avoid silence during the interview

**Now work in pairs. Describe the last interview you had, when it was, what
you discussed and if you were successful.**

3.27 🔟 **Listen to a talk and match 1 – 6 with A – H.**

1 traditional interview
2 behavioural interview
3 case-study interview
4 warm-up
5 information exchange
6 conclusion

A a strategic conversation
B talk about the future of the company
C get facts from the candidate
D to show a candidate's intelligence
E show a candidate's skills
F an opportunity to repeat interest in the job
G ask the candidate common-ground questions
H show a candidate solves problems.

Achieve IELTS: listening and note-taking

When a question asks you to complete notes or a sentence ...

1 make sure you know how many words you have to complete the question – you will lose marks if you go over the word limit.

2 quickly read the title and the notes. Try to think what you already know about the topic – this will help you understand the listening passage. Try to predict what information may complete the notes.

3 listen carefully to the beginning of each section – you will hear a description of the situation you hear in the listening passage.

4 check your spelling and grammar where necessary. You will lose marks for incorrect spelling. Both US and UK English spellings are accepted.

5 re-read the notes at the end of the test and make sure what you wrote makes sense.

3.27 **Now listen again and complete the notes. Use no more than three words for each answer.**

JOB INTERVIEWS AND INTERVIEW TECHNIQUE

Traditional interview: aims to evaluate how well a candidate (1) _____ description.

Behavioural interview: employer wants the candidate to offer (2) _____ to show their skills. STAR framework: Situation; (3) _____, Action, Result.

Case study interview: employer wants the candidate to analyse a (4) _____ and present a solution.

Warm-up: the employer gets a first and (5) _____ of you. It is an opportunity for candidates to describe their background and (6) _____ in the job.

Information exchange: the candidate's aim is to (7) _____ that they have the correct skills and experience. This part is not objective, but a highly (8) _____ encounter .

Personality, (9) _____ a positive attitude and good communication skills are important.

If you are not sure (10) _____ to a question, ask them to repeat it.

Do not be worried about (11) _____ , you may need some time to answer a question.

Try to illustrate your answers with (12) _____, but make sure you avoid (13) _____ and phrases like *you know.*

Try to express yourself in a (14) _____ and do not criticise a former employer or (15) _____ on other companies.

Conclusion: use the opportunity to (16) _____ for the interview. The last impression is as important as (17) _____ .

🔟 **Work in pairs. Discuss the questions.**

1 Are interviews the same in your country?
2 Which things from the listening passage do you do in interviews?
3 Which advice is also useful in the IELTS Speaking test?
4 What is the best way to practise for the Listening and Speaking tests?

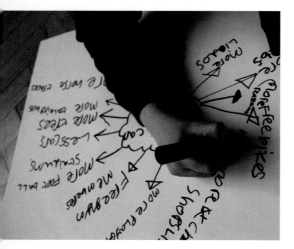

Writing

❶ Put the stages of writing an essay in order.

A _____ brainstorm ideas to include in the essay

B _____ read the essay again and check for corrections

C _____ reject irrelevant points and concentrate on four or five main points

D _____ transfer the essay onto the Writing Test Answer sheet

E _____ think of supporting points and examples

F _____ read the title, underline the key words and decide what you think about the subject

G _____ read the essay and make any corrections to spelling, grammar and punctuation

Now say how much time you should spend on each stage.

❷ Read the title and underline the key words.

> **Write about the following topic:**
>
> *Technology today is transforming the way people work and the way companies do business. Workers, and graduates in particular, in all areas of life need to be able to use this technology. To what extent do you agree or disagree with this statement?*
>
> **Give reasons for your answer and include any relevant examples from your own knowledge or experience.**
>
> **Write at least 250 words.**

Now follow stages 2 – 7 in activity 1.

❸ Read an essay and mark it (out of 9) for ...

1 task fulfilment – how well does the essay answer the question? How relevant, developed and supported are the main points? How clear is the writer's opinion?

2 coherence and cohesion – how well is the information linked and put into paragraphs?

3 vocabulary – is a wide range of vocabulary used accurately?

4 grammatical range and accuracy – is a wide range of structures used accurately?

Improvements in technology changed our life dramatically. In business, we cannot avoid using technology anymore. Example, the popularisation of the Internet has significantly reduced time in collecting information and in comunications. On the Internet, there are a tremendous number of websites

5 providing all kinds of information. When we connect to the Internet, we can get almost any kind of information within a very short time. E-mail reaches to receivers within seconds. It could be said that if we resist using the internet, we will not be able to compete with other buisnesses in the future. All workers need to be able to use technology in their work.

10 However, this does not the same in our private life. We do not have to use technology in our private lives, if we do not wanna. For example, a large number of people do not have the Internet facilities in their homes. Some of them may not know how to use it, however there may be others who deliberately choose not to have the Internet in their house. These people,

15 often say they are too tired to use because they have been using it the whole day in their office They may say that they do not want to be annoyed by too much information coming through the Internet into their home. We should not overlook the fact that too much technology causes tiredness among some people.

20 We mostly have no choice but to use technology in business, however, we can choose using technology or not by ourselves in our private lives.

4 **Read the essay again and find ...**

1 two punctuation errors
2 seven grammatical mistakes:
   one tense error
   two grammar errors
   two missing words
   two extra words
3 two spelling mistakes
4 one error of formality.

Now correct the mistakes.

5 **Use the notes you made in activity 2 and write an essay for the title. You have 40 minutes.**

Speaking

❶ Look at the picture and say what is happening.

Now read the passage and answer the questions.

1 What is the *milk round*?
2 What are its advantages and disadvantages?

The milk round

The *milk round* is the name of the annual recruitment programme when employers visit universities to give presentations and interview finalists. The name milk round comes from the service where a milkman delivers milk to your door – in the same way companies deliver jobs to the university. The milk round can be a great opportunity to meet an employer. It can help you to make your mind up about whether certain jobs and organisations are right for you. It takes place close to you and it can be much easier to get an interview during the final term than in summer, when many of their vacancies will be filled. However, there are some disadvantages: using the milk round will take time out of your final year – how much time will you be able to spend to attending presentations, making applications and attending interviews? You need to be organised – there will be many presentations to choose from each evening, and you must know what you want from a job. Recruiters aim to persuade you to apply to their organisation; these events are about careers in specific organisations, not about careers in general. Many firms are represented in areas where graduates are regularly recruited like banking but not much coverage is given to fields such as arts or publishing.

❷ Work in pairs. Ask each other the questions.

1 Have you ever been to a careers fair?
2 Do you know what career you would like in the future?
3 What are your plans for the immediate future?
4 What are your plans for the long-term future?

3.28 ❸ Listen to a conversation and complete the table.

	type of work	reasons
Marta	(1) _____	(2) _____
Michie	(3) _____	(4) _____
Tomas	doctorate	(5) _____

Express yourself: talking about plans

Complete the expressions with the words in H.

1 *What are you _____ to do?*   2 *What are your _____ ?*

3 *Have you got anything in _____ ?*   4 *I'm _____ to spend a year in France.*

5 *I don't want to _____ a real job just yet.*

6 *I'm _____ to go over and do seasonal work.*

3.29   **Now listen and practise.**

H get into
planning (x2)
hoping
plans
mind

Achieve IELTS: reformulation and checking

In the discussion …

you may want to check your understanding of a question.

in other words   to put it another way   so what you're asking is

you may want to clarify terms and definitions.

by research I mean …

you may want to ask the examiner to clarify the question.

Could you explain what you mean by … ?

Can you give me an example of what you mean?

You will not lose marks if you need to ask these questions and may even gain marks.

Pronunciation

3.30 **4** **Listen and practise the phrases for reformulation and checking in *Achieve IELTS*.**

5 **Work in pairs. Student A, you are the examiner – interview Student B. Student B, you are the candidate – answer the questions.**

Part 1: Let's talk about students in your country.

1 *At what age do students go to university in your country?*

2 *How many years do students spend at university?*

Part 2: Describe your opinion of work.

You should say:

  – *what kind of job you would like to do*
  – *what qualifications you need to do the job*
  – *what qualities people need to do this type of work*
  and explain why you would choose this type of employment.

Rounding off questions

1 *Is it normal for students to take a year out?*

2 *Where would you go for a gap year and what would you do?*

Part 3: Let's consider first of all how work has changed over recent years.

1 *What are the effects of industry on the environment?*

2 *Are many people self-employed in your country?*

Finally, let's talk about your plans for the future.

What are you planning to do in the next five years and how do you hope to do this?

Now change roles.

Assignments

1.1 Students A and B

Ask Student C the questions and make a note of their answers.

1 What's your name? (Can you spell it for me?)
2 What subject are you applying for?
3 Why you want to study in (the UK)?
4 What qualifications do you have?
5 Why you want to take the course?
6 Where do you see yourself five years from now?
7 What are your main responsibilities in your job?
8 How you do you think you will benefit from taking the course?

2.1 Key to quiz

Mostly As
You don't have much control over your finances – if you continue spending it could lead to a big debt.

Mostly Bs
You don't plan your spending or manage your finances well. As a result you're never sure how much money you have or how much you have spent. You need to be more careful with planning, saving and spending.

Mostly Cs
You enjoy spending money, but don't spend money for pleasure. You are reasonably in control of your finances, but a little advice on financial planning could help you.

Mostly Ds
Your greatest love in life is saving money. You are happiest with money in your pockets, not in the shopkeeper's.

3.1 Student B

Concorde	
built by	Britain and France
capacity	100 passengers, 2.5 tonnes cargo
range	6,880 km
speed	2,150 kph
weight	185 tonnes
engines	4
route	Paris – New York / London – New York

3.2 Student B

Correct Student A. Use these words.

elephant   Amsterdam   two   highways

Now read the sentences to Student A.

1 The front window of a car is called the radiator.
2 Tankers carry passengers on cruises.
3 The capital of New Zealand is Auckland.
4 People who can't walk often use a wheelbarrow.

4.1 Best and worst inventions (according to a UK survey)

Best inventions	Worst inventions
1 Bicycle – 70%	1 Atomic/Nuclear Weapons – 31.5%
2 Radio – 5.5%	2 Landmines – 21.5%
3 Computer – 4.5%	3 Internal Combustion Engine – 11%
4 Penicillin – 4.5%	4 Plastic Bags – 8%
5 Internal Combustion Engine – 4%	5 Speed Cameras – 7.5%
6 Internet – 3.5%	6 Mobile Phones – 7%
7 Light Bulb – 3%	7 Car alarms – 6%
8 Cat's Eyes – 2%	8 Television – 3.5%
9 Telephone – 1.5%	
10 Television – 1.5%	Source: BBC

5.1 Student A

Give Student B directions from:

- Columbia University to the American Museum of Natural History
- the American Museum of Natural History to the Soldiers and Sailors Monument
- the Soldiers and Sailors Monument to the Cathedral of St John

5.2 Student A

Read the instructions to Student B. Time Student B and stop him or her after two minutes.

I'm going to give you a topic, which I'd like you to talk about for one to two minutes. Before you start, you will have one minute to think about what you are going to say. You may make notes if you wish. Here is a pencil and some paper. I'd like you to talk about an activity you enjoy doing in your spare time.

6.1 Student A

Ask Student B questions to find out the words in Australian English. Answer Student B's questions.

British English	Australian English	British English	Australian English
banana	nana	lots of money	1 _____
sweets	lollies	woman	2 _____
trousers	daks	sausage	3 _____
sheep	jumbuck	shoe	4 _____
kangaroo	roo	swimsuit	5 _____
toilet	john / dunny	city	6 _____
sunglasses	sunnies	afternoon	7 _____
food	tucker	lots of money	8 _____

7.1 Student A

Write about the events again in this order.

1 called security
2 discovered the laptop was stolen
3 had a shower
4 went back to the room, couldn't find her keys, called the porter
5 went to the kitchen and spoke to Keith
6 the porter opened the door
7 looked for keys
8 went to lecture

Start like this: *Ester called security as soon as she had discovered someone had stolen her laptop. Before this she ...*

8.1 Check your answers with the key.

Key

Mostly As
You take care when you shop and try to look after yourself, your community and the environment.

Mostly Bs
You try to balance concerns about the environment and producers against your shopping budget.

Mostly Cs
Your shopping budget is your main concern – getting the best value for money at the cheapest shops.

8.2 Student A, begin ...

This is a person who ...
thing that ...
subject which ...
organisation which ...
place where ...

Use these words or think of your own examples.

a politician   a bank   business studies
a shareholder   a volunteer

9.1 Student A

Part 3 Discussion questions

1 What do you feel are the main differences between men and women, and how does this affect their lives?

2 Would you agree that women who work are less feminine than those who do not work? Why do you feel this way?

9.2 Student B

Part 3 Discussion questions

1 Men have greater physical strength, but women have more endurance. How does this affect their choice of career?

2 Do you agree that educated women make better mothers? In what ways might this affect the children?

10.1 Student B

Think of three places to eat. Invite Student A to have lunch with you at one of the places.

If Student A does not want to go there, suggest another place – give reasons for your suggestion.

a fast food burger outlet   the college refectory
a coffee bar   a street food seller

11.1 Himalaya quiz answers

1 b   2 a   3 c   4 a   5 b

6.2 Student B

Answer Student A's questions. Ask Student A questions to find out the words in Australian English.

British English	Australian English
lots of money	big bickies
woman	sheila
sausage	snag
shoe	kanga
swimsuit	bathers
city	big smoke
afternoon	arvo

banana	1	_____
sweets	2	_____
trousers	3	_____
sheep	4	_____
kangaroo	5	_____
toilet	6	_____
sunglasses	7	_____
food	8	_____

7.2 Student B

Write about the events again in this order.

1 the porter opened the door
2 looked for keys
3 discovered the laptop was stolen
4 called security
5 went to lecture
6 went to the kitchen and spoke to Keith
7 had a shower
8 went back to the room, couldn't find her keys and called the porter

Start like this: *When the porter opened the door, Ester looked for her keys and then ...*

Listening passages

Introduction
Track 1.1

Mohammed: My name is Mohammed, I'm from Amman – the capital of Jordan. I'm a postgraduate student in Total Quality Management, and my first degree was in Industrial Engineering. I took IELTS because I wanted to study here in Britain and all the universities asked for IELTS. What I found most difficult thing about the test was the writing part because the subject didn't interest me very much, so I really had to think hard about what to write and try to get as many ideas as I could about the subject, so it took me a long time to plan the essay and not so much time to write it. The most enjoyable part was the interview where you can experience having a conversation with an examiner from Britain or Australia and you can hear the English language before you come to Britain. My IELTS score was 6.

Pol: Hi, my name is Rattapol, I come from Bangkok, the capital city of Thailand. I took the IELTS test because I wanted to study in Australia, the IELTS score is one of the requirements that the universities in Australia needed to decide whether or not I could come to study here. The test has four sections that test all my language skills in English so I could see where my weak and my strong points are. What I found most hard about the test was the speaking test because I couldn't communicate with the examiner effectively. Sometimes I couldn't understand the question. But the most enjoyable part of the test was the listening test because I prepared very well for this part. I worked very hard to get a good score in the test and my final score was better than I predicted it would be – I got 6.5 points.

Zhang Tien: Hello, my name is Zhang Tien and I come from China. To come here I took the IELTS test. The reason I took it was that I wanted to go abroad to study further and the test was necessary to get a place in the course here. I chose to do IELTS because it is flexible – what I mean by this is that some parts of the test need your own answers and opinions. During the test, to be honest I didn't like the reading test because I found it hard to complete the task within the time limits and I couldn't complete some of the questions. The most interesting part for me was the speaking test. It was a very pleasurable experience to speak with a native speaker and the listening part was also very nice because it contains pictures, graphs in the questions, so that is more like a game than a test and I nearly forgot that it was a real test. My score was 6 points.

Unit 1
Track 1.2

Liz: Hello, come in. Please take a seat.

Füsun: Thank you.

Liz: My name's Elizabeth Clark, most people call me Liz, and I work at the British Embassy and this is Christopher Hobbs from the British Council.

Christopher: Hello. You can call me Chris if you like. It's short for Christopher.

Füsun: Hello Liz, Chris.

Liz: And you are Füsun. I'm sorry, I'm not sure how to pronounce your last name.

Füsun: That's okay, a lot of people have problems with my name. It's Kiliçoğlu.

Liz: OK thanks. Let me just write that down. That's K …

Füsun: K-I-L-I-Ç, that's c with a dash underneath it, O-Ḡ with a line above it L-U.

Liz: I'll just repeat that to make sure I've got it right. K-I-L-I-Ç – C with a dash below it, O-Ḡ with a line above the G, L-U.

Füsun: And my first name, Füsun is spelt F-Ü, the U has two dots above it, S-U-N.

Liz: Now before we begin the interview I'd just like to check your details to make sure they are accurate. Let's start. What's your marital status? You're …

Füsun: Single.

Liz: Single, so do you prefer Miss or Ms as your title?

Füsun: I think Ms is okay, put Ms.

Liz: And your address for correspondence?

Füsun: I'll give you my parents' address, they live in Izmir and are sure to send anything on to me. It's Daire – that means apartment 11 D.

Liz: Just a second – how do you spell *daire*?

Füsun: Just as it sounds, Turkish isn't like English – we say words the same way we write them.

Christopher: Yes, English spelling can be a bit confusing.

Füsun: So it's D-A-I-R-E.

Liz: 11 D.

Füsun: That's correct. 1738 Caddesi, Karsiyaka.

Liz: Could you just spell Cad ..

Füsun: Yes, of course. It's C-A-double D-E-S-I, and Karsiyaka is spelt K-A-R-S, with a dash underneath it – I without the dot – Y-A-K-A. And that's Izmir.

Liz: Right, I think I've got that.

Christopher: And you're currently working at the moment, I see.

Füsun: That's right. I'm working at The Aegean University in the Faculty of Engineering, in the Department of Bioengineering.

Liz: So you are well qualified already.

Füsun: I'm quite well qualified, my first degree is in biomedicine, and from that I became interested in bioengineering and took our higher diploma in bioengineering and then I got my research assistant position in that subject. At the moment I'm studying English and I'm learning Spanish too.

Christopher: So, why do you want another degree in a similar subject? You put down here that your preferred choice is an MSc in Biomedical science. Can you tell us why you're applying for a scholarship to do this?

Füsun: Yes, I'm applying for a scholarship for several reasons. First of all, the course I'd like to do is different from bioengineering – it's much broader and contains a module in management: management of laboratories in particular.

Christopher: Why does this interest you particularly?

Füsun: At the moment I manage a lot of work in the labs, and I think that it's really important to understand it better.

Liz: I understand. How long have you studied bioengineering?

Füsun: Altogether, about six years studying and another two years as a research assistant.

Christopher: So how could you benefit by doing the course – is it a way of making progress in your career?

Füsun: Yes, it will help me to move into management. More importantly though, I can learn about the newest ideas and research in my subject and bring this information back to my department.

Liz: Yes, I see. Why do you want to study in Britain at this university?

Füsun: I'd like to study at that university for a number of reasons: firstly, because the course is one of the best in Europe. Secondly, because Britain isn't so far from home, so I can come back quite easily and lastly because I want to improve my English and visit more of the country.

Liz: So you've been to Britain before.

Füsun: I visit Britain as often as I can. I've been there four times now on conferences and on holidays.

Christopher: That's great. Finally, where did you hear about the course?

Füsun: I saw the course advertised in the British Council library, and I also saw this scholarship advertised there.

Liz: Well, I think that's all – anything else, Chris?

Christopher: No, nothing else. Is there anything you would like to ask us?

Füsun: Yes, I'd really like to know when the results of the scholarship are sent out.

Liz: It usually takes between seven to fourteen days.

Füsun: One to two weeks then.

Liz: Yes, that's right.

Füsun: Thank you. That's all I wanted to know.

Christopher and Liz: Thank you very much.

Track 1.3

that's c with a dash underneath it
you can call me Chris if you like
G with a line above it
people call me Liz
the U has two dots above it
it's short for Christopher
i without the dot

Track 1.4

Helen: Hello, welcome to the university. Let me introduce myself, my name's Helen Brown. I'm the International Office administrator and I'm responsible for looking after students here on scholarships, in particular Chevening scholars. Perhaps you could introduce yourselves to me.

Ansgar: Hi, I'm Ansgar, from Graz, in southern Austria.

Magali: And my name's Magali. I'm from a town near Montpellier, France.

Helen: It's a pleasure to meet you.

Magali: Pleased to meet you too.

Ansgar: Nice to meet you.

Helen: So, let's get started. I'm going to tell you about the schedule for today. Today is your orientation day at the university and it's going to begin in half an hour at 10 o'clock with a speech from the Vice Chancellor welcoming you to the university.

Magali: That's very nice: where is it?

Helen: It's in the main hall on floor 3.

Ansgar: OK, but how do we get there?

Helen: From here, the International Office, go down the corridor, past the lecture theatre and student common room. Then you'll be at the main entrance and you'll see the lift to your left. Take the lift to floor 3 and the main hall entrance is after the buffet.

Magali: OK, floor 3 after the buffet: I can always find my way to food, so we'll be able to find the main hall, no problem.

Helen: So after the Vice Chancellor greets the new students, then 30 minutes later, the Mayor will welcome you to the city. Together it should be about an hour so it's not too much of a drag.

Ansgar: And what happens then?

Helen: After that you'll have a meeting with a representative of the British Council and she will brief you on life in Britain and what your sponsor expects and of course doesn't expect from you.

Magali: It will be nice to meet them. Is that in the main hall too?

Helen: No, but it is on floor 3 again: with your back to the main hall go down the corridor, past the labs.

Ansgar: Sorry?

Helen: The laboratories, on your right and the computer cluster rooms on your left and at the end of the corridor are seminar rooms 1 and 2. Your meeting is in seminar room 2.

Magali: Did you mention what time that is?

Helen: No, I didn't – it's at 11.15, and it should last about half an hour. You'll meet her a number of times during your studies, so it's important to go to that meeting.

Ansgar: OK, I'll make sure Magali is on time.

Magali: Ansgar, I'm always on time.

Helen: Very well. Now for the final part of the morning and lunch, you'll be with your department.

Ansgar: We're both doing biomedicine.

Helen: Oh, that's interesting.

Magali: But we're not sure how to get to our department.

Helen: Well, you don't need to go very far from seminar room 2: the laboratories and seminar rooms all belong to your department. So basically you need to turn left out of seminar room 2 and go past the next two teaching rooms. Your departmental office is on the left.

Ansgar: Will someone be there to meet us?

Helen: Oh, but of course. At 12.00 the course administrator will meet you at the departmental office and introduce you to members of staff and the head of department: Professor Heanue.

Magali: Heanue? How do you spell that?

Helen: H-E-A-N-U-E. He will tell you about the department and your course, the course work and academic life in Britain. Have you both got reading lists?

Magali: Yes, I have.

Ansgar: I'm afraid I haven't.

Helen: You can get one at that meeting. Then finally, as it's your first day, you'll have lunch with the department staff in the refectory from 1 to 2.

Ansgar: Oh, that's really nice.

Magali: Great.

Helen: There's just one more thing. In the afternoon you have the chance to meet other international students in the main hall again and you can ask them about their time at the university. That's from 2.30 onwards.

Ansgar: I'm looking forward to that.

Track 1.5

Let me introduce myself
Perhaps you could introduce yourselves
Nice to meet you
Pleased to meet you too
It's a pleasure to meet you

Track 1.6

Professor Heanue: That's about all I want to say about the course and coursework: as you heard, it's very intensive and there's a lot of work to do. So, how to deal with all the work – it's really important to make sure you have good study skills – it makes the difference between failing, just passing or doing well on any course. There are workshops given by student service counsellors on study skills, but I just want to put you in the picture with a quick overview of useful study skills. There are five points I want to make here. The main thing is to get organised, the first thing you need to do as soon as you get your timetable and reading list is to draw up a plan of study – time management is what all students are bad at. Unfortunately, it's what they need to be very good at. Make up a timetable and put in all the things like lab work, lectures, seminars and tutorials that you will attend. Make a note of exactly what work you will do for each of your courses.

Ansgar: Where do we get that from?

Professor Heanue: Your lecturer will tell you exactly how you will be assessed at the end of the course. Make sure that you add in time for reading, preparing seminars and so on. Put

deadlines into your study plan and put these deadlines into your computer to remind you when they are. With deadlines you need to be realistic and know yourself. Are you the kind of person who leaves things to the last minute? If you are, make sure you remind yourself about deadlines well in advance: don't leave things to the last minute.

Magali: That sounds like me.

Professor Heanue: Aim to have a balanced life of academic work, a paid job if you need one and social activities. As a rough guide, you should be doing 40 hours of academic work per week and five to 15 hours for a part-time job, no more. The second point is don't be late or miss lectures: remember the person giving the lecture is probably the same person who sets your exams. In lectures you hear information from the person who will be testing you on it. You will take much longer to gather it from other sources – classes offer an opportunity to ask questions about difficult material, and you won't miss extra information. Thirdly, make sure that you regularly re-read your notes from lectures, books and handouts: this will help you remember what you have done. Finally, two more important points – we expect you to work long hours on your own. The information we give you in tutorials and lectures is just a starting point, often comprising the main points of themes of the subject. After this it's up to you to go into detail about the topic and be familiar enough on certain points to give a seminar on it if asked. The next and last point is this: you need to think about what you read and any information you get on a topic. We are looking for students who can evaluate material critically – students who can think critically. Students who simply read and remember information do not make as good progress as students who think about the subject and form their own opinions on it based on looking at the subject from all points of view.

Magali: So we're not just learning facts and figures.

Professor Heanue: Facts and figures are an important part of learning, but not the most important thing – it's what you do with them that is critical.

Track 1.7

Ahmed: Oh, Joanna and Anna, I'm afraid I'm just useless at studying. I've sat here for three hours now and it's just not going in. I guess I'm just not patient enough. You're both good at studying. What qualities do you think are the most important in a good learner?

Anna: It helps if you're patient, but I think other characteristics are more significant.

Ahmed: Such as?

Anna: A good student needs to be organised – I think that's absolutely essential. For example, take you, Ahmed. If I ask you to find your notes from the last lecture, how long will it take to find them?

Ahmed: About two hours: it's in that pile of paper there.

Joanna: You see, Ahmed, you lose two hours study time looking for a paper and then you're not in the mood for studying.

Ahmed: But if a student is intelligent – like me – then they can remember the lecture and not need to look for notes.

Joanna: You know Anna is right. It's really important to be organised, probably more important than being intelligent, but in my opinion the vital thing is motivation: you know – having the motivation to get up in the morning to go to the library and learn.

Anna: I really agree with that, but I think there's more than that. Organisation and motivation are fundamental to good learning, but the crucial factor is determination.

Ahmed: Determination?

Anna: Yes, the ability to get up and learn, not just once a week or twice a week but every day, day after day until you get where you want.

Joanna: Anna's right – a good learner is organised, motivated and determined to succeed.

Ahmed: But isn't intelligence the main thing for a good learner?

Anna: Without the other things, intelligence doesn't really matter.

Track 1.8

other characteristics are more significant
I think that's absolutely essential
It's really important to be organised
the vital thing is motivation
Organisation and motivation are fundamental to good learning
the crucial factor is determination
isn't intelligence the main thing

Unit 2

Track 1.9

Student advisor: So you're thinking of opening a bank account with us?

Han: That's right.

Student advisor: And you are an international student at the university?

Han: Yes, I am.

Student advisor: And how did you hear about us?

Han: From student services – they gave me a list of banks near the university and I chose this one because you have a branch near campus and a student advisor at the bank.

Student advisor: Yes, I'm part of the student advice team – there are three of us here. Right, now I'll go over the services we offer to international students, and then we can go through a few details before we set up your account.

Han: OK.

Student advisor: We can offer you a current or cheque account and a savings account.

Han: Do you pay interest on the current account?

Student advisor: We do, but not very much – about 1.5%. You get a much better interest rate on the savings account, around 4%. We also give you a free overdraft facility.

Han: I'm sorry?

Student advisor: If you run out of money, we allow you to spend more money then you have in your account – that's the overdraft. But you can only take out up to £100. If you need more than £100, then you must tell us before you take any more money out.

Han: I see.

Student advisor: Now, once your current account is open, then you can set up direct debits for any regular payments you need to make.

Han: Could you tell me how that works?

Student advisor: Well, for instance, let's take your mobile phone. You have to pay a certain amount every month for it.

Han: Yes.

Student advisor: So, you can tell us to pay that amount each month and we'll do it automatically for you.

Han: I see.

Student advisor: As soon as your account is open, we will send you a debit card, which you must sign immediately and keep in a safe place. Then a day or two later we'll send you a personal identification number.

Han: A PIN number.

Student advisor: Yes, and you must keep the number secret. You can change it, if you like, when you use it for the first time, but if you change it you must remember the number. If you forget or lose the number, then we have to send you out a new card and a number for security reasons.

Han: OK.

Student advisor: The next thing you could do is open a savings account. If you know you have to save a certain amount of money to pay your accommodation or course fees, we can open a savings account for you to put aside some money each week or month.

Han: How can I do that?

Student advisor: You can manage your accounts in one of four ways. You can come into the bank here on the university campus and tell us what you would like to do, or you can call us on 08457 004 004 and instruct us what to do over the phone – that's 24-hours a day, seven days a week. Alternatively, you can manage your account over the Internet.

Han: I see.

Student advisor: You have to go online and register at our website at www.hsbc.co.uk/online-banking before you can use the service. Finally, if you have a digital TV, you can use TV banking by pressing interactive on your digital TV remote control.

Han: Oh really? I don't have a digital TV, unfortunately, but I can do the first three things.

Student advisor: Now do you have any insurance?

Han: What's that?

Student advisor: For example, if you lose something or one of your possessions is stolen, we will cover the cost of it.

Han: How much does that cost?

Student advisor: It's £24 a year, so it really is worth thinking about.

Han: I don't need to think about that – I'll take out insurance.

Student advisor: I'll arrange that for you as soon as your account is open. Now, would you like to go ahead and open an account with us?

Track 1.10

Student advisor: Now have you got all the documents we need?

Han: Let me see. I've got a letter from my department saying which course I'm taking. Here you are.

Student advisor: Thanks. You're with the School of Management then. And you're from?

Han: Hong Kong. I'm Chinese.

Student advisor: Then I'll need to see your passport.

Han: Is my university card okay?

Student advisor: No, I'm afraid not. I need to see your passport.

Han: My passport – here it is.

Student advisor: Thank you. And have you got a letter or bank account statement that shows your permanent address?

Han: This letter shows my parents' address, is that okay?

Student advisor: Yes, that's fine. Now, the final thing I need to see is your application form.

Han: Here you are. I filled it out with a black pen and in capital letters, but I'm afraid my handwriting isn't very neat.

Student advisor: Oh, you're right – it is a bit difficult to read. Can we go over it just to check I have the details correct?

Han: Yes, go ahead.

Student advisor: So title: is that Mr?

Han: Yes, it is.

Student advisor: And forename, Han. H-A-N?

Han: That's right.

Student advisor: And your surname. How do you spell that?

Han: It's Li. L-I.

Student advisor: Thanks. Right, now home address.

Han: I put my parents' address, is that okay?

Student advisor: Yes, that's fine. So, house number, street name and town, all there. Now hall of residence – that is ...

Han: University hall, flat number 11B.

Student advisor: How long have you been there?

Han: Oh sorry, I missed that box. I came here in July to do the summer English course before my course started. The pre-sessional course started on July the 14th, and I arrived a few days before that on the 10th.

Student advisor: So, here's your home number. Have you got a mobile phone?

Han: Yes, I got it two days ago. The number is 07860 556 469.

Student advisor: I'll just read that back to you: 07860 556 469. And your land line in the UK is 01274 235650.

Han: That's correct.

Student advisor: And e-mail? We need that so if you get near to your overdraft limit we can send a note to tell you.

Han: My university e-mail address is han.li@bradford.ac.uk, and my personal e-mail is han_21@yahoo.co.uk.

Student advisor: So, your university e-mail is han.li@bradford.ac.uk and your personal e-mail address is han_21@yahoo.co.uk. Now I'd like to ask you for a few details about your course. The course starts in September this year and ends in June 2009, so you're an undergraduate student.

Han: Yes, I'm a first year undergraduate. What about those boxes? I wasn't sure which to tick.

Student advisor: Well, these are for us to contact you with special deals and promotions. Do you want us to telephone you about any offers?

Han: No, no thank you – I don't like talking on the phone very much.

Student advisor: What about contacting you on e-mail or by post?

Han: Yes, you can do that.

Student advisor: And can we pass your details on to other parts of our business?

Han: I'd rather not for the moment – maybe later.

Student advisor: Well that's fine. We'll have your account open within 5 – 10 working days.

Track 1.11

han.li@bradford.ac.uk
www.hsbc.co.uk/online-banking
han_21@yahoo.co.uk

Track 1.12

Bank assistant: Good afternoon.

Alice: Hello.

Bank assistant: How can I help you?

Alice: I'd like to make a transfer, please.

Bank assistant: You want to transfer some money. That's fine. Let me just bring up some details. Right. Here we are. Can you tell me your name please?

Alice: It's Alice Deltour.

Bank assistant: OK, and your date of birth?

Alice: 20 February 1982.

Bank assistant: Right and for security, can I have the first letter of your password?

Alice: It's B.

Bank assistant: And the fifth letter?

Alice: That's F.

Bank assistant: Fine. Now, where do you want to make the transfer to and from?

Alice: I'd like to send money from my current account abroad.

Bank assistant: Which country are you sending it to?

Alice: To China – my boyfriend is on holiday there and he's run out of money.

Bank assistant: Oh dear. China, okay. Now there are several ways to do this. We can do it by credit card, by electronic transfer, by cheque or by banker's draft.

Alice: Erm, I'm not sure – what's the best way?

Bank assistant: Well, that all depends. The simplest way is by cheque really.

Alice: I just write the cheque and send it.

Bank assistant: Yes, but it can be very slow and take a long time for the money to clear, between three to four weeks – how soon do you need the money to get there?

Alice: I'd like it to get there in the next couple of weeks.

Bank assistant: So really sending a cheque is going to be too slow.

Alice: Yes, I think so.

Bank assistant: Let's look at electronic transfer then. This usually takes between two and five working days.

Alice: That's two to five days.

Bank assistant: Working or business days, if you send it on Friday it will get there the following Friday at the latest.

Alice: I see, that's much better.

Bank assistant: Yes, but we do charge a fee for this. We charge a flat fee of £21, and on top of that the receiving bank may charge a fee and

an agent may also charge you for transferring the money between banks.

Alice: So how much is it altogether?

Bank assistant: We can't give you an exact amount – you need to check it with the receiving bank and any agents that they use.

Alice: I see.

Bank assistant: Also you can send it in sterling or dollars from here, but there will be an additional fee depending on the exchange rate when you convert it into Renmimbi.

Alice: So there will be another charge too?

Bank assistant: I'm afraid so.

Alice: Does it make any difference if I send it in dollars or sterling?

Bank assistant: It could make a difference according to which currency has the best exchange rate. The other difference is this: if you send dollars, the amount goes through the US clearing system: we send the money to our branch in London, they then send it to our branch in New York and the New York branch sends it to the bank in China.

Alice: It goes all around the world then. What about if I send sterling?

Bank assistant: In that case we send it to our branch in London, from there it may go directly to China unless the bank in China has an agent in London in which case we transfer it to the London agent and they send the money on to China.

Alice: So how do I proceed with the transfer?

Bank assistant: OK, first we'll need some details about the beneficiary from you.

Alice: The who?

Bank assistant: The beneficiary: the person receiving the money.

Alice: OK – what do you need to know?

Bank assistant: We'll need the full name of the beneficiary and their account number.

Alice: OK.

Bank assistant: You need to tell us the name of the bank in China and the address of the branch. We also need the bank's sort code and the SWIFT number.

Alice: What's a SWIFT number?

Bank assistant: Basically it's an inter-bank code: it helps banks identify each other through a unique code number.

Alice: OK, and that's spelt … ?

Bank assistant: S-W-I-F-T, swift. And the final thing we need is the reason for sending the money.

Alice: You need a reason from me? I just told you, my boyfriend's run out of money.

Bank assistant: Well, we don't need a reason – the receiving government needs to know why the money is entering the country and we have to be able to tell them.

Alice: OK. So from me you need: the bank's name, the address of the branch, the sort code and SWIFT number; the beneficiary's name and account number and a reason for sending the payment.

Bank assistant: Yes, that's correct.

Alice: OK, so I'll check these out and come back to you with them so we can go ahead with the transfer.

Track 1.13

Hello everyone, I'm Sue Booth, from the Student's Union Finance office, and I also act as the Student Finance advisor. This workshop's on managing on a student budget, or in other words, managing a budget as a student. In this talk, I'll go over some ways you can help yourself save and plan your finances.

Let me give you a few facts and figures first. As you already know, life can be very expensive when you are a student. Not only is it expensive with fees, accommodation, books and so on, students find they have very little time to supplement their income with work. The average living costs for home students are £8,400 in London and £7,317 outside London – this is for home students only, international students have higher fees. Much of this total comes from the cost of accommodation, with students spending around £2,800 in London and £2,000 elsewhere.

Due to high costs like this, it means that many students have to work to fund their education. Currently the National Union of Students estimates that 42% of students work part-time, but other estimates are higher with some figures saying that 60% of students work to cover their basic cost of living. Of course, this can have a negative effect on studies: according to the National Union of Students 38% of students missed lectures because of working part-time and 21% missed deadlines for giving work into their department. However, for many students even working part-time is not enough to cover their expenses. So here are a few ways to keep down your costs.

Firstly, if you have a student account with a free overdraft, withdraw the maximum amount of money and put it into a savings account where it will earn interest: putting £1,500 in a savings account giving you 4.5% interest could earn you around £69 a year. This doesn't sound like much but according to estimates from the National Union of Students, this is about 7% of students' annual food bills.

Cutting down on your household costs can help too. Keep an eye on your fuel bills – by lowering the heating in your house you could save £30 a year, and by changing your light bulbs for energy efficient lights, you can save £10 a year on electricity. Check the prices of your energy suppliers regularly and change supplier if you find a cheaper one. You could buy a pre-pay fuel card to pay your bills, these often give you a slight discount on your energy bill. If all this doesn't sound like very much you could save up to £700 on transport by investing in a bicycle, and you'll get fitter with this too.

You can make another major saving by buying your books second-hand: the average cost of books is £367. Check out the departmental notice board for students leaving the department and selling their books. Alternatively you can go to the second-hand bookshops near the campus or even buy second-hand books over the Internet.

Now let's look at shopping. The Students' Union has negotiated student discounts at several different places including clubs, theatres, cinemas, bookshops and stationery shops, so make sure that you know where these places are and that you use your discount. Try to do your shopping weekly and if possible do it with other students so that you can take advantage of offers at the supermarket. Finally, try to avoid making cash withdrawals more than once a week and after you have made your weekly withdrawal, leave your cash card at home.

Unit 3

Track 1.14

Lu: All right, so here's the map of Europe. We've got two weeks, nearly three. Where do you want to go?

Makiyo: I want to see as much as possible. I'm going back to Japan in the summer and I might not get the chance again. I must see Paris and Madrid.

Lu: OK, we can start in Paris. We'll take the Eurostar from London.

Makiyo: The Eurostar?

Lu: Yes, that's the train that goes under the sea, between England and France. We can get a discount with our railcards, then use the ISIC for discounts on flights and accommodation after that. If we stay in hostels, it won't be too expensive.

Makiyo: Good. We don't need to stay in London – we can go there anytime. I think we should just stay two nights in each place. I'm so excited!

Lu: Me too. But it will be difficult to choose. After Paris, I want to go to Amsterdam. Amsterdam is very exciting. You can visit the Rijksmuseum. You love modern art.

Makiyo: And what are you planning to do?

Lu: Oh, you know, just have a look around. I'm sure there's plenty going on there. You can choose the next place.

Makiyo: Berlin, definitely. Oh, but what about Prague? Prague is so beautiful. I've seen pictures of the Charles Bridge.

Lu: You have to choose between them, but I've heard that Prague gets really crowded at Easter. It's quite a small city.

Makiyo: It has to be Berlin, then. There is so much to see there.

Lu: Next I would like to go to Budapest. Katrina says it's wonderful in the spring. There are lots of swimming pools and perfect weather. It's bigger than Prague, and parts of it are just as pretty. I'll choose Budapest.

Makiyo: Fine. So the next place is mine. How many more can we choose?

Lu: Only two. We already have five places.

Makiyo: Athens? Rome?

Lu: Let's take a look on the website. Hmm ... There isn't any cheap accommodation listed, and it's a long way from Budapest.

Makiyo: Yes, I suppose it might be too expensive, even with the discounts. I must see Madrid. The Prado museum is there. That means you can choose one more place.

Lu: Then it's Rome or Bern, in Switzerland. Switzerland has beautiful scenery.

Makiyo: But Rome is so much more famous and exciting. Please?

Lu: All right, you win. Rome it is. Now we'd better start making our bookings. You book the Eurostar, and I'll contact the Student Travel Association.

Track 1.15

Recorded message: Welcome to Eurostar International customer relations. For English, please press one. Thanks. Your call will now be placed in a queue, and answered as soon as an agent becomes available.

Agent: Which journey would you like to make?

Makiyo: London to Paris, return.

Agent: And what is your date of travel please?

Makiyo: The 21st of March, coming back on the 6th of April.

Agent: What time of day would you like to travel?

Makiyo: Around midday is best for me.

Agent: There is one departing at 12.09 from Waterloo station.

Makiyo: Pardon? Could you repeat that, please?

Agent: 12.09.

Makiyo: Nine minutes past twelve.

Agent: Yes, nine minutes past twelve, gets to Paris at 15.59.

Makiyo: Right. I need to check the times of the trains coming back as well, on the 6th of April. The latest I can get back to Waterloo is 9.15 p.m. What's the last one I could catch to get back by 9.15?

Agent: How about if you arrive at 21.53? Is that OK?

Makiyo: I think that would be too late because the last bus is at 9.30. Could you give me the one before that, please?

Agent: Yes, I'll give you that. 19.19 from Paris, arrives London at 20.54.

Makiyo: Sorry, what time was that from Paris?

Agent: 19.19, erm, nineteen minutes past seven.

Makiyo: Sorry, I'm getting a bit mixed up. Could you run that by me again?

Agent: Yes, of course. The train departs from Paris at 19.19, and it arrives in London at 20.54.

Makiyo: Got that. That will be fine. I'll need two tickets. Can we get a discount with our ISIC student cards?

Agent: Yes, of course, if you are under 26 you can get a discount making the price £59 for the round trip.

Makiyo: I'm afraid I didn't quite catch that. Could you say it again?

Agent: £59 for each return ticket. Subject to availability.

Makiyo: All right, well please could you book those now?

Agent: Yes. How would you like to pay?

Makiyo: I'll pay with my Visa card.

Agent: Could you give me the name on the card, and the number please?

Makiyo: The name is M Kumada, K-U-M-A-D-A. The number is 4929 8935 7321.

Agent: Can I repeat that back to you? M Kumada, 4929 8935 7321.

Makiyo: That's correct.

Agent: And what is the expiry date on the card?

Makiyo: It's 07 – 07.

Agent: 07 – 07. Thank you. That's fine. Would you like the tickets to be sent by post, or will you pick them up at the check-in at Waterloo?

Makiyo: We'll pick them up at the check-in.

Agent: Please remember to bring proof of your age with you when you travel.

Makiyo: Just one more thing, please. I am from Japan, and my friend is Chinese. Do we need visas to travel in Europe?

Agent: I'm afraid I don't know. You will need to contact the embassies of the countries you are going to.

Makiyo: All of them? Oh, dear.

Agent: Thank you for your call.

Makiyo: Goodbye.

Agent: Goodbye.

Track 1.16

Pardon?

Could you repeat that, please?

Could you run that by me again, please?

Sorry, what time was that?

I'm afraid I didn't quite catch that.

Can I repeat that back to you?

Track 1.17

Interviewer: The Airbus A380 is a revolution in aircraft technology. Today I have as my guest Mr James Carr, who worked on the project. Mr Carr, when did you start working on the Airbus A380?

James: I started working on the A380 project at the beginning of 2003, about a year after the first real construction began, although work on the plane began in 2000.

Interviewer: Can you tell us something about the plane?

James: It is the biggest passenger jet in the world, with a capacity of 550 – 600 seats. It is over 24 metres high and has a wingspan of around 80 metres. It has 20 wheels and weighs 421 tonnes without passengers, and has a range of 14,800 kilometres.

Interviewer: What exactly did your job involve? Were you working on the fuselage?

James: No, I was working on the wing assembly, at Broughton in North Wales. The fuselage and tail fins were made in Germany and Spain, and the final assembly took place in Toulouse, France. My job was to work on the computer-controlled wing panel assembly machines. These wing panels are not just sheets of metal but have reinforcing stringers which are long pieces of metal running along their length. The stringers are needed for strength. For the A380, Airbus invested heavily in automated machinery to fit these. The wing panel assembly machines cost around US$12 million each and there are now 6 of them. The machines required control programs to operate them, which told them where to go and what to do. I was responsible for the control programs.

Interviewer: How many people were working on the wing assembly?

James: It involved around 1,000 people, but this was a small percentage of the total, and they weren't all working at Broughton. Before the wing assembly took place, the wing had to be designed. This required massive amounts of research. The wing must be strong enough, but the weight must be kept to a minimum for safe take off and landing. The take off speeds for large aircraft can exceed 330 kph.

Interviewer: What was the factory at West Broughton like?

James: Very big. The part I worked in was as high as a six- or seven-storey building. On some days, there were clouds inside the main building. There were other buildings – offices and departments – inside the main buildings. Workers used bicycles, trucks and vans to get around inside. The building is the size of six and a half football pitches.

Interviewer: How did you test the wing?

James: The wings went through several tests to confirm design and stress predictions. For the new aircraft, we tested one set of wings to destruction to find the strength. In other words, we completely destroyed the wing. We used another set of wings for fatigue testing. Fatigue testing is where we move the wings up and down repeatedly over a long period to check that they perform well and that no cracks appear. There were also test aircraft that pilots flew to check flying performance, fuel economy, loading and safety.

Interviewer: How did you feel when the first plane was finished?

James: The A380 is the most significant commercial aerospace project in over 30 years and so it was good to be involved with something so important. On 27th April 2005 we watched as the A380 test aircraft flew for the first time, and there was a real sense of achievement.

Interviewer: Did you have any problems during the construction?

James: We didn't attempt a project of this size without expecting some problems. The whole thing was a problem-solving challenge from start to finish. Nothing was predictable, for example while we were developing the programs, the robots nearly put holes in the wrong place, and we had to start again. All these problems cost the company millions of dollars along the way.

Interviewer: How much did the whole project cost?

James: I would guess it cost around £8.4 billion or €12.6 billion.

Interviewer: Thanks for talking to us, Mr Carr.

James: Not at all.

Track 1.18

OK, so I'm going to tell you about the longest journey I've ever made, and I actually went nowhere at all! Well, in fact I did go somewhere, but I never arrived at that place. Well, not really. Let me explain. It was in the end-of-term break, we had two weeks' holiday, so my family and I – I mean my host family, the people I stay with in this country – decided it would be nice to go to Ireland. Not Northern Ireland; I meant to say Eire, which is Southern Ireland. I saw some pictures in a magazine and it looked really beautiful – you know, green fields and friendly people. So, we planned our journey the cheapest way that we could, because we all wanted to save money. The ferry went from Solyhead – no, sorry, it was Holyhead – to Dublin, so we could use the train to get there. There is no station in Buckingham where I live, so we had to get the bus to Oxford, which takes one hour, and we decided to take a taxi to the bus stop because we had quite a lot of luggage. That is to say, my host family had a lot of luggage, I just had one backpack. So, we all got in the taxi and we were very excited. It took about four hours on the train and we were all asleep by the time we reached the ferry. Then we had to wait another two hours for the next ferry and finally we got on. That was another three hours. Finally, the boat arrived at Dublin and we all got ready to get off. I was really looking forward to our holiday, but when we went through passport control the officer asked where I was from. When I said I was from Japan he asked to see my visa! I didn't have a visa – I thought my visa for England would be OK for Ireland too. So, I had to get right back on the ferry and go all the way back home. My host family offered to come back with me but I said

no. Well, you can imagine how I was feeling. Just terrible. And that was really the longest journey I've ever made.

Track 1.19

Well, in fact I did go somewhere
I mean my host family
Not Northern Ireland; I meant to say Eire, which is Southern Ireland
That is to say, my host family had a lot of luggage
No, sorry, it was Holyhead

Track 1.20

1 Cong is **flying** to Taiwan next Tuesday.
2 Cong is flying to **Taiwan** next Tuesday.
3 **Cong** is flying to Taiwan next Tuesday.
4 Cong is flying to Taiwan next **Tuesday**.
5 Cong is flying to Taiwan **next** Tuesday.

Unit 4
Track 1.21

Jibing: Dona, come over here.

Dona: What is it Jibing?

Jibing: Look at this poster.

Dona: Student Quiz night in the Students' Union bar at 9 o'clock. Why did you want me to look at that?

Jibing: Well, we could go along. I'm not doing anything on Thursday.

Dona: I'm not working on Thursday evening, and we don't have to give in any essays until next Monday, or prepare for any seminars.

Jibing: And there are no lectures on Friday so we don't need to get up early.

Dona: Yeah, why not, it might be nice to go and watch.

Jibing: Go and watch?

Dona: Yes.

Jibing: You haven't been to a quiz night before, have you Dona?

Dona: No, I don't think so. No, I haven't.

Jibing: Because it's not something you sit and watch – you join in.

Dona: Hang on a minute, you mean that we're going to go to take part in a quiz?

Jibing: Yes, why not?

Dona: Oh no, not me, I'm not getting involved in that.

Jibing: Dona, it's just for fun, it's nothing serious. Come on, just have a go.

Dona: Not till you tell me exactly what happens.

Jibing: Students who want to join the quiz pay a small amount of money – it says here it's one pound for each person – and they get a sheet to write their answers on.

Dona: So they get a sheet of questions and they write their answers on a piece of paper. Sounds like exam practice – not a lot of fun in that. No, I think I'll watch TV instead.

Jibing: Just let me finish. You don't do it individually and you don't get a sheet of questions. You do it in teams – in this quiz it's teams of four people.

Dona: So we need to get two more people.

Jibing: Ahmed has already agreed to come.

Dona: So you've already arranged it!

Jibing: Of course not Dona, I've just been asking around, that's all and someone said that your general knowledge is really good.

Dona: Oh really?

Jibing: Yes, you should at least have a try.

Dona: So we're in teams and we can discuss the questions.

Jibing: And the questions are given by a quizmaster who shouts out the questions to all the teams.

Dona: Well, that sounds a bit more interesting.

Jibing: We should give it a go. All the teams are in competition, lots of our friends and classmates will be there and it'll be a lot of fun.

Dona: And it's nothing serious?

Jibing: Not really.

Dona: So what kind of questions do they ask?

Jibing: Usually general knowledge questions, questions about sports, current events, trivia and they often have music questions where they play a bit of music and you have to say who sang or wrote it.

Dona: What does *trivia questions* mean?

Jibing: Questions about things that aren't really important, like *Who invented Coca Cola?*

Dona: Dr Pemberton.

Jibing: Sorry?

Dona: Coca Cola was invented by Dr Pemberton.

Jibing: How do you know that?

Dona: Never mind. You know, quiz night sounds like the kind of thing I could do.

Jibing: You can do it. You'd be good at it. What do you say?

Dona: What happens at the end then?

Jibing: At the end of the quiz the quizmaster shouts out the answers, and we mark our own answer sheets. Then each team says how many they got correct. The winning team has to show their answer sheet to the quizmaster and they say if that team really has won or not. The team that wins are given a prize.

Dona: Oh yes, what is it?

Jibing: The prize is ten pounds in cash.

Dona: Ten pounds! It's not much but you can count me in.

Track 1.22

Come on, just have a go.
You can do it.
Give it a go.
At least have a try.

Track 1.23

Quizmaster: Hello, everyone, is everybody ready for the Thursday night quiz? We've got five teams tonight, and three rounds of questions, so pencils ready and we'll get started. OK, round one with questions on art and literature. Question one: who painted *Guernica*? Which famous painter did *Guernica*?

Dona: Does anyone know this one?

Ahmed: I think he was French or Spanish.

Dona: So not Kandinsky?

Ahmed: No, definitely not Kandinsky.

Emi: It's Picasso, I'm certain of it.

Dona: OK. We'll write Picasso.

Quizmaster: OK everyone, next question. Who wrote the great novel, *War and Peace*?

Emi: I know this one. It's Zola, Emile Zola.

Dona: Are you sure?

Emi: Positive. One hundred per cent sure.

Dona: Right. Emile Zola.

Quizmaster: All right everyone, and the final question in this round. When was *The Great Wave* by Hokusai produced?

Jibing: Come on Emi, you're the artistic one, you should know this.

Emi: I'm thinking, I'm thinking. It was produced in the eighteenth century.

Dona: So we think it's the eighteenth century. Is that what I'm writing?

Ahmed: Well, I don't have a clue, so put the eighteenth century.

Dona: OK, eighteenth century.

Quizmaster: Let's move on now to the next round and it's science and technology. Here's the first question. Who was the World Wide Web invented by?

Jibing: Does anyone know this?

Ahmed: I think I do – wait a minute, it's coming to me: Tim Berners-Lee invented the World Wide Web.

Dona: Are you sure?

Ahmed: Positive.

Dona: All right. The World Wide Web was invented by Tim Berners-Lee.

Quizmaster: Next question. What is the science of engineering small things called?

Dona: Ahmed.

Ahmed: I'm sorry – my mind's gone blank.

Dona: Any guesses?

Jibing: I think it is called miniaturisation.

Emi: No, no, it's not called miniaturisation – it's called minimalism.

Dona: Minimalism. Right – everyone OK with that?

Jibing: OK.

Quizmaster: Next question. Where – or in which country – was the world's largest particle accelerator built?

Ahmed: The world's largest particle accelerator was built in Houston, Texas.

Dona: No, it's not. It was built in Geneva, Switzerland.

Jibing: Dona's right. It's also where Tim Berners-Lee invented the World Wide Web.

Quizmaster: OK teams, let's move on to round three now: sports. Which country has won the football World Cup the most times? Is it A Germany, B Italy or C Brazil?

Jibing: C, Brazil.

Dona: Brazil, OK.

Quizmaster: Next question. In which country were the 2000 Olympics held?

Dona: The year 2000 Olympics were held in Greece.

Ahmed: I don't think so. The 2004 Olympics were held in Greece. The 2000 Olympics were held in Sydney.

Emi: I think Dona is right, Ahmed.

Ahmed: No, she isn't. It's Sydney, Australia.

Dona: Jibing, what do you think?

Jibing: Well, I just don't know.

Dona: OK, so it's two against one in favour of Athens. Sorry, Ahmed, I'm going to put Athens.

Quizmaster: Final question now. How many events are included in the heptathlon?

Dona: Any ideas anyone?

Ahmed: Not really, I'm pretty hopeless when it comes to sport. Don't you know, Dona?

Dona: It could be seven or five, I'm not sure.

Emi: We can't lose anything by trying.

Dona: OK. I think five events are included in a heptathlon. We'll put five events.

Quizmaster: And that's also the end of the competition, so I'll take a short break and then I'll give you the answers. And remember – no cheating.

Track 1.24

All right everyone. The moment you've all been waiting for – it's time for the answers. Now, I'll read the answers out and see who's won then I'll check their answers and give the winners the grand prize tonight of ten pounds, in cash. Right, the answer to number 1, who painted *Guernica*, is Picasso, of course. Question 2, the writer of *War and Peace* was Tolstoy, Leo Tolstoy. Number 3, *The Great Wave*, was produced by Hokusai in the eighteenth century. Now on to the science questions, the World Wide Web was invented by Tim Berners-Lee. Question 5 – the science of engineering small things is called nanotechnology. The next question, the world's biggest particle accelerator was built in Geneva, Switzerland. Number 7, the World Cup has been won the most times by Brazil, of course. The 2000 Olympics were held in Sydney – that's the answer to question 8. And the final question, how many sports are in a heptathlon? The answer is seven. So anyone with all nine points?

Track 1.25

And so in today's talk I'm going to look at the history of inventions and some of the questions about ownership of copyright, or who owns the rights to new ideas and the impact this is having on today's global economy.

So, let's start at the beginning with the original purpose of patents. The original purpose was to encourage innovation and growth by encouraging inventors to give details of their inventions in exchange for a limited monopoly on sales of the product. That is, they would get the profits from single ownership of a product for a limited time only, then other companies would be free to manufacture the same item. But individual countries were able to choose whether or not they followed the same rules as other countries. There was a time when countries could go their own way on copyright so that they could introduce legal protection for inventors whenever they thought it appropriate. For most of the 19th century, the United States provided no copyright protection for inventors, arguing that it needed the freedom to copy in order to educate the new nation. Similarly, parts of Europe built their industries by copying the inventions of others, a model which was also followed after the Second World War by both South Korea and Taiwan.

Today however, developing countries do not have the luxury of deciding whether or not to allow people to copy the inventions of others. As part of a trade deal, countries joining the World Trade Organisation also signed up to an agreement that set minimum standards for the legal protection of inventions. The agreement puts down rules describing the protection that a country must provide for inventions from other countries. Copyright applies no matter whether the products are imported or locally produced and applies to all products – domestic or foreign. Companies like pharmaceutical firms spend a lot of time and money researching and developing new products and need the money from these products to finance future research and development. This includes also firms that produce computer programs and new plant varieties. However, all of these were not protected in most developing countries.

But this new development raised interesting moral and ethical questions which can be put in the form of two questions: which comes first – public good or private profit, and should Western companies be allowed to patent natural products? Let's look at the first question. Many countries feel that the World Trade Organisation agreement gives them a bad deal and developing countries such as India and Brazil are making their opinions known when it comes to the battle between Western patent protection and matters of public interest such as health and farming. Much of the recent debate has centred on the issue of access to expensive medicines. Many developing nations simply cannot afford the price of patented Western medicines and have started to make their own cheaper versions. Developing countries made a statement at the World Trade Organisation meeting asserting the importance of public health over Western companies' copyrights and of course, profits from these products.

But perhaps the biggest conflict between rich and poor countries over copyright comes from the patenting of traditional knowledge such as ancient herbal medicines. In 2003 it was estimated that in Africa 80% of the people use traditional medicines. However, companies from developed nations have been given patent rights for these medicines. For example, the turmeric patent – turmeric being a yellow coloured powder made from the roots of a herb. In March 1995, a patent was granted in the United States for the use of turmeric in wound healing. However, in India, the wound-healing properties of turmeric powder are well known, and have been applied to the scrapes and cuts of generations of children. The traditional medicines sometimes find their way into Western products without the agreement of or compensation to the people who have used them for generations. So now developing countries are trying to produce databases of traditional knowledge (India is already doing this) so as to protect patent rights to these resources. This, however, costs millions of dollars to countries that could be using the money for other things.

Track 1.26

A: OK, which inventions and discoveries have we got? Bicycle, internal combustion engine …

B: The car engine, in other words.

A: Look, this must be the most important invention – it's saved so many people's lives over the years and was our first antibiotic – Alexander Fleming discovered it. Don't you agree that it's the most important thing?

C: I don't think it's unimportant, it's certainly an important invention, but I'm not really sure it's the most important. It's true that it can cure you when you're ill, but isn't a much better invention something that keeps you fit?

B: Like?

C: Like this. It's low technology at its best: it keeps you fit, it helps people get around, it doesn't pollute the atmosphere and it's fun.

B: Just what is fun about that? It's hard work, it's cold and it's murder when you have to go up hills. No, that is not one of the best inventions. This is.

A: Oh no, really.

B: I'm serious. In fact, can you imagine life without it? It wasn't the first mass media, but nowadays it's certainly the most important. It gives us news, sport and entertainment. People watch it for hours and hours and soon we'll be able to watch it in our cars and even on our mobile phones.

C: Oh great. Personally I think it's one of the worst inventions – such a waste of time.

B: No way, it gives people a way of relaxing and something to talk about with their friends.

A: You know, he's got a point, and it's not nearly as bad as something like nuclear weapons.

B: Or something as evil as landmines. You've got to admit that although it may have some bad points, all in all it does have a lot of good points.

Track 1.27

such a waste of time
he's got a point
all in all
it's certainly an important invention

Unit 5
Track 2.1

A: Hi, good morning.

B: Good morning.

A: I wondered if you could help me?

B: Sure, go ahead.

A: I need to get to the Low Memorial Library at Columbia University, and I'm not sure how to get there.

B: Well, getting around New York is generally very easy. Public transport is good: there are buses, the metro and even ferries, and there are lots of cabs.

A: I was thinking about walking actually: I've got quite a bit of time before the conference.

B: Well, that's not too difficult either. In New York we have a grid system: most roads run either north to south or east to west.

A: Yes, I know, it's very difficult to get used to.

B: Really – where are you from?

A: London: the streets and roads are not straight at all there.

B: OK, well here the north–south roads are called Avenues. Go out of the hotel, cross Riverside Drive and head east down the crosstown road West 80th Street.

A: Excuse me? Crosstown road?

B: Crosstown roads run from east to west across the city. These are mostly called streets.

A: So streets go east–west and avenues run north–south.

B: You got it. So go down West 80th Street one block east till you get to the lights.

A: One block east?

B: Yes, we tend to give directions by north, south, east or west. And by blocks, blocks of buildings, not by streets or roads.

A: I see.

B: Then at the corner of West 80th and West End Avenue turn north and head uptown for upper Manhattan.

A: But I thought I already was uptown.

B: You're in upper Manhattan. But being in upper Manhattan and travelling uptown are different things. Upper Manhattan contains Central Park and the areas north of it. Then lower Manhattan runs from the south to about 14th Street. Finally, there's the midtown area. Midtown stretches from 30th Street to the southern Central Park.

A: OK, but what about uptown and downtown?

B: Basically, this depends upon where you are standing: north of where you are is uptown and south of where you are is downtown.

A: So I want to go uptown to the University.

B: That's correct. So at the corner of West 80th and West End Avenue, head …

A: Uptown.

B: Then turn north and keep going for about twenty minutes till you reach the intersection of West End Avenue, Broadway and West 108th Street. From there the Avenue becomes Broadway, so keep following it north, over the junction with Cathedral Parkway through Morningside Heights until you get to West 116th Street. Turn right into West 116th Street and Columbia University is on your left.

A: Let me just go over that again: east from here until I get to West 80th Street and then turn left into West End Avenue.

B: That's right.

A: Then I just keep going for about a mile and a half until I see the University.

B: That's correct. It should take you about forty minutes in all.

A: Thank you very much.

B: Can I give you a map in case you get lost?

A: No, that's all right – I've got a very good sense of direction.

Track 2.2

A: Excuse me, I'm trying to get to the Low Memorial Library at the University of Columbia. I'm going to a conference there.

B: Oh right.

A: Could you tell me how to get there?

B: Well, you're quite close, about fifteen minutes away.

A: Fifteen minutes away. I've just walked half an hour from West 80th Street.

B: You must have taken a wrong turn. We're here on the crossroads of Central Park North and Central Park West. Go north six blocks to West 116th Street and turn left. Go past Manhattan Avenue on to Morningside Avenue.

A: So I go six blocks along Frederick Douglas Boulevard and then take a left on to West 116th Street, continue down there till I get to Morningside Avenue.

B: That's right, then you'll see Morningside Park. Cut through the park, past the statue and back on to West 116th Street. The University is straight in front of you.

A: I see.

B: Keep going down 116th and cross Amsterdam Avenue, on your left is Hamilton Hall and Kent Hall is on your right. Go past Kent Hall and you'll see Low Plaza on your right, with the Alma Mater statue and the entrance to the Library in front of you.

A: Thank you – you've been very helpful.

Track 2.3

A: Hi.

B: Hello.

A: How can we help you?

B: Is this the Office of Institutional Real Estate?

A: Yes, sir. My name's Alice Baum and I'm a University Housing Supervisor.

B: Oh, good, I wonder if you could help me?

A: I'll certainly try, sir.

B: I'm hoping to rent an apartment from September when I begin here and I'd really like some advice on where to rent and how to rent a place.

A: Advice on renting in Manhattan. We've got plenty of advice about that. The first thing to think about are the prices. New York is an expensive place to live and Manhattan is the most expensive place in New York – everyone wants to be here. In most areas of Manhattan, you will have great difficulty finding a studio apartment for less than $1,300 – $1,400 per month. But, there are areas just outside Manhattan (within a 30 – 40 minute commute) where you can find a decent studio apartment to rent for $850 – $1,000 per month.

B: That's a big difference. But then there are travel costs on top of that.

A: Yes, there are. If you're prepared to make compromises in your choice of accommodation, perhaps you can find an apartment you like and can afford. Monthly rents also depend on two other factors: apartment size and then amenities.

B: Can you tell me a bit more about that?

A: Basically bigger flats get higher rents, so if you can live without a lot of space, it's much cheaper. And if you are willing to take a flat which has street noise or doesn't have much natural light, then you may save some more money.

B: I see.

A: However, you could go the other way and get a bigger flat and share it with another student. You can cut costs by sharing a large bedroom. To find a roommate, check the listings for apartment shares in the Housing Registry.

B: Share a flat – I hadn't given that idea much thought.

A: Lots of our students do that.

B: What about amenities? Can you explain that a bit more?

A: You need to decide what facilities you really would like and what you can do without. For example, do you want a doorman? Would you like an elevator? These kinds of things put the prices up.

B: I don't think I need a doorman. Is there anything else I should know?

A: Yes, remember, the housing market is very competitive, especially for affordable apartments. You need to be prepared to make decisions quickly and be flexible with your plans. Don't start your search earlier than four weeks before you want to move in because tenants only need to give landlords 30 days' notice of their departure.

B: OK.

A: And make apartment hunting your life for two or three weeks – that should be enough time to get familiar with the market and find what you are looking for.

B: What's the best way of finding a place?

A: There are really only two ways – you do it yourself or you get someone else to do it for you.

B: That sounds interesting. How do I do that?

A: There are property brokers who will find a place for you. They can guide you to the property of your choice and help you with the paperwork.

B: Well, that sounds great.

A: But they do charge you a commission fee. In Manhattan, expect to pay between 12% and 15% of the year's rent. That means if your rent is $1,000 a month, the broker's fee works out to $1,800.

B: Oh, maybe not a broker then. And what's the other option again?

A: Do the leg work yourself: look in the classified ads, call landlord companies and do online searches – check out our website first.

B: You mentioned paperwork, could you tell me something about that?

A: Sure. To rent an apartment, you may be asked to complete an application, by your prospective landlord. You may also be asked to pay between $50 and $200 for credit reports – landlords want to see evidence of steady income and good credit.

B: I see.

A: Because you are a full-time student most landlords will require a guarantor, someone to guarantee you will pay the rent on time. And when the landlord approves your apartment application, be prepared to pay the first month's rent and the deposit when you sign the lease.

B: That's a lot to think about and it sounds like a lot of hard work. Thank you very much for the advice.

A: You're very welcome, and good luck.

Track 2.4

Can you tell me a bit more about that?
Can you explain that a bit more?
What's the best way of finding a place?
How do I do that?
What's the other option?

Track 2.5

At the beginning of the last century new technologies and rapid urbanisation were transforming the way people in the West lived. In the quickly expanding cities, new ways of working with steel and glass were offering architects new ways to create radically new buildings. In America, architects were creating skyscrapers in Chicago and then New York, like the Flatiron building in 1902 – designs that would eventually redefine the urban landscape throughout the world, and it was from these new breakthroughs in architectural engineering and ideas in Europe that the modern movement was formed. The response of European architects to the Americans' technological advances (including bridges and other building forms as well as skyscrapers) would lead to the development of Modernism.

The modern movement believed that the new age needed a new architecture to reflect the age of machines. The most important of the European architects was the Swiss-born architect Le Corbusier. Le Corbusier declared that the house was a machine for living in. He began to develop new thinking in design, space and mass-production in architecture. The Modernists began their mission to make architecture not simply about the building of buildings, but rather about the construction of a new way of living.

For Le Corbusier and his colleagues, Modernism was not just a new way of building – it was a new idea, a movement through which architects could construct a better life for everyone and thereby change society forever. By the 1930s architects like Le Corbusier and Ludwig Mies Van Der Rohe were established architects in Europe promoting the ideas of Modernism. In 1934 the revolutionary Lawn Road flats were built in London – also known as the Isokon building. It was an attempt to build a housing block for professional people and had all the comforts of modern living including a restaurant, called the Isobar, a laundry, central heating and even a central shoe polishing service. In 1952 in Marseille, France the *Unité d'habitation* brought together Le Corbusier's vision for communal living with the needs and realities of post-war France. Up to 1,600 people lived in a vertical village surrounded by an area of park land complete with an internal shopping street halfway up the building, a recreation ground and children's nursery on the roof.

The starting point for Modernism, however was not beauty – this would follow naturally from creating rational, efficient buildings – it was about building a better life for people, to improve the lives of ordinary working people. This was the beginning of building social housing for the workers, as Berthold Lubetkin said in 1938 *Nothing is too good for ordinary people.*

The Second World War had changed the world forever – socially, economically and politically. The end of the war left Europe in ruins, and a massive rebuilding programme was necessary. But this also provided a new opportunity and optimism. Modernist town planning was heavily influenced by Le Corbusier's plan of 1933, which promised a future of sunshine, fresh air and greenery for city-dwellers. Le Corbusier's new city would consist of giant white apartment blocks divided into zones, separated by green spaces with wide roads running between them. This was a powerful vision in the immediate post-war years, when re-housing families from slums to clean, modern apartments was a political priority. By the 1960s, Modernism was the dominant style of architecture. Schools, offices, homes, and even entire towns were all being constructed using, to a greater or lesser extent, methods first advocated by Le Corbusier, Mies Van Der Rohe and other Modernist architects.

During the1960s and 70s politicians liked the Modernist solutions to the problems of aging slums in the form of high density housing in tower blocks like Trellick Tower built in 1972. But soon Modernist architects began to be blamed for destroying communities and over the next twenty years, public criticism of modernist architects became louder. The idea of building a better society through architecture was almost agreed to have failed and by the start of the 1990s, the modern movement which promised an international architecture seemed to be over.

However, in the first decade of the 21st century the reputation of the modernist movement was restored. Modernist buildings became modern icons, with homes in modernist buildings being sold for large sums. In 70 years the landscape of modern cities has changed dramatically and much of the change can be attributed to Le Corbusier and other pioneers and the modern style has been developed further into the Hi Tech style by architects like Sir Norman Foster who designed the Swiss Re building in 2004. However, what is left is more than just a collection of Modernist buildings – there remains the idea that architects, through their work should try to improve the quality of life of their fellow citizens.

Track 2.6

1

This city is located in the south-east of Poland in central Europe. It is situated between the Jura uplands and the Tatra Mountains, and is on the banks of the River Vistula. It has one of the best-preserved city centres in Europe. It is comprised of two main parts: the old town and the new town. The old town is the part I like best with Wavel castle on the hill overlooking the river and the market square where you can sit and have a coffee and meet people. It has the oldest University in Poland so it has lots of students and the nightlife is great. I hope that it doesn't change at all, because it is so beautiful and that's what has caused the biggest change: tourism. Lots of people now are visiting the city from all over the world and UNESCO has made the old quarter a World Heritage site.

2

I'm going to talk about a city I lived in for about three years. It's a relatively modern city located in the south-east of Australia and some people classify it as a world city. It's on the coast and looks over Port Phillip bay in the immediate south and the Indian Ocean. It's a commercial and industrial centre with seven universities. It's also the country's largest port. The city has been growing since it was founded in 1835 and many new public buildings have been built recently including a new exhibition centre. I love sports, and the thing I like best about the city are the sports facilities and the wide variety of sports you can watch there.

3

I've lived in this city since I was a child and my home is still there. It's on the coast, with the Persian Gulf to the north and the desert to the south and it's the trading capital of the UAE. It is divided into two main districts – Deira and Bur Dubai which are divided by Khor Dubai or Dubai Creek. Deira contains many markets or souks like the spice souk and the gold souk, while Bur Dubai has the mosque and a museum. Dubai has changed probably more than any other city in the world. In the early 20th century it was a small trading city, but during the last century it has developed into a major centre for tourism and commerce and now has the most amazing and expensive hotels in the world. I hope the city will continue to expand in trade and tourism with state of the art buildings, but the part of the city I like best is the old town with the white houses on the banks of Dubai Creek.

Track 2.7

state of the art
developed into a major centre
capital of the UAE
so it has lots of students
recently including a new exhibition centre

Unit 6

Track 2.8

Monica: Hi there Ivan. You look a bit fed up. What's wrong?

Ivan: I feel like an alien here. I thought I could actually speak English but now I'm not so sure. I don't seem to understand what local people say to me. It's a whole new different language out there on the street! They use words I haven't even heard before!

Monica: What do you mean? Which words exactly?

Ivan: Well, I was in a café today – just around midday. I was feeling really hungry and I wanted more than a cup of coffee and a sandwich. So, I was having a look at the menu and this man said to me 'The chook and vegies are bonzer here, mate'. I just didn't understand his accent. I felt really stupid. I had no idea what he was saying to me and I certainly didn't know how to reply!

Monica: Oh, don't worry, Ivan. It takes time to get used to a new accent and a new set of words of course. Actually chook is what Australians say for chicken and vegies are vegetables.

Ivan: So, *chook* and *vegies* means chicken and vegetables? I didn't know. He was speaking so quickly too.

Monica: Never mind. Just think – you'll recognise these words when you hear them again. And remember you can always ask people to explain a word like chook if you don't understand. And you can also ask them to speak more slowly too. People are very friendly here in Oz, you know.

Ivan: Oz?

Monica: Yes, Oz. It means Australia. Now he said the chook and vegies were *bonzer*, didn't he?

Ivan: Yes, what does *bonzer* mean?

Monica: It means something is great or excellent. Australians have other words like that. We can say that something is *grouse* or *ripper* as well.

Ivan: So, grouse, ripper or bonzer all mean great? These are useful words to know.

Monica: Yes, so when this man said that the chook and vegies were bonzer he was recommending them to you.

Ivan: So, he was just being friendly then?

Monica: Yes, that's right. As I said before, Aussies are really friendly people.

Ivan: Aussies?

Monica: Yes, an Aussie is an Australian. Now, this Aussie called you mate, didn't he? We often use this word when we greet each other. We say *G'day, mate.* Just that means the same as *friend.* Now we can also say sport or cobber. Both of these have the same meaning as mate or friend. So you can greet someone with *G'day cobber* or …

Ivan: G'day sport!

Monica: That's right. You see, you can do it! And we say *hooroo mate* too when we want to say goodbye. People can also say ta-ta for goodbye. The word *Ta* on its own means thank you.

Ivan: These are useful words to know. I remember the waiter said hooroo when I left the café and I didn't say anything. He must have thought that I was really unfriendly.

Monica: Never mind. Don't let it get to you, Ivan. Next time someone says ta to you, just repeat and say it back. So, ta, mate. Thanks! It's easy when you know how.

Ivan: But there are so many new words. I don't think I can learn them all.

Monica: Don't worry about it. You'll get used to it. It's just a matter of time. After all, it takes time to get used to a new country and …

Ivan: … a completely different language.

Monica: Yes. You'll be all right. You can do it. You are a Sydneysider after all.

Ivan: A *Sydneysider*? What's that?

Monica: A Sydneysider is someone who lives in Sydney. So you and me are …

Ivan: Sydneysiders?

Monica: Yes! that's right. Now I reckon this café will be a bonzer place to meet some Aussies and practise the language. And I'm feeling quite hungry now. How about going there for a sanger?

Ivan: A sanger? What's that?

Monica: It's a sandwich!

Track 2.9

Never mind.
Don't worry.
Don't let it get to you.
It's just a matter of time.
You'll be all right.
You'll get used to it.

Track 2.10

Interviewer: Welcome to the last programme in the series *Language Matters*. Now, did you know that there are 6,000 languages in the world? It sounds like a lot, doesn't it? But, according to linguists, about half of the world's languages are going to die out within the next hundred years. This means that there is a language dying out somewhere in the world every couple of weeks or so. So, our languages are at risk of extinction and linguists like my guest Jan Petersen are involved in a race against time to save them. Jan, welcome to the programme. Now, when exactly does a language die?

Jan: Well, in very simple terms a language dies when the last person who speaks it dies. Now, there are about fifty languages in the world today with only one speaker left. And interestingly enough, the majority of these languages are here in Australia. Now, to give you a very recent example, a colleague of mine was doing some field work in Cameroon, Africa a few years ago and he came across a language called Kasabe, which linguists like us had never studied before. It had just one speaker left, a man called Bogon. Unfortunately, the linguist had no time on that visit to find out much about the language so he decided to go back to Cameroon a year later. Unfortunately, he went back only to find that Bogon had died a few weeks earlier.

Interviewer: So, one week Kasabe existed as one of the world's languages and the next week it did not.

Jan: That's absolutely right. Today, Kasabe is an extinct language. However, there is nothing unusual about a single language dying. Communities have, after all, come and gone throughout history, taking their languages with them. But what we are seeing now is a considerable increase in the rate at which our languages are dying out.

Interviewer: So, why are they dying?

Jan: Well, many things can kill a language. It can, for example, die out because of natural disasters. A few years ago an earthquake in Papua New Guinea killed over 2,000 people and displaced thousands of others. Entire villages were wiped out and around one third of the population were killed. The people in those different villages had been identified as being different from each other in their speech. This means that in effect they spoke separate languages. So, as a result of the earthquake, the number of speakers of these languages has gone down dramatically. Languages may also die as a result of cultural assimilation.

Interviewer: What exactly do you mean by cultural assimilation?

Jan: Well, many of our languages are at risk of extinction as a result of cultural assimilation. That is to say – big cultural movements that began 500 years ago. This was when colonialism spread a small number of dominant languages around the world.

Interviewer: So minority languages are taken over by dominant languages such as English and French, for example?

Jan: That's right. Now when one culture assimilates another, there is a sequence of stages that affect the endangered language. The first stage is that there is great pressure on the people to speak the dominant language. The second stage is a period of bilingualism. This means that people become proficient in the new language and at the same time hold on to their old language. Then, and often quickly, bilingualism starts to decline with the result that the old language gives way to the new. This leads to the third stage, in which the younger generation increasingly finds its old language less relevant. For example, Breton, which is spoken in north-west France, is a good example of a language that has declined dramatically in recent years. In recent times, this has already happened to two other Celtic languages in Northern Europe – Manx, which used to be spoken on the Isle of Man, and Cornish. Both these languages are currently attracting support and attention but once a language has lost its last native speaker, bringing it back is extremely difficult. However, all is not lost. The language of Breton can be saved if enough effort is made – the kind of effort, in fact that has already helped the language of Welsh get over a dramatic decline. In fact, nowadays Welsh is very much a living language, with around half a million speakers!

Track 2.11

Interviewer: So, it is never too late to save a dying language?

Jan: Well, we certainly can't save all our languages. We certainly can't do anything to help those languages where there are too few speakers and where the communities are too busy just trying to survive. However, many other languages are not in such serious danger – for example, those 5,000 languages where there are fewer than 100,000 speakers. Now, languages with this number of speakers will not die next week or next year, but they may not exist in a couple of generations' time. So even a language with 100,000 speakers is not necessarily safe.

Interviewer: So what can we do to save our languages?

Jan: Well, first of all the communities themselves must actually want to save their languages. And, of course, society in general needs to have a respect for minority languages. In practical terms this means supporting the community with both linguists and language teachers and providing materials such as grammar books and dictionaries for use in schools. Examples of reversing the trend of declining languages have already been achieved in parts of Australia, North America and Europe.

Interviewer: But at the end of the day is it worth all this effort to revive dying languages? Is language death such a bad thing? If a few thousand languages survive, that will be enough, won't it?

Jan: No, the loss of languages is a disaster. We should care about language extinction for the same reason that we care when a species of animal or plant dies. Language loss reduces the diversity of our planet. In the case of language, we are talking about intellectual and cultural diversity, not biological diversity, but the issues are the same. Diversity enables a species to survive in different environments. And we know that the strongest ecosystems are those which are most diverse.

Interviewer: So there is a need to maintain linguistic diversity?

Jan: Absolutely. Linguistic diversity is essential because cultures are mainly transmitted through spoken and written languages.

Interviewer: But what can we learn from language?

Jan: Well, sometimes what we learn is practical, such as when we discover new medical treatments from the folk medicine of an indigenous people. And sometimes this knowledge is intellectual. By this I mean that languages can tell us something about early civilisations. And of course, very often it is linguistic. So, we learn something new about the language itself – the way the language works. They enable us to understand the behaviour that makes us truly human and without which there would be no communication at all.

Interviewer: Well, we will certainly be talking more after this short break. Stay with us …

Track 2.12

Monica: So, Ivan, what is important to you when you are learning a language?

Ivan: Oh, that's a good question. I've never really thought about it before. So give me a moment to think about it. Well, I certainly think it's important to know a lot of words.

Monica: So, by words, you mean vocabulary.

Ivan: Well, yes. For example, you need words to do simple things, like understand a menu in a restaurant. I remember when I first arrived in Sydney I didn't know words like *chook*, which means chicken, of course. So, for me vocabulary is the key to learning a language. In fact, I carry my dictionary everywhere with me so that I can learn as many words as possible. What do you think?

Monica: Just a minute. Let me see. Yes, I agree that words can be immediately useful when you learn a language. But I certainly want to learn to speak correctly. I feel really embarrassed when people don't understand me because of my grammar. So learning grammatical rules and speaking accurately are

also important for me. In fact, I actually like it when people correct my mistakes. Is that the same for you?

Ivan: Let me think. That's a good point, but to be honest with you, I find it really embarrassing when people correct me a lot. I mean, if my teacher corrected every single mistake I made, it would take too long for me to communicate what I actually wanted to say. I think it is important to just get out there on the street and talk to people and try not to worry too much about making mistakes. I think it is just as important to have a go and just experiment with language!

Monica: So for you it is more important to be fluent?

Ivan: Absolutely. Is there anything else that is important in learning a language or have we thought of everything?

Monica: Just a second. Give me a moment. Actually yes, there is something else. What about knowing how to say a word and where to put the stress in a word or a sentence?

Ivan: You mean, pronunciation? Yes, that's important too. I like to borrow videos, listen to the voices and try to copy how they speak. And, of course, I can stop the tape, rewind and listen again. Now, is there anything we've forgotten to mention?

Track 2.13

I've never really thought about it
For example, you need words to do simple things
I couldn't even order a meal
grammatical rules and speaking accurately are also important
a word or a sentence

Unit 7
Track 2.14

A: Hello, Security.

B: Hi. I'm sorry about calling.

A: That's not a problem. How can I help you?

B: I'd like to report a burglary, I think.

A: Very well, madam. Can I take some details from you first of all? Your name and student number are …

B: My name's Ester.

A: Ester …?

B: Toporek.

A: Can you just spell that for me, please?

B: T-O-P-O-R-E-K. Student number UC 339.

A: And your place of residence?

B: I'm in halls – in Western Hall, room E86.

A: And is this where the burglary took place?

B: Yes, it is: my laptop was stolen from my room.

A: That's your personal computer?

B: No, I've got a separate desktop PC, it's my laptop that was stolen.

A: And are you missing anything else?

B: I can't find my keys anywhere.

A: The keys to your room?

B: Yes, I just can't see them anywhere.

A: When was the last time you remember seeing them?

B: I last saw them before I went to the bathroom for a shower, I think, but I can't be sure.

A: I understand. We need to get as much information from you as possible. What had you done before you took a shower?

B: Before I went to the bathroom I'd been with Keith in the kitchen having a chat for a few minutes. We talked about a few things like the concert he'd been to the night before and the lecture we'd attended earlier in the afternoon.

A: So you could have left your keys in the kitchen when you went for a shower.

B: I suppose so, I'm not certain.

A: How well do you know Keith?

B: Oh, he's a really good friend, it's nothing to do with him.

A: Did he see your keys in the kitchen?

B: No, I asked Keith before I rang you, he hadn't seen my keys – he'd gone back to make a coffee about fifteen minutes after we'd compared notes.

A: Fifteen minutes later.

B: Yes, more or less.

A: E floor is on the ground floor isn't it?

B: Yes, why?

A: Was the kitchen window open?

B: I'm not sure, it might have been, I'm not 100% positive. I didn't pay much attention to it.

A: Did you go straight from the kitchen to the shower room?

B: Yes, but when I went back to my room I couldn't get in, I was locked out.

A: So, had you locked the door before you went to the kitchen?

B: I'm pretty sure I did – I usually lock my room door. As soon as I'd discovered I was locked out I called the porter and he let me back in to my room.

A: And you discovered your laptop was missing when you went into the room.

B: Well, no. The first thing I did was look for my keys so that I could lock my door. When I couldn't find my keys, I thought that I'd left them somewhere in the hall and decided to go to lost property the next day. Later, after the porter had opened the door, when I decided to correct my lecture notes and needed my laptop I couldn't find it. I looked everywhere.

A: OK, madam. Have you called the porter's lodge to report it?

B: Er, no, not yet, I didn't think of that.

A: Could you call them immediately after this? The thief may still be around or they may have filmed him on the security cameras. One last thing, madam.

B: Yes.

A: Did you mark your property with your student number?

B: Yes, I did.

A: And is it insured?

B: I'm almost certain it is, but that's not the point. I've got my dissertation on it and a lot of my work from this year is on it.

A: I see. I'll send someone over in about 30 minutes, and in the meantime we'll contact the local police station.

B: Thanks.

Track 2.15

I can't be sure.
I'm not certain.
I'm pretty sure I did.
I suppose so.
I'm almost certain it is.
I'm not 100% positive.

Track 2.16

1

A: Hi, I'd like to return these books.

B: Thank you very much, er Susan.

A: You can call me Sue.

B: Er, OK. I'll just be a second. Right, the first five are fine, but this one's overdue.

A: Overdue? How much is there to pay on it?

B: There's three pounds 50 to pay.

A: But the due date was Sunday the 13th. I couldn't bring it back then.

B: Why not?

A: Well, the library is closed then.

B: No, the library is open seven days a week, twenty-four hours a day.

A: Well, I mean I was in London at the weekend and I needed it for the previous week for an essay so I couldn't bring it back on time.

B: You know, you could have renewed the book online from London or even from your hall of residence.

A: Really! Nobody told me I could renew the book online. If I'd known that, I would have renewed it before the due date, honestly.

B: Well, I'm afraid that's out of our hands. You need to pay three pounds 50 fine on this, and there's another four pounds twenty on the other book.

A: Another four pounds. Why's that? I've only had it for ten days.

B: Exactly, that's the problem – it's an overnight loan book only. All journals and reference books are overnight loans only, you have to return them the next day or we charge you 40p per day.

A: I'm sorry, I didn't see that – I'd have returned it the following day if I'd seen it was overnight only – really.

B: I'm afraid it's up to you to know what kind of books you have and how long you can keep them.

A: Look, it's nearly the end of term and well, you know how tight things get with money: could you forget about the overnight loan and just charge me for the other book?

2

A: Hello, Mohammed. Welcome back to the exams office.

B: Hello, Elizabeth. Thanks.

A: How can I help you today?

B: I've just got my marks back from the dissertation.

A: Oh yes?

B: And I've noticed that some points were deducted for lateness.

A: Yes, that's correct.

B: Em, ten marks were taken away.

A: Yes, that's correct. Students should hand in their work on time.

B: But I was only three days late handing the essay in.

A: Four days – you were four days late, Mohammed. If you had made arrangements with your tutor to hand in your essay late, we wouldn't have taken off any marks.

B: But you still took off ten marks – I thought you would only reduce the score by five points.

A: Yes, we would have only reduced it by five if you had given it in with a cover sheet and if it hadn't had coffee stains all over it. If the tutor had been able to read all of it we wouldn't have taken away five more points.

B: My tutor couldn't read it?

A: Not the parts with coffee all over it, no.

B: I'm so sorry.

3

A: Oh no, look at that.

B: What's up, Sema?

A: Look at this, they've clamped my car.

B: What do you mean?

A: They've put a lock on my car wheel.

B: Who did that?

A: It must be University security.

B: Why would they do that? It's a University car park; you're a student at the University. Have you got a parking permit?

A: Yes, look, there in the windscreen – I wouldn't have parked here if I didn't have one. And if I hadn't parked here where would we have parked? The car park is full and we only had five minutes to get to the tutorial. If I hadn't parked here, we would have been late for the lecture and we would be in Mr Hoban's bad books again.

B: And what does Vice Chancellor mean?

A: You know very well that the Vice Chancellor is the head of the university, now is not a good time to ask stupid questions.

B: Well, I wouldn't have asked, if you hadn't parked in her space.

A: I've parked in the Vice Chancellor's parking space?

B: It says here: reserved for Vice Chancellor.

A: Oh no.

Track 2.17

If Mohammed had handed in his work on time, he wouldn't have lost any marks.

If Susan had renewed her books, she wouldn't have paid a fine.

If Sema had not been late, she wouldn't have been in a rush and would have parked her car in a student parking space.

Mohammed would not have lost any marks if he had included a cover sheet.

Sema would not have parked in the Vice Chancellor's place if she had seen the sign.

Track 2.18

Good afternoon and welcome everyone. My name is Emily Sutherland and I'm here to give today's talk on causes of crime and relate them to theories of crime. I'm going to look at three broad perspectives on crime: rational choice, biological determinism, and finally sociological determinism.

Let's look at the earliest theory of crime: rational choice. This is often referred to as the classical theory and was developed in the eighteenth century by philosophers like Jeremy Bentham and Cesare Beccaria. They believed everyone is capable of committing crime – crime, they thought, is an activity of total free will and individuals weigh the consequences of their actions against the possible punishment. That is to say, anyone would commit a crime if they thought they would not be punished for it. Therefore, in their view the way to prevent crime must be to make the cost of crime greater than the benefits – make punishment harder, for example. Although this is an old idea, it is still popular today, with over two million people in America, for example, in prison.

In the nineteenth century, science began to play a part in criminal theory and biological determinism grew as a theory of the cause of crime. Various theories of this kind have existed for well over a century and argue that crime is caused by psychological or physical factors that the criminal cannot help. There have been theories that try to explain criminal behaviour by analysing overall body type, by focusing on the appearance of the face, and even by looking at bumps on the head. While the more extreme examples of these theories may sound silly and outdated, some forms of biological determinism are still with us today and some scientists are looking for the criminal gene – a gene that causes some individuals to become criminals. In effect, if we can find the criminal gene then we can use medicine to stop criminal behaviour.

In the early twentieth century more mainstream, society-based theories of the causes of crime were developed. The three main theories which are still with us today are: learning theory, strain theory and control theory. I'll describe briefly each of these in turn before going into them in more depth in later lectures. Learning theory was developed during the 1920s and 1930s and believes that crime, like any other behaviour – is learned from the people around you. When people around you think crime is an acceptable form of behaviour, criminality becomes a normal way of life. The second one – strain theory – sees crime as the result of a capitalist economy in which people are encouraged to get a good job and a good education. However, not everyone has the opportunity to get a good education or a good job, and this causes stress or strain as people cannot reach their aims by legal means and try illegal methods instead. The third social theory is control theory which looks at an individual's relationship with people who tie them into society, such as parents, family or teachers and looks at the criminal's usually poor self-image. The important consequence of these social theories is that they see criminals as people who were poorly or badly socialised. With proper treatment, or re-socialisation, they can live a normal or non-criminal life. In effect, criminals don't need punishment, they need to be taught.

Now let's look at the earlier theory of the causes of crime in more detail. Philosophers like Bentham and Beccaria were really more concerned about the legal system than why people commit crime …

Track 2.19

Jan: What have we got here then?

Walter: Well, the first case is a man who was drunk in a city centre bar.

Marie-Claude: Nothing unusual there – a fine, I think.

Jan: No, I'm sorry, I don't agree with just a fine. If you look at the details you'll see that he was threatening people – verbal abuse. This is clearly more than just being drunk – he was drunk and abusive.

Walter: I'm afraid I agree with Jan, a fine is not enough.

Marie-Claude: We could fine him quite a lot – say £200.

Jan: You've got to think about the other people: the bar owner, the customer he threatened, the other customers. This kind of behaviour makes everyone feel uncomfortable and unsafe, don't you agree, Walter?

Walter: I completely agree, I think a £200 fine and excluding him from city centre bars and pubs for one month.

Marie-Claude: A fine and an exclusion order – that's a bit heavy.

Jan: Marie-Claude, it's the only way to stop him doing it again.

Marie-Claude: I still don't agree fully with you, I think you're being too hard, but if you've made up your minds, then a fine and an exclusion it is.

Jan: OK, next one.

Walter: The next one is vandalism – a 15-year-old boy smashed a shop window and sprayed graffiti around.

Marie-Claude: It's just his age – anti-social behaviour. What do you want to do about him? Jan?

Jan: You know, he's too young to take real action against, but I feel very strongly about this kind of thing.

Walter: I agree with you Jan. If we allow this kind of behaviour now, just think what will happen in the future. I think we need to come down hard on him.

Marie-Claude: Oh, come on you two – he's just a boy, it's his age, and his parents are just as responsible for his behaviour.

Jan: I think you're right Marie-Claude. The parents are responsible too.

Walter: Let's tag him – let's put an electronic signal on him so that we know where he is and say that he cannot go outside the house after 7 o'clock.

Marie-Claude: Tagging him? Walter, you're treating him like a criminal and he'll become a criminal if you treat him like one. I totally disagree with that.

Jan: I can't agree with you either this time, Walter. Don't you think you're being too hard?

Walter: Well, let's compromise – how about 50 hours community service? He can clean the graffiti and help the community.

Marie-Claude: OK.

Jan: And let's not forget his parents. As Marie-Claude said, they are equally responsible.

Walter: £50 fine for his parents?

Marie-Claude: You're fining his parents too?

Jan: I'm in complete agreement – community service and a £50 fine for the parents. Who's next?

Walter: The next case is shoplifting – a 22-year-old woman, a first time offence.

Marie-Claude: As it's a first time offence, I think a warning is enough.

Jan: I'm sorry, I couldn't disagree more. Shoplifting is a serious offence: it puts shops out of business and raises the price of things for everyone. In my opinion she should go to prison.

Marie-Claude: Prison! Walter, tell me you're not on Jan's side.

Walter: Well, I'm afraid that I think it's a serious offence too, but I don't entirely agree with Jan because it is the first time she has done this. I think we should put her on probation and recommend that she sees a counsellor.

Marie-Claude: I agree in part with that, particularly seeing a counsellor for help with the problem, but I still think that probation is quite hard. It will give people she knows a bad opinion of her.

Jan: I'm afraid we have to agree to disagree on this one Marie-Claude. I believe a short prison sentence will make sure she never does this again and if we can't put her in prison then we should put her on probation.

Walter: Do you agree on probation, Marie-Claude?

Marie-Claude: No, I don't, but if the alternative is prison, then I'll go along with you on this.

Unit 8
Track 2.20

Emi: Oh, Marta – I'm so glad I caught you. I'm just off to town to pick up a few things, but I wanted to ask you about it first.

Marta: Fire away – what is it?

Emi: Look, I need to get a load of things before the semester starts, but I don't know where the best places to get them are.

Marta: OK, what kind of things are you going for?

Emi: Well, the first thing I need is clothes. It's always raining, this is the only jacket I've got and it's wet through. Melbourne's much wetter than I thought it would be.

Marta: Oh, it's not that bad, you need to remember that Melbourne has quite a wet climate, so we do get a lot of rain. But you should get a good wet weather jacket because you'll need it. What about a DRIZ-A-BONE jacket?

Emi: What's that and how much are they?

Marta: They're a popular waterproof coat and it really depends on how much money you want to spend: if you've got about a hundred or more dollars, you could go to an outdoor shop. They sell jackets that keep out the rain, but they are quite expensive and you'll need to shop around to get the best price – there's one in the shopping centre and I think there's another in the retail park.

Emi: A hundred dollars – that's a lot, I can't afford that much.

Marta: There's an alternative.

Emi: What is it?

Marta: Charity shops.

Emi: I want a waterproof coat, not charity.

Marta: But that's where a lot of students get things like coats and jackets from. In fact we sometimes call charity shops *Op shops*, short for *Opportunity shops*. Op shops sell clothes that other people can't use or don't want. You can pick up a real bargain if you look. The other place is the army store.

Emi: Army stores?

Marta: Yes, they're usually quite cheap – they sell ex-army gear – a lot of students go there for things like waterproof jackets.

Emi: Oh, really? It's an idea, maybe I'll go to all of them to check out the prices.

Marta: Yes, that's always a good idea, but remember it's very usual for students to go to charity shops and they also sell things like Fair Trade coffee, CDs, books and lots of other things.

Emi: OK, I'll definitely check it out. Do they sell course books for students?

Marta: Is that the next thing you need?

Emi: Yes, we got the reading list yesterday and I calculated that if I bought all the books new it would cost me nearly $500. Just one on Total Quality Management costs $50.

Marta: Phew, that's a lot of money.

Emi: It is, but I need it – it's a set book, what can I do?

Marta: Well, the first thing you could do is look in a second-hand bookshop – there's one just next to the University. When students finish their studies, a lot of them go there and sell their course books, so the next year's students can buy their old books at a reduced price.

Emi: That's a good tip, I'll certainly pop in there. So, clothes, books, and – stationery. Where can I get that?

Marta: There are a couple of places you can get stationery: you can get general things like pens and notebooks from a newsagent's, or the Student's Union Shop. If you want anything like a punch or stapler, you could go to an office supply shop – there's one in the retail park, but that's a bit out of town. The other place you could try is the stationery shop in the precinct. You can get things for drawing and art there too if you're into that. I think there's a sale on there at the moment, you could find what you want with a discount.

Emi: I'll certainly go there then. And, the most important thing – I need some food.

Marta: Food shopping. Well, there are several supermarkets around here. There are the usual supermarket chains where you can buy almost everything and there are discount variety chain stores where food tends to be cheaper but with less variety.

Emi: I don't mind – that's good for me.

Marta: But let me give you a really good tip: go to the market, the food's fresh and it's often cheaper than you buy at the supermarket.

Emi: When is it open?

Marta: The central market is open at the weekends and I think on Tuesdays, but during the week it closes at 5.30.

Emi: I don't think I'll have time to make it there, I'll have to go to the supermarket.

Marta: Or you could go to the milk bar near the campus and get something quick and easy to eat, ready to eat food.

Emi: That's not a bad idea, thanks Marta.

Track 2.21

a discount
I can't afford that much
You can pick up a real bargain
check out the prices
I'll certainly pop in there

Track 2.22

1

A: Excuse me, can you help me, I'm looking for a binder and dividers – do you have any?

B: Yes, of course, what colour binder are you looking for?

A: Well, what colours do you stock?

B: There's black, of course, and we also have blue and red. We also have ones with the University crest on it.

A: Oh, that's nice. I'll take one of those please.

2

A: Can I help you at all?

B: Oh, sorry I didn't see you there. No, it's OK, I don't need any help, I'm just browsing.

A: Are you looking for anything in particular?

B: I'm looking for books on management – total quality management.

A: I see, well, the business section is over there, you should be able to find something.

B: Thanks.

A: If you need any help or if you find anything you like, just give me a shout.

B: Will do.

3

A: Hi, how are you doing?

B: Hello, I'm looking for a waterproof jacket, the only coat I've got is this one and it's not at all waterproof.

A: The waterproof jackets are over here. Let's see. What size are you?

B: I'm never sure if I'm small or medium.

A: Well, you look like you're a medium size to me. Do you want to try this on for size?

B: I'll have a go. No, it's a bit too large.

A: How about this one? It's the smaller size.

B: OK. Yes, that's much better.

Track 2.23

A: Excuse me, could I have a minute of your time please?

B: I'm sorry, I'm really busy at the moment.

A: I'll only be a moment – I won't hold you up too long.

B: What … what's it about?

A: I'm a student at Monash University with the Faculty of Business and Economics and we're doing research into people's shopping habits and ethical issues. So we're taking a survey about people's attitudes for the project and I wondered if you could spare five minutes of your time to answer a few questions and to complete this questionnaire.

B: Well, only if it takes five minutes, I'm on my way to an appointment.

A: Five minutes great, I won't keep you any longer – promise.

B: All right then.

A: That's great. First can I get some particulars from you?

B: I suppose so.

A: Are you aged between 20 to 30, 30 to 40, or 40 to 50?

B: 20 to 30.

A: What's your marital status?

B: Why do you need to know that?

A: It's so we can compare shopping habits between population samples.

B: OK, I'm single.

A: And do you live alone or with other people?

B: I live with other people.

A: That's great, now I'll just ask you a few quick questions about your shopping habits.

B: OK.

A: When you're shopping for food, which things do you check: the price tag; the ingredients or if it is fresh or processed food?

B: I never really check the price, but I do tend to look at the ingredients: if there are lots of E-numbers I usually avoid it, so I don't really eat processed food. I prefer to buy fresh food if I can, although it goes off quicker than the other stuff.

A: So, can I tick B for ingredients as your first choice?

B: No, I think you should tick box A – freshness for me.

A: OK, I'll just change that. There, now do you like to shop at the local market, the local shops or at a supermarket?

B: Well, I don't much like shopping to tell you the truth, so the nearer the better. I'm not organised enough to get everything I need on the one day that the market is open, so not the local market. On the other hand, to get to the supermarket you have to drive there or get on a bus and the cost of getting there means that you don't save anything. So I guess I usually go to the local shop.

A: I see, so not the market or supermarket, you chose B.

B: Yes.

A: When an item is getting old, like a computer for example do you keep working with it, try to upgrade it, or throw it away and buy a new one?

B: I often keep things I work with because it takes time to get to know how to use it properly and if you buy new things, you have to spend a lot of time reading the instructions and so on. Besides I don't earn enough to throw things away and buy new all the time. So I guess the answer is A, keep the old one, rather than try to upgrade it or the last option.

A: OK, got that. Final question now. When you're buying cleaning products do you go for the cheapest, the best on the market or environmentally friendly products?

B: For me the best thing for the job is the one to buy. I'd like to buy environmentally friendly products, but the fact is they don't do the job as well as the best ones. I think I wouldn't buy the cheap one, because they are just as bad as the environmentally friendly products at cleaning and still harm the environment.

A: Well, that's all.

B: OK then, good luck with your findings.

A: Thanks a lot.

B: You're welcome. Goodbye.

Track 2.24

Before we begin with this week's lecture on international trade, I'll quickly recap on the main points from last week's lecture. You will remember that I talked about the power of multinational companies or TNCs – transnational companies and the role of the WTO, or World Trade Organisation and its influence on intellectual property, investment and protection of interests of richer countries. I also talked about the way these organisations set up trade rules that actually favour richer countries: one example I gave was agricultural subsidies. Rich countries spend $1 billion every day on subsidising their own farming industry, but when developing countries export their products to rich markets they face tariff barriers which put up the price of their goods. I'm going to continue with these themes, but take another angle on the theme of international trade and look at alternative ways of trading. Today I'll be talking in particular about a network of not-for-profit organisations who are cutting the middle men out of international trade and giving the profits earned from products directly back to the producers of these goods. I am, of course, talking about Fair Trade.

So, let's take a closer look at Fair Trade. I'm going to kick off by giving a brief description of the background to Fair Trade. Fair Trade aims to alleviate poverty in the South by providing producers in Africa, Asia and Latin America with opportunities to access Northern markets. It aims to build sustainable direct relationships between these producers in the South and consumers in the rich parts of the world. Over the past 40 years, Fair Trade in Europe has grown from its Dutch origins to a global network of producers and suppliers. In terms of economic value, the total for products sold under Fair Trade labels is estimated to be about $258 million and this is growing year on year. So as we can see this sector of international trade is small, but significant. For a definition of Fair Trade I'll refer to the one given in 1999 by a group of the four biggest Fair Trade organisations. They define Fair Trade as an alternative approach to conventional international trade. It is a trading partnership which aims to give an alternative model of international business by providing sustainable trade between poor producers and rich consumers. Therefore, Fair Trade is about much more than making profits and paying shareholders. That's enough about the background and definitions, let's explore these aims in more detail.

I'd like to turn now to look at these three aims individually. Fair Trade has six main goals. Firstly, to improve the livelihoods and well-being of producers by improving market access, paying producers a better price and providing continuity in the trading relationship. In effect, paying a decent price over a longer period in order to improve the lives of the small farmers and producers. Secondly, to promote development opportunities for disadvantaged producers, especially women, and to protect children from exploitation in the production process. Thirdly, to raise awareness among consumers of the negative effects on producers of international trade so that they can exercise their purchasing power positively. Fourthly, they want to set an example of partnership in trade through dialogue, transparency and respect – that is to say, to give an alternative model of international trade. Fifthly, to campaign for changes in the rules and practice of conventional international trade, and this returns to my point about the WTO. Sixthly, to protect human rights and good environmental practice. So much for the goals of Fair Trade, I'd like to move on to describe the main types of Fair Trade organisations.

There are at least three types of Fair Trade organisation. First of all are producer organisations which cultivate or produce a wide variety of products – food products like coffee and handicrafts including jewellery – and export them to the market countries. We can say that the producers are at the heart of Fair Trade. Following on from these, are the second kind of Fair Trade organisation: importing organisations which buy products from producer organisations. These importing organisations pay producer organisations a price that enables them to live adequate lives. In their home countries these importing organisations act as wholesalers or retailers. In their home markets they sell most of the products through specialised shops (called *world shops*). Many of them sell products through supermarkets. Thirdly, as I have already mentioned, Fair Trade products are sold directly to the public through World Shops. They are mostly run by volunteers and are not-for-profit organisations. These shops also have educational and campaigning functions and help promote the ideals of Fair Trade to the wider public. To sum up this part of the lecture: Fair Trade is being set up as a commercial, political and social alternative to international trade. At this point I'm going to go into more detail about world trade, Fair Trade and how this is affecting the economies of individual countries with particular reference to the European countries.

The first country I'm going to talk about is Holland …

Track 2.25

I'm going to tell you about this. I bought it in Antakya, which is a very ancient city, when we were on holiday. I bought it from a carpet dealer as a souvenir of our holiday travelling around Turkey. It's not very large, about one metre wide by two metres long. It's handmade from a region of Turkey called Kars, and the reason I bought it really was for the design, it's something similar to star shapes on it. It's got a very strong design with nice colours in it. At the moment, the rug is on my living room floor and whenever I look at it, it reminds me of our trip.

This was a gift from my friend who lives next door, she needed some help decorating her new flat. I went over there and we spent the whole weekend painting and decorating, moving furniture, clearing rooms and so on. In return she cooked and made tea, which was very nice, so all together it was quite an enjoyable weekend and we got the flat decorated quite quickly. She gave me this for helping her: it's quite big with large flat green leaves and in summer it has these beautiful red flowers a bit like a rose which come out around June and stay open until September, so I remember all the hard work and fun we had.

Now, look at the one which is – it's got a stone base with a little gold label showing the date and what it's for and at the top of it is a small gold figure standing up with his arms across his chest, looking very proud with his right leg on a football. It's only a small statue which is made of brass or some other metal that isn't very valuable. But there are two reasons I really like it. First of all, I got it as a prize from a football competition, which we entered for fun, last summer. We couldn't really play football, but we came second in the competition, much to everyone's surprise. Secondly, I like it because of the expression on the little footballer – he looks very proud and professional but we came second and we couldn't play very well. Anyway, it always brings to mind the day when we nearly won a football competition.

Track 2.26

I bought it from a carpet dealer
whenever I look at it, it reminds me of our trip
she gave me this for helping her
I got it as a prize
I remember all the hard work and fun
it always brings to mind the day we nearly won a football competition

Track 2.27

1 This was a gift from my friend who lives next door

2 the day when we nearly won a football competition

3 I bought it in Antakya, which is a very ancient city, when we were on holiday

4 a football competition, which we entered for fun, last summer

Unit 9
Track 3.1

Kamaal: Hi Joanna. What's the matter? You look a bit depressed.

Joanna: Hi Kamaal. I've just been reading this article in the newspaper about how difficult it is for sociology students to get a job after they graduate. They always want people with work experience. How do you get work experience if they won't give you a job? It's an impossible situation.

Kamaal: Yes, I know. It's a real problem.

Joanna: And the article says that some people spend a year or more living at home, doing unpaid voluntary work just to get something to put on their CVs. Really boring stuff like photocopying and addressing envelopes. I don't want to do anything like that. I want a real job.

Kamaal: It's the elections for the Students' Union committee posts next month here at the university. All the positions are up for election: academic officer, sports officer …

Joanna: What's your point?

Kamaal: And the position of Equal Opportunities Officer is coming up for election.

Joanna: I'm still not sure what you're getting at.

Kamaal: Why don't you stand for it? The post starts in June, you're well known at the university and I think you would be good at it.

Joanna: Equal Opportunities Officer! That sounds great. Isn't that the Students' Union officer who promotes equality within the university?

Kamaal: Yes, that's right. They raise awareness of equal opportunities for everyone in the university and promote the issue around campus.

Joanna: I'd love to do something for women on campus. But what about my studies?

Kamaal: It's a paid sabbatical post.

Joanna: Sabbatical?

Kamaal: Yes. That means you take a year off and then start your studies again. Meanwhile, you get really good work experience, and you can earn money at the same time.

Joanna: That sounds really interesting. But how do I get elected?

Kamaal: You go to the Students' Union, fill in an application form and just give it to the Union. Then, I guess, you need to put together a manifesto and try to get people to support you. I'll help you with your campaign, and I'll help you with publicity materials like posters for the notice boards and leaflets to hand out to everyone.

Joanna: It sounds really exciting. What exactly does the Equal Opportunities Officer do?

Kamaal: I'm not really sure. Let's have a look at the Students' Union website. There it is. Hmm. The Equal Opportunities Officer is responsible for anything which concerns women and equal rights and is responsible to the Students' Union executive committee for making sure that any racism or sexism is dealt with. Students' Union officers have to be available for students to talk about any problems they have, and to try to help them.

Joanna: I would love that part of the job, giving help and advice to students. The whole reason I want to work in Social Services is to help people.

Kamaal: That would be very good experience. It's a big responsibility, too. It also says that you're in charge of a budget and you would be responsible for managing a team of people. It's good experience for a management position in the future.

Joanna: Now I'm getting really excited! What about the day-to-day responsibilities?

Kamaal: It says here that the Equal Opportunities Officer acts on any health and safety issues. The Equal Opportunities Officer represents all the students on university committees like the Safety committee and the Equal Opportunities committee. Lots of meetings then.

Joanna: I don't think I would enjoy all those meetings quite so much. My first aid certificate might be useful for safety issues.

Kamaal: Very useful. And you would supervise the running of the crèche, make sure that students with young children have access to child care, that sort of thing. Oh, look, the Equal Opportunities Officer also has responsibility for the University Bus Service.

Joanna: Perhaps I could even get it to run on time.

Kamaal: Now, don't be too ambitious. We have to get you elected first. Let's take a walk to the Union office. Maybe we can meet the Equal Opportunities Officer and talk to her about the job.

Joanna: Great. Let's go.

Track 3.2

they are responsible for anything which concerns women

they are responsible to the Students' Union executive committee

you would supervise the running of the clinic

you're in charge of a budget

The Equal Opportunities Officer represents all the students

Track 3.3

caring	patient
aggressive	bad tempered
loyal	good humoured
quiet	hard working
gentle	organised
selfish	intelligent
bossy	generous
lively	disorganised

Track 3.4

I'm going to talk about a person I admire and respect – Arzu. This doesn't mean that she doesn't have any bad points, but on the whole she's got more good than bad points. She was my Biology teacher three years ago, and we have kept in touch and become good friends since then. She's a really nice person, very caring and extremely lively, there's never a dull moment around her. This is great if you're in the mood, but she can get on your nerves a bit because she's always up to something. She'll do anything for you if you're in trouble or if you need something, she's a very loyal person. However, she can be very bossy – always telling you what to do or organising other people, which is a laugh because she's the most disorganised person I've ever come across. I'll give you an example …

Track 3.5

on the whole she's got more good than bad points

there's never a dull moment around her

she can get on your nerves a bit

she's always up to something

She'll do anything for you

she's the most disorganised person I've ever come across

Track 3.6

Presenter: Hello and welcome to *You and Your Life*. Now, wouldn't it be wonderful to have our own helper around the house – a nanny? Nannies look after children and do the housework for people with more money than time. In our report today, Abby Simpson travels to New York to meet a new kind of nanny. Traditionally this is a job done by women, but in today's report we meet Bill, a male nanny or *manny*.

Abby: For eight-year-old Jake, going to school is always fun with his 29-year-old *manny*. Back home, there's homework to do for Jake and his older brother, Justin. Bill is helping them with it. He was studying for a Masters degree in drama therapy, but gave it up to become one of Manhattan's first male nannies. Mum Lauren is home, but working in her study. Dad is still in the office. With two energetic boys, Lauren says Bill is the ideal nanny.

Lauren: He grew up as a little boy. I'm a woman, I was never a little boy. Any other female nanny was never a little boy, and some things that I think are just outrageous, he says, *Hey, I did it too*, and I look at him and I think, *Well, he's a good guy, so I guess they'll be OK*. And so that gives me a really different perspective on my children.

Abby: According to Tim Kahn, author of *Bringing up Boys*, men are more likely to feel comfortable with rough-and-tumble play, which is great for girls and pretty essential for boys. He says that a man's boundaries around danger tend to be more relaxed: a man's more likely to let a child walk on top of a wall. He told me that if a child played in this way at three, four years old the spirit of adventure and curiosity stayed with him for life. Being a male nanny doesn't worry Bill either. He's always worked with children.

Bill: I can provide the same things that a female nanny could provide. I mean, I don't think there are any differences in the care that's given. Besides this, I think the other thing I can provide is a male figure in the home.

Abby: In the United States, parents are employing young *mannies*, sometimes to care for babies, but more often as active role models to get junior away from the TV and computer. From rollerblading to summer surf *mannies*, these are the big brothers who are always willing to play largely because they're paid for it.

But it's not all play. Bill has domestic duties too, like making the beds. The agency that placed Bill with his family told me that they are now actively recruiting male nannies. They said that here in New York they couldn't keep up with demand. They told me that many families wanted a male figure in the home because there were a lot of single mothers and busy families with parents who were working long hours and had very busy careers and didn't have enough time to be with their young children. Jake's dad works long hours too, and he told me how he felt about Bill playing a fatherly role when he's away. He said that he had a good relationship with his children. He said they loved him very much and that he didn't think that he would be replaced by anyone else as their father figure. In fact Bill, he says, has made their lives better. Still, dad always tries to be home for a bedtime story. I asked Bill how he became a male nanny.

Bill: You have to go on a course. Friends laughed when I started studying. They said that they had been sure that I wouldn't complete the course. But I did it, even though I was the only man among 70 women on my course.

Abby: And the course is tough. Bill told me he had trained in first aid, child development and, of course, nappy changing. When I questioned him about the worst part of the course, he smiled and didn't say anything. So what about the future of male nannies? Across the Atlantic in Britain up to 180,000 new childcare workers are needed in the next three years. But just two per cent of those in the childcare industry – nursery nurses, childminders and nannies – are men. Ministers said that the industry could not afford to exclude men. And what does Bill think? He feels that more men would be attracted if childcare was recognised as a career. Finally, I asked him whether he really liked his job.

Bill: I really enjoy it. It's much freer than a structured office job, and you can see children develop and grow. It's very rewarding.

Track 3.7

Part 1

Professor: Right. Everybody seems to be here. Who's leading the seminar today?

Peng: Erm, it's me. Peng Zhang.

Professor: And what areas of social studies are you going to talk about today?

Peng: I'm going to talk about women in the workplace. I have some slides here which will help to explain, but please stop me and ask me if there's anything that isn't clear. I'm going to concentrate on the overall British public today, which includes ethnic minorities. I will look at those groups separately later in the term. To give you a general overview of things, to give you the big picture that is, we can see from this slide that the population of Britain is 57.5 million. 64% of this number are of working age, that is, between 16 and 64 years old. That 64%, roughly 37 million, is composed of equal numbers of men and women, which means that there are 18.4 million women of working age in this country. 67% of this number of adults of working age, or around 12.3 million, do some kind of paid work. If we look now at gender, of the men, 79% are in employment. Now I'll go on to briefly talk about education.

There are more women than men in full-time higher education at the moment. That means they are doing a degree at university. There are currently 486,300 females, compared to 429,000 men. Women consistently have better results in state examinations, across all ethnic groups. One would expect this to carry through to the world of work: that is we would expect women to earn equal if not better salaries and hold equal if not better positions than men. But in reality how many of these women go on to work in highly paid jobs?

Part 2

Peng: From this chart here, we can see the percentage of women employed in a range of professions. It is clear that the majority of women work in low-paid jobs, despite their academic superiority. The question I would like to address is whether this is a matter of preference or not and if not, are there other reasons for this? Much research is being done in this area and I'd like to begin by looking firstly at an overview of some of the careers, especially the lower paid careers, women move into. Some women, such as home carers, have no choice, because they have sick, disabled or elderly people to look after. 88% of all care workers are female. There is however a profession with more women: an even higher percentage of hairdressers are women: 89%. If we look at catering and the leisure industry 73% of workers in restaurants or cafes are women. Turning to more general employment, 83% of office workers are women – but not in a management position. Moving over to the well-paid jobs, we can see that the percentage of women who work in the legal profession is fairly high, at 42%. The second highest is medicine, with 39%. Numbers working in marketing and IT are lower: 25% and 32% respectively. Overall, it seems that the greatest number of women are employed in the caring or service sectors.

Let's now move on to a very important indicator of equal opportunity in the work place: money. Despite the equal opportunities policy in Britain, it is clear from this final chart that there is still a gap in earnings between males and females, although not necessarily for doing the same job. The gap between men and women calculated by the hour is 18% for full-time and 13% for part-time workers. On a weekly basis, men generally receive an average of £129 more before tax, which is a 25% difference. To sum up, there are an equal amount of men and women of working age in this country, but a higher number of men in the workforce. Despite a higher level of education, more women work in jobs in the caring and service sectors than men, which tend to be lower-paid. This may be the reason why salaries for women are generally lower. That's all for today. I expect you've heard enough statistics for one afternoon. Are there any questions, please?

Unit 10

Track 3.8

A: I'm glad that's over. That was difficult, I had to take loads of notes. It was a hard lecture, what did you think?

B: Really difficult, the concepts in total quality management are hard to grasp sometimes.

A: Well, I'm glad it wasn't just me that found it difficult to understand.

B: Look, why don't we grab lunch and talk it over, it might make things clearer for us.

A: That's a great idea, but I've got a seminar now with Dr Mellor from 12 to 1 but I'm free after that.

B: OK, I'll go to the library for an hour, review my notes from the lecture and see if I can find any books from the reading list.

A: You mean you didn't read anything about it before you went to the lecture?

B: No, why, did you?

A: Not really.

B: Maybe that's why we didn't understand it then.

A: That could be it.

B: Anyway, it's just gone 12 now, let's get together at say ten past one.

A: OK, where do you want to meet?

B: How about at the central reception in the main foyer?

A: That's good, but let's make it 1.15: it'll take me ten minutes to get there and if the seminar overruns I may need five minutes more.

B: That doesn't matter, I'll just hang on for you to get here.

A: Where do you want to go?

B: How about something light, just a snack? What about going to the Fair Trade Café for a bite to eat? Is that OK for you?

A: I'm quite hungry at the moment, I'll be starving by 1.15. I think I'll need more than just a snack.

B: Do you want to go to the main refectory? We can get a three-course meal there quite cheaply and they have different kinds of foods there.

A: Yes, they had a Thai food promotion there last week.

B: That's right – real English style Thai food.

A: Ha, it's better than fish and chips all the time.

B: True.

A: Look, I have to rush, see you in the main refectory at 1.15 …

B: No, main reception … don't forget!

Track 3.9

Why don't we grab lunch?

Let's get together at say ten past one.

How about something light?

What about going to the Fair Trade Café for a bite to eat?

Do you want to go to the main refectory?

Track 3.10

A: Hi Greg, just in time.

B: Hi Caroline, how was the seminar?

A: It was really good. Simon …

B: Who?

A: Dr Mellor, I mean, took us through the main points of the lecture again and we were able to ask about anything we didn't understand the first time.

B: Feeling hungry now?

A: Yes, I am a bit, what about you?

B: I'm starving – let's see what they've got.

A: Let's see now. Do you want a starter? They've got tomato soup or mushroom pâté.

B: No, I'm not bothered about a starter. What's the main course?

A: Grilled fish, roast beef, vegetable lasagne for the vegetarians and salad niçoise as the healthy option.

B: Never mind that, what's for dessert? Profiteroles – yummy!

A: Profiteroles! You're not really going to eat that, are you?

B: You bet I am, I love profiteroles.

A: What about the main course?

B: I suppose if I'm having profiteroles for dessert, I'd better have the healthy option for the main course.

A: Salad niçoise, then?

B: Yeah. OK, let's go and order.

C: Hello, good afternoon. What can I get you today?

A: I'll take the vegetable lasagne, please.

C: Which vegetables would you like with that?

A: Could I have broccoli and boiled potatoes, please?

C: Certainly. Here you are.

B: And I'll have the salad niçoise, please.

C: Any side dishes with that?

B: No thank you, but I'll take some garlic bread please.

C: Here you are.

B: Lovely, thank you very much. And I'll have some profiteroles, please.

C: Here you are. Enjoy your meal.

B: Thanks. I'll get this.

A: No, no. We'll pay for our own.

B: No, it's OK, it's on me, it's my treat.

A: I couldn't let you pay, no, really.

B: Caroline, I insist – as long as you tell me what your tutor said about total quality management.

A: Well, OK. I'll buy next time.

B: It's a deal. Can you take for both of these please?

C: Both together, that's £6.25.

B: Here you are.

A: Thanks Greg, next time lunch is on me.

Track 3.11

B: I'll get this.

A: No, no. We'll pay for our own.

B: No, it's OK, this one's on me, it's my treat.

A: I couldn't let you pay, no, really.

B: Caroline, I insist.

A: Well, OK. I'll buy next time.

B: It's a deal.

Track 3.12

Hi, my name's Jo Mulhearn and I'm the International Students' Welfare Officer with the University of Dublin. In the second of our talks, I'm going to give you some hints and advice about what to do if you go for dinner with other Irish and British students. While you're over here for your studies, there will be a number of dinners you will be invited to attend, like the end of term dinner, or student society dinner, and there will be a number of informal occasions when you will get an invitation for lunch or dinner. Today I'm going to give you a bit of advice on what happens when you get a dinner invitation, and things you should avoid doing. All right?

OK, let's get started. When you get an invitation to a dinner, you need to reply within one or two days. If you get an invitation letter, it will say RSVP at the bottom and this means you need to reply in writing. You may get invited to eat out at a restaurant – when this happens, whoever extends the invitation to dinner, regardless of whether they are male or female, will pay for the meal. In view of this, it's polite not to order the most expensive meal on the menu, but to go for something mid-price. However, if the invitation is from a classmate or friend it is most likely assumed that you will each pay for yourself. This is often called *going Dutch* – each person pays for their own meal. When you accept a dinner invitation, tell your host if you have any diet restrictions – if there is anything you don't eat, or if you are vegetarian for example, or if there is anything you are allergic to.

Dinner usually starts at seven or eight p.m. We are usually quite time-conscious, and being on time is very important. When an appointment is made, you are expected to arrive within fifteen minutes of the appointed time. If you are invited to dinner at seven p.m., you should try to arrive at five past seven. When you are invited to a party or event, especially at someone's home, an appropriate gift could be a bottle of wine, flowers or chocolate. If you are invited to a birthday party, a small gift is appropriate and make sure you take a birthday card.

When you enter the dining room, your host will tell you where to sit, or you can ask where you are sitting. When the meal starts, wait for others to start eating, this is usually when all the people are at the table or when the host says something like *Go ahead, Tuck in* or *Help yourself.* When you are asked if you would like a serving of a particular dish, do not refuse out of politeness. If you want something, you should accept. We usually try to leave little, if anything, on our plate at the end of the meal, so don't take more than you can eat. After you have had enough, it is appropriate to politely decline additional servings. If you would like more of some food and it is not right in front of you, say, *Please pass the,* for example, *potatoes.* Don't reach across the table or in front of someone to get something – that is considered rude. Ask them to pass it to you.

When you are finished eating, say something like *What a delicious meal. Thank you so much.* Never burp at the dinner table, it's really rude even if you can't help it. When you have finished, place both the knife and the fork side by side diagonally across your plate and wait for everyone to finish before leaving the table. A note or card sent to thank the host for the nice time you had at the party or event is not necessary, but it is a nice gesture (and may get you invited again). Finally, smoking. If you do not see ashtrays in a home, then your host probably does not want visitors to smoke in the house. Otherwise, ask your host's permission before smoking. If your host does not want you to smoke in the house, you may excuse yourself for a few minutes to go outside to smoke.

Track 3.13

A: So, today following from the lecture on nutrition, Harald is going to tell us about different views on eating healthily. Over to you, Harald.

Harald: OK, everyone. We all know that good health starts with a healthy diet and good nutrition. Incorporating sensible eating habits into our lifestyle helps us maintain our future well-being and today I'm going to look at three different approaches to diet: the western approach, the oriental approach and the naturopathic approach.

C: I'm sorry Harald, what does that last one mean?

Harald: The naturopathic approach? Basically it sees food as a kind of medicine and bases its diet approach on this. So, food as medicine, which I'll come to later.

C: Thanks.

Harald: I'd like to look at the western approach first of all as it's the approach we're all most familiar with here. Western approaches to nutrition focus on getting a balance of protein, carbohydrate, fruit, vegetables and fibre, plus a balanced intake of vitamins and minerals. In general, western nutritional therapists recommend that we should eat five portions of fruit and vegetables a day; use organic and free-range produce whenever possible; decrease our intake of fast and processed foods and consume fresh food every day; limit your intake of tea, caffeine and alcohol; drink plenty of water; limit your intake of red meat and dairy products but make sure you get enough essential acids found in oily fish, nuts and seeds.

D: Sorry, Harald. Did you say that we need to limit our intake of water?

Harald: No, no – just the opposite, we need to drink about two litres of water each day. Now I'll move on to the next approach, the oriental approach. In oriental medicine, the approach to nutrition is quite different. It focuses on eating seasonal foods and balancing them according to their properties. For example, in summer, it's recommended that lots of salads, vegetables grown above ground (such as peas and beans) and soft fruits are eaten. In winter, root vegetables like turnips and carrots and other vegetables grown below ground are eaten. It is believed that eating out of season – for example, eating imported tropical fruits in winter – is not good. All foods are classified according to their properties and their effects on the body, such as whether they are warming or cooling foods. If too many cool foods, such as tropical fruits, are eaten during winter, they will cool the body making it more susceptible to things such as poor circulation, colds or weak digestion. Taking lots of warm foods in summer, on the other hand, will overheat the body and may cause conditions such as certain types of skin diseases and liver problems.

C: So if someone has a hot condition like a skin disease, in oriental nutrition, they should eat cool foods.

Harald: Like soft fruits and lettuce and so on, yes. And if they have a cold illness like a cold they are given warming foods like meat and vegetables. Food preparation and cooking methods are also important. Boiled, grilled or fried foods, casseroles and soups are considered warming, while raw, cold and refrigerated foods are considered cooling.

A: That's very interesting, Harald. Can we move on to your third category and then the other students can ask you questions? They are obviously very interested in the subject.

Harald: The final approach is the naturopathic approach. As I said, this approach sees food as a medicine and like the oriental approach the method of preparation is important, as is the way food is eaten. Naturopaths recommend the following good eating habits: eat slowly and chew food thoroughly to help digestion; take meals in a calm and quiet environment (don't eat in front of the TV); don't do any other activity, such as reading, while eating; always leave a portion of the stomach empty at the end of a meal to allow for digestion; avoid overeating and don't take heavy meals in the evening. When it comes to preparing and cooking food, naturopaths say we should include raw food in our meals and cook food as little as possible. Specific foods are also used as medicine in naturopathy. For example, raw potato juice is used to treat stomach problems because it's very alkaline. There are of course many other different views on healthy diets and I've chosen only three, but I hope it was interesting.

A: Thanks very much Harald, now I'm sure the other students have lots of difficult questions for you …

Track 3.14

1

A: Excuse me, I'm looking for a place to eat around here.

B: Well, the nearest place is just past the gate, it sells sandwiches, snacks and jacket potatoes.

A: That sounds fine, what's it called?

B: I'm not really sure, but look at the prices – it's very cheap: most things are under a pound.

A: Thanks very much for your help!

2

A: Where would you like to go for lunch?

B: I'm a stranger round here, where do you recommend?

A: There's a great place on Low Petergate, it sells pasta and Italian food.

B: Oh, but I eat Italian food all the time at home.

A: OK, what about vegetarian food? Do you like that?

B: Yes, I do.

A: Then I can recommend a nice little place just around the corner with a good selection of really tasty food.

B: Fine, let's go, I'm starving.

3

… and there are lots of places to eat in and around the College of St Johns, so you don't need to go hungry. I can't officially recommend any, but I'll tell you about one of my favourites. It's a traditional pub, with an open fire and traditional beers. It's quite near here and although it's in the shopping precinct on Goodramgate it's very cheap and it does a great beef burger. Also the other good thing is that it's open late on Thursday, Friday and Saturday.

Track 3.15

just past the gate

most things are under a pound

you don't need to go hungry

just around the corner

Friday and Saturday

Unit 11
Track 3.16

Good evening and welcome to the news at ten. World scientists have called on their governments to take urgent action against climate change. They have agreed that all countries should cut carbon dioxide emissions. They say that action taken now to reduce the build up of greenhouse gases in the atmosphere will lessen the rate of climate change. However, some countries still dispute that climate change is a reality, pointing to evidence from scientists in other …

Welcome to *Crossing Countries*, my name is Jeremy Moss and I'm reporting from Kazakhstan in central Asia. Here, just 40 years ago, the waters of the Aral Sea lapped up against the shoreline. Today the waters have receded so much, that there is no water as far as the eye can see. The former Soviet Union diverted the Ama Dariya and the Syrdariya rivers, which fed the Aral Sea, to grow cotton in the desert. But they created an ecological and human disaster. What was the fourth biggest inland sea is now mostly desert. What appears to be snow on the seabed is really salt. The winds blow this as far as the Himalayas. All of this was done in the name of cotton – grown where it would not grow naturally.

Hello and welcome to the six o'clock news. Today's main stories: a report from the World Wildlife Fund has claimed that melting glaciers in the Himalayas could lead to shortages of water for hundreds of millions of people in future. The Himalayas contain the largest store of water outside the polar ice caps, and feed seven great Asian rivers. In the report, the WWF says India, China and Nepal could experience floods followed by droughts in coming decades. Scientists have been calling for immediate action against climate change in order to slow down the rate of melting, which is increasing every year.

Track 3.17

Monica: Hi, Karl, are you OK? You don't look very well.

Karl: Oh, it's just the weather. This heat is really getting to me. My head feels very heavy. There's just no air outside.

Monica: Oh, I know what you mean. It's almost too much isn't it? Actually, it may turn out to be the third hottest summer on record so far you know.

Karl: Really?

Monica: Apparently, yes. But it's been just as hot as this all over the world. Have you not heard about it?

Karl: No, I haven't. What's been happening then?

Monica: Well, fields have been turning yellow and drying up all over France. And, forest fires have been burning out of control there too. It was so dry that it just all went up in flames – just like that! Did you not see those French firefighters on television the other evening? They've been trying to put all those fires out for a week.

Karl: No, I didn't know. I must have been having a cold bath at the time trying to cool down!

Monica: Well, try to cut down on that water if you can! Have a shower next time! Baths use up much more water and water's a pretty scarce resource these days. Rivers have actually been disappearing. This has been happening in Italy, in fact. Can you imagine? They have actually been drying up altogether! And lots of people have been falling ill and even dying because of the heat all over the world.

Karl: Yes, I remember now. There was that terrible heat wave in India where many people died. And droughts have hit parts of China too. Many people have been going without water there. Some of their glaciers have been receding too.

Monica: Yes, I know. The same thing's been happening in Switzerland. This summer they've been melting ten times faster than they usually do. And apparently glaciers in Italy are around 20% smaller than they were ten years ago! Just think about that!

Karl: Well, frankly, I'm not surprised. Just look at the weather out there. It's absolutely boiling. I can't stand it.

Monica: Yes, it's a real scorcher. In fact, they say it's going to go up even more before it comes down! But, you do know why it's all happening don't you? Basically, it's all due to global warming. And that's caused by the build-up of greenhouse gases by human activities. So, our planet is hotting up because of you and me. That means it's your fault that you've got a headache!

Karl: Oh, I'm not so sure about that.

Monica: You don't mean it could all be down to the forces of nature and absolutely nothing to do with us humans whatsoever? Get real!

Karl: Well, it's possible that global warming could be the result of natural phenomena. Perhaps changes in solar activity or volcanic eruptions. You know, volcanoes – that kind of thing. And of course it could just be caused by long term cyclical changes in our climate.

Monica: Come on! The world's oceans have been warming up over the last 40 years! And everyone knows that climate models based on ocean temperature are much more reliable than models based on air temperatures. All the evidence is there in our oceans. They are warming up and there's just no way that can be put down to Mother Nature!

Karl: Well, I'm not so sure about that. I think it's possible. But anyhow, we just don't know enough about it, do we?

Monica: Well, interestingly enough, we can find out more if we want. There's a talk on Global Warming later this week. They've been putting posters up all over campus. I read about it in the refectory this morning. The title is *Global Warming – Fact or Fiction?* Do you fancy coming along? It should be interesting.

Karl: What's the title again? Fact or what?

Monica: That heat must definitely be getting to you. The title is *Global Warming: Fact or Fiction?*

Karl: Yeah, I'd like to go for that. That way we can decide which of us is right and who is wrong.

Monica: And you know global warming is a hot topic.

Track 3.18

This heat is really getting to me.
It's almost too much.
Just look at the weather!
It's absolutely boiling!
I can't stand it.
It's a real scorcher.

Track 3.19

Dr Marianne Meffen: Good evening, everyone. Thank you all very much for braving the heat wave outside to come to this talk on global warming! I'm absolutely delighted to welcome Dr Ken McArthur, who is one of the world's leading climatologists and we are delighted that he has found time to join us this evening to tell us more about his pioneering work. Over to you now, Ken.

Dr Ken McArthur: Thanks for that warm introduction, Marianne. Well, I am going to start off by outlining what is actually happening in the Himalayas. I'll then be moving on to talking about how the experience there fits into the larger scheme of things – the bigger picture of global climate change. So, hopefully by the end of the evening we will all have a greater understanding of the need to take the pressure off our planet. Now, the Himalayas contain the largest store of water outside the polar ice caps and they feed seven great Asian rivers including the Mekong and the Ganges. But as you can see from the images coming up on the screen right now, today this vast area is in crisis. Some would view it as nothing short of a catastrophe in fact. The glaciers, which regulate the water supply to these rivers, are melting and they are melting fast. In fact, they're retreating at a rate of about ten to fifteen metres every year. Now, the rapid melting of these glaciers will first increase the volume of water in rivers, causing widespread flooding. As you can imagine, these raised water levels will leave those many people living on flood plains particularly vulnerable. However, in a few decades this situation will change and the water level in rivers will decline. So, in effect the peoples of India, China and Nepal could experience flooding followed by droughts in coming decades. So what does this mean for the future of those hundreds of millions of people throughout China and the Indian subcontinent? After all, most of them live far from the Himalayas themselves. Well, the reality is that these people rely on water supplied from these rivers. Vast numbers of farmers of course need regular irrigation to grow their crops successfully. Glacial melting, in effect, means massive eco and environmental problems for the peoples of Western China, Nepal and Northern India.

So where does glacial melting in the Himalayas fit into the wider debate on global climate change? Well, we know that ice is receding everywhere. And this is because our planet is heating up. Nepal, China and India are already showing signs of climate change. We know, for example that Nepal's annual average temperature has risen by 0.06 degrees Celsius. We also know that three snow-fed rivers have shown signs of reduced flows. And the water level in China's Qinghai Plateau wetlands has affected rivers, lakes and wetlands. And recent research indicates that India's Gangotri glacier is receding by 23 metres (75 feet) each year.

So our planet is indeed under pressure. In fact, the temperature of the Earth could rise by two degrees Celsius above pre-industrial levels in a little over twenty years. And projections for 2100 are that the Earth will have got warmer by between 1.4 and 5.8 degrees Celsius. Well, what does it mean for us? Well, it will certainly mean drought where major water sources are fed by snow or glacial melt. We know for example that two thirds of the world's people will be living in areas of acute water stress by 2025. And as for animal life, the consequences will be even more serious. The natural habitats of animals such as polar bears, seals and walruses will shrink fast, putting them well on the road to extinction. In fact, in global terms, scientists have predicted that one in ten animals and plants will have become extinct by 2050. That means one million species will have disappeared completely. So, in order to slow down the rate of melting which we know is increasing year by year, we need to take immediate serious action on climate change. This image is a representation of the Earth as it is today – a fossil-fuel driven planet. So, serious action means converting to progressively cleaner technologies. By that I mean switching to technologies that produce little or no greenhouse gases combined with the active removal of carbon dioxide from the atmosphere. And I think that governments need to take a leading role in this. After all, they have to carry a great deal of responsibility for the state our planet has got itself into in the first place! Dealing with climate change at government level also involves following international agreements. But there are plenty of things that we as individuals can do that could make a dramatic difference. How did you all travel here for this talk this evening?

Did you make the journey by car by any chance? We know that if every driver took just one fewer car journey a week, it would cut down on carbon dioxide emissions from traffic by 13%. There are many other things we can do – all of which involve very little effort on our part – which can really make a difference. For example, we can recycle our household rubbish and remember to dispose of our household chemicals carefully. And by that I mean not doing things like pouring paint down our sinks! So you see, we do have the power to make change and save the future of our planet. And that's fact not fiction. Thank you very much indeed. Now, do we have any questions from the floor?

Track 3.20

1.4 – 5.8°C
0.06°C
13%
10 – 15 metres per year
2050
1 in 10
2100
CO_2

Track 3.21

Karl: Hi there Monica, what are you up to?

Monica: Oh, I'm reading this really interesting article about a woman who set up an eco-team and …

Karl: An *eco-team*? I've never heard of that before. What do you mean by that exactly?

Monica: Well, an eco-team is a group of people who get together to learn about how they can lead more environmentally-friendly lives.

Karl: What do you mean by environmentally friendly?

Monica: Well, learning how to live in a way that doesn't harm the environment. Well, as I was saying, this woman called Helen set up this eco-team in her town. She got in touch with people who she thought would be interested in joining. Then she got together with this co-ordinator and together they …

Karl: Could I interrupt you there? I'd like to know what this co-ordinator does.

Monica: Well, the co-ordinator is the person who provides the eco-team with all the support and resources they need, like books and equipment for …

Karl: What kind of equipment exactly?

Monica: Well, I was just about to talk about that. You see the co-ordinator gave the team equipment such as hippos that'll save water …

Karl: Wait a minute, can I butt in here? Hippos? Now what on earth are they?

Monica: They are kind of bags that you put in the toilet cistern. They reduce the amount of water you use when you flush the toilet. I wouldn't mind getting one of these hippo bags myself, in fact.

Karl: Yes, that's not a bad idea. It sounds like a really easy way to reduce water waste.

Monica: Anyway, as I was saying, her team got some other equipment too. They got some radiator panels and …

Karl: What are radiator panels? Can you explain what they do?

Monica: Well, these radiator panels go on the wall behind the radiator and deflect the heat back into the room. So they stop the heat escaping. Now this eco-team is also doing things like recycling their household rubbish. So they do things like re-use their old plastic bags when they go shopping. To be honest, I've never even thought of doing that before!

Karl: Oh, I always re-use mine. I've got lots of them at home.

Monica: Really? Well, can you give me a couple of them so I can start re-using them myself?

Karl: What do you mean?

Monica: I've just told you. Because up to now I've been throwing them all away!

Karl: OK, I'll see what I can do.

Monica: Now, the team also tries to cycle or walk to the shops instead of going by car. But we both do that already, don't we?

Karl: Well, that's mainly because the shops are so near campus.

Monica: And if the eco-team wants to go to markets or supermarkets out of town, they try to car share.

Karl: Car share? Can you explain that?

Monica: Well, a few of them travel together in the same car instead of travelling separately. It's a good idea but until I actually learn to drive and you buy yourself a car that kind of energy-saving strategy will just have to wait!

Karl: Yeah, right!

Monica: Now what was I saying? Oh yes, the team also tries to eat healthy food so they go together to markets and buy organic food.

Karl: Can I just stop you there for a second? Organic food?

Monica: Well, I was just about to explain what that is. Organic food is food that doesn't contain any artificial chemicals. Anyway, this woman Helen says that there is a link between health and the environment. And she's absolutely right of course. After all, if we look after our environment, we also look after our health and the health of future generations.

Karl: I'm not so sure. But anyway, where can we get all this organic food then so that I can find out? I've never thought of doing that before.

Monica: Me neither! But, apparently there's an organic farmer's market once a week on Saturdays just outside town. We could go take a look this weekend if you fancy it. We could both do with eating a bit more healthily!

Karl: Yes, but how exactly do we get there without a car? I'm not sure about the buses at the weekend.

Monica: Buses? On your bike! We can cycle there of course. Then you can find out for sure if there is a link between our health and the environment.

Karl: Right.

Track 3.22

Anyway, as I was saying …
Can I just stop you there for a second?
Can I butt in here?
Could I interrupt you there?
I was just about to explain what that is …
I was just about to talk about that …
Now, where was I?

Unit 12
Track 3.23

Marta: Hey, Michie, Tomas. I wondered when you two were going to show up. It's a great party, all the department's here.

Michie: We're a bit late. We stopped at the supermarket to get a bottle of lemonade and a bottle of cola. Is that Professor Weller over there dancing?

Marta: I think it is – she's really getting into the swing of things. And all the guys are here too: Susie's over there talking to Simon, there's Lucy and Caroline's chatting to Cathy and Graham by the bar. The drinks are over there and there are some snacks and things to eat over there by the wall.

Tomas: That's good, I'm a bit hungry.

Marta: We haven't seen each other since last week. What have you guys been up to since the exams?

Tomas: If you really want to know, I've been recovering. That was the hardest month of my life. I've been watching TV, playing video games and calling home. And that's it.

Michie: Me too, I was asleep for three days, I was exhausted.

Marta: I know exactly what you mean. Ten tests in two weeks. That was hard.

Michie: But you know, it wasn't really the tests that were hard – once you got into the exam room and opened the paper then the questions were quite fair. It was all the hard work before the tests.

Marta: And the tension, you know, not knowing what to expect. I was really nervous before the first exam.

Tomas: Yes, it was a bit frightening when we got the timetables.

Michie: I get very stressed by exams and I could hardly concentrate.

Marta: I find exams stressful too. So what did you do to keep calm?

Michie: I tried to be as relaxed as possible by doing exercises like T'ai Chi and Yoga. I found that breathing exercises were relaxing. I couldn't really study until I felt calm so I spent about an hour a day doing the exercises and then I found that it really cleared my mind.

Marta: That's interesting. I enjoyed studying for the tests.

Michie: You thought the tests were enjoyable! No way, Marta.

Marta: No, I didn't enjoy the tests, I enjoyed studying for them. I really liked having the time to study by myself and revise and have the time to think about the subject and what we were taught.

Michie: I can understand that. It can be good to have time to yourself, but didn't you get nervous before the test?

Marta: Not really. You see I was well prepared. I'd been practising my French with friends, reading newspapers and books in French and I even went to Paris for a long weekend just before the test, so I really knew it inside out. It gave me a lot of confidence. What about you Tomas, how did you prepare?

Tomas: Well, I was really cool about it I didn't do a thing.

Marta: You didn't do anything?

Tomas: Not a jot. I didn't lift a finger.

Marta: I don't believe a word of it, you're one of the best students. I bet you're going to get a distinction.

Tomas: No way, but about revising, in my opinion if you don't know it by now you never will. You know, you see people who just spent all term having a good time then panic at the last minute and try cramming for exams. They ask you for notes from classes they missed, they want your old essays and they think they can cram three years into three weeks. I think that if you stay on top of things then you don't really need to get into a last minute panic.

Michie: Oh come on Tomas, you're the exception rather than the rule. Everyone gets nervous before an exam.

Tomas: No, I don't believe in getting nervous. I was looking forward to it in fact. You know Michie, the examiner isn't trying to fail candidates – they're on your side, but you've got to prove yourself.

Marta: That's true, but I think it also helps to be prepared, that way if you have a bad day, you still stand a chance of passing.

Michie: I agree with you Marta, Tomas is too big for his boots sometimes – preparation, confidence and calmness is what you need.

Tomas: And a positive attitude: go and get it!

Track 3.24

it really cleared my mind
I really knew it inside out
I didn't lift a finger
if you don't know it by now, you never will
stay on top of things

Track 3.25

Tomas: How about that – we did it, we're university graduates.

Marta: It's unbelievable. Who would have thought that we could pass a difficult subject in a different language?

Michie: But we did do it. Congratulations everyone. How did you feel when you went up for your degree, Marta?

Marta: Personally speaking, I'm just glad it's over. I was petrified. I was so wound up in the assembly before the ceremony, I couldn't speak to anyone. Just the thought of walking through the Main Hall with all our friends and family there. I just kept imagining the worst.

Tomas: Like what?

Marta: Oh, just stupid things like I'd miss it when my name was called out, or I'd fall over going up to the stage and my gown would get caught on a chair. You name it, I'd imagined it.

Michie: Oh Marta, I never knew – you looked so relaxed and happy when you went for your degree.

Marta: I really didn't feel like it, I was shaking like a leaf. The experience of standing up in front of all those people was petrifying. What about you Tomas? I bet you were excited too.

Tomas: No, not me. I was cool about it. I thought it was just very enjoyable – most of it anyway.

Michie: What do you mean you were cool? I saw your face, you looked really tense and stressed.

Tomas: Well, I admit I was feeling a little nervous during the assembly – I had butterflies in my stomach. But when the ceremony started and the procession began I could see my mum and dad – they were smiling from ear to ear at me and I became a lot happier. They were delighted and it made me feel glad.

Michie: So, what didn't you like?

Tomas: It was just the Vice-Chancellor's address, his speech to the new graduates. He really does like the sound of his own voice. He went on and on and on and I got a bit bored. All I wanted to do was to get out of the hall and be with my folks.

Marta: Yes, it did drag on a bit. Although it was boring, he said some good things. Now, Michie, don't tell me you didn't panic either.

Michie: Overall I think I enjoyed it. I had mixed feelings at the time though. I did feel a bit panicky as I was going up the stairs to the stage. I just kept telling myself to pull myself together and keep my eyes on the person in front and just keep going. And when I got to the stage and saw my tutor there smiling at me I nearly burst into tears! Can you believe it? When I came off the stage it was such a relief.

Marta: You wouldn't be the first person to cry on their graduation day, anyway.

Tomas: Well, it's been an emotional day. How about going for a quick coffee and a chat about what we're going to do next?

Michie: You're on. Coffees on Tomas everyone.

Track 3.26

I nearly burst into tears
it was such a relief
I had butterflies in my stomach
I was shaking like a leaf
I was so wound up … I couldn't speak
they were smiling from ear to ear
I had mixed feelings

Track 3.27

Good afternoon everyone, I'm Gerhard Holliger from the Munich Investment Bank. The University asked me to come today to give you some advice and help on how to be successful in an interview situation. Today I'm going to talk you through the types of interview you may have, how to prepare for these, the kinds of questions interviewers may have and how to deal with them. As you can see, there's a lot to do in the time we have so I'll get started immediately. There are at least three basic types of interview which I'll term traditional, behavioural and case-study. To begin with I'll go over the interview type we're probably all most familiar with: the traditional interview.

In a traditional interview the aim is to get factual information from a candidate and evaluate how well they fit the job description. Typical questions include, *Why did you choose your degree subject? Do you have any weaknesses and what are they? Why are you interested in this position?* The second type of interview is the behavioural interview where

the employer requires you to offer concrete specific examples to show what skills you have. They may ask questions like, *Can you tell me about a time when you worked in a team? Could you give me an example of a time you had a challenge and how you dealt with it?* When answering this kind of question, use the STAR framework: talk about the situation; say what your task was; state the action you took and finally say what the result was. The final kind of interview is the case-study interview. In this kind of interview the employer requires you to analyse a problem or situation and present a solution to it. An example question might be, *What would you do in a situation where a customer complained about bad service?* This is the kind of interview we often give at our company as a second interview at the company building. Let's look now at the basic structure of an interview.

Interviews follow a pattern of warm-up, information exchange, and conclusion. During the first few minutes of the interview in the warm-up phase, an employer will be getting a first, and perhaps lasting, impression of you. To help you feel at ease, a practised interviewer might ask common-ground questions about your interests or where you live or your journey to the interview. Some interviewers might start by saying *tell me about yourself.* This is simply an opening for you to briefly describe your background, skills, and interest in the position, but it's a question you need to prepare for. So on to the information exchange.

This is the main part of the interview. It is when you are asked the most questions and learn the most about the employer. If you are prepared for the interview, you will be able to predict the kind of questions you will be asked and be able to respond with full answers. During this stage it is important to remember that a job interview is a strategic conversation with a purpose. Your goal is to persuade the employer that you have the skills, background, and ability to do the job and that you can comfortably fit into his or her organisation. You can strongly influence the interview outcome if you realise that an interview is not an objective process in which the employer offers the job to the best candidate based on merit alone. But rather, an interview is a highly subjective encounter in which the interviewer offers the job to the qualified person who he or she likes best. Personality, confidence, enthusiasm, a positive outlook and excellent interpersonal and communication skills count heavily.

Here is some general advice on how to do your best in the information exchange part of the interview. Show enthusiasm in your responses to the employer's questions. Think about your tone of voice and body language. Look the interviewer in the eye, sit up straight, control nervous habits and smile when you enter the room. If you are unsure how to respond to a question, ask the questioner to repeat it. This will buy you time and ensure that you answer the question asked. Don't be afraid of short pauses. You may need a few seconds to think of an answer or the interviewer may need time to formulate an appropriate question. It is not necessary to fill up every second with conversation. Try to give examples to illustrate your answers. Avoid colloquial language and repeating phrases like *y'know, know what I mean.* Answer questions honestly and if you really don't know what response you should give, say so. Remember that whatever questions you are asked, however probing they may be, there is always a way of expressing yourself in a positive way. Never criticise a former employer or organisation and do not comment negatively on other companies – doing this gives people a negative impression of you. Employers do not want

excuses or bad feelings about a negative experience. If you are asked about a low grade job, a sudden job change, or a weakness in your background, don't be defensive. Focus on the facts and what you learned from the experience. Employers want people with a positive attitude.

Eventually the employer will probably say, *Do you have any questions?* This means that the interview is moving to the conclusion stage. Always ask questions because this gives you the opportunity to demonstrate your research and interest in the job. The employer may also ask you if you have anything else you would like to add or say. Again, it's best to have a response. You can use this opportunity to thank the employer for the interview, summarise your qualifications and restate your interest in the position. This last impression is almost as important as the first impression and will add to the points discussed during the information exchange.

Finally, there is no magic to interviewing: it is a skill that can be learned and improved upon with practice. So practise with friends and family before the interview – the more practice you get, the better prepared you will be on the day.

Track 3.28

Tomas: What are you planning to do after we get the results, Marta?

Marta: Do you mean what am I planning after I pass the exams?

Tomas: You're very confident, aren't you?

Marta: Not really, I'm just trying to be positive. So, to answer your question about what I'm planning to do, I'm hoping to spend a year in France.

Michie: Have you got anything lined up?

Marta: Not really, but I don't want to get into a real job just yet. I think I need a lot more practice to become really fluent in French, so I'm planning to go over and do seasonal work, visit friends and just go where I fancy.

Tomas: Seasonal work, like fruit picking. That sounds like a really nice way to spend a year.

Michie: I wish I had enough confidence to do that, never mind time and money. Who are you going with?

Marta: No one, I'm going to take off by myself.

Michie: You're going alone?

Marta: Why, do you want to come along?

Michie: No, I was just curious if you were going with anyone.

Tomas: Why, what are your plans, Michie?

Michie: I need to get as job as soon as possible. I'm thinking about going to the careers fair next week to meet employers, find out about them and go to some of their presentations.

Marta: Do you know who's going to be there?

Michie: There are a couple of companies that I'm interested in, large department stores I'd like to work for.

Marta: What line of work do you want to do?

Michie: I've decided that I'd like to be a buyer for a department store.

Tomas: Could you explain what you mean by *buyer*?

Michie: Yes, a buyer is someone who buys things for large organisations like department stores. They meet producers and negotiate prices and terms with them, and then buy the products if they can agree. That way I can use my languages travelling around the world, meeting producers and negotiating terms and contracts.

Tomas: You made a decision? When did that happen?

Michie: Are you trying to say that I'm indecisive?

Tomas: To put it another way, you're not known for being the most decisive person in the department.

Michie: Well, I've made my decision all right. What about you – have you got anything in mind?

Tomas: Well, actually yes. I'm hoping to stay.

Michie: In other words you're going to do a PhD.

Marta: A doctorate. Tomas, you're so secretive – you didn't say anthing about this. So if I understand you correctly, you're going to be here for another three years.

Tomas: At least three years, but I'll have a lot more time to myself because there isn't so much coursework – most of it is time studying and researching. By research I mean I want to follow my own ideas, testing some theories I have and gathering data to prove them.

Michie: That's really great.

Marta: Well done. Can you give me an example of what you mean by one of your theories? I'm sure we're interested in what Dr Tomas has to say.

Track 3.29

What are you planning to do?
What are your plans?
Have you got anything in mind?
I'm hoping to spend a year in France.
I don't want to get into a real job just yet.
I'm planning to go over and do seasonal work.

Track 3.30

in other words
to put it another way
so what you're asking is
by *research* I mean …
Could you explain what you mean by … ?
Can you give me an example of what you mean?

Acknowledgements

Photographs
Cover left ©Purestock/Alamy, middle ©Blend Images/Alamy, right ©Pacific Press Service/Alamy; p.4 top ©Marshall Cavendish, left ©Luis Harriso; p.6 ©Ian Shaw/Alamy; p.11 ©Ed Bock/Corbis; p.12 ©David R. Frazier Photolibrary, Inc./Alamy; p.18 top ©Keith Dannemiller/Corbis, 2 ©Reg Charity/Corbis; p.22 ©Satoshi Kambayashi, used with kind permission; p.25 ©Louis Harrison; p.26 ©Royalty Free/Corbis; p.30 left top to bottom ©E J Images/Alamy, ©Interfoto Pressebildagentur/Alamy, ©Authors Image/Alamy, ©Jayne Fincher.Photo Int/Alamy; p.32 ©Mark Ralston/Reuters/Corbis; p.36 ©f1 online/Alamy; p.37 ©Sally and Richard Greenhill/Alamy; p.39 ©Corbis Sygma; p.41 Holly Harris/Getty Images; p.42 ©Marshall Cavendish; p.44 ©Christian Darkin/Science Photo Library; p.45 top ©Kenneth Eward/Biografx/Science Photo Library, bottom ©Eric Heller/Science Photo Library; p.48 ©Vintage Images/Alamy; p.49 ©Doug Houghton/Alamy; p.50 1 ©Andrew Drysdale/Rex Features, 2 ©Cordelia Molloy/Science Photo Library, 3 ©George D. Lepp/Corbis, 4 ©Annebicque Bernard/Corbis Sygma; p.54 ©ComStock Images/Alamy; p.55 top-bottom ©Ian Davidson Photographic/Alamy, ©Alex Segre/Alamy, ©Ambient Images/Alamy, ©Chuck Pefley/Alamy, ©Black Star/Alamy; p.57 ©Getty Images; p.58 1 ©Andrew Holt/Alamy, 2 ©Philippa Lewis; Ediface/Corbis, 3 ©Henry Westheim Photography/Alamy, 4 ©Paul Cooper/Rex Features, 5 ©Arcaid/Alamy; p.59 top ©Roger-Viollet/Rex Features, bottom ©Roger-Viollet/Rex Features; p.60 left to right ©John Foxx/Alamy, ©ImageState/Alamy, ©nagelestock.com/Alamy, ©Helene Rogers/Alamy; p.61 ©Popperfoto/Alamy; p.62 ©London 2012/Handout/Reuters/Corbis; p.63 top to bottom, ©Cephas Picture Library/Alamy, ©allOver photography/Alamy, ©Jon Arnold Images/Alamy; p.66 ©The Image Bank/Getty Images; p.71 ©National Geographic/Getty Images; p.72 ©Times Newspaper/Rex Features; p.73 top ©Lebrecht Music and Arts Photo Library/Alamy, bottom ©Hulton Archive/Getty Images; p.74 ©Louis Harrison; p.75 ©Edward Bock/Corbis; p.78 ©Chuck Savage/Corbis; p.81 1 ©Varie/Alt/Corbis, 2 ©Phototake Inc./Alamy, 3 ©Royalty Free/Corbis; 4 ©Mehau Kulyk/Science Photo Library; p.84 top ©Jason Timsoon/Rex Features, left©Zave Smith/Corbis; p.87 © BananaStock/Alamy; p.90 ©2002 Getty Images; p.92 ©David Wall/Alamy; p.93 ©Marshall Cavendish; p.97©The Image Bank/Getty Image; p.98 a ©Ferruccio/Alamy, b ©Fairtrade Foundation, used with kind permission, c ©Marshall Cavendish, d ©Sue Cunningham Photographic/Alamy; p. 100 1 ©David Copeman/Alamy, 2 ©CheapShots/Alamy, 3 ©Profimedia.CZ s.r.o./Alamy, 4 ©Hugh Threlfall/Alamy, 5 ©Royalty-Free/Corbis; p.104 ©Fred Prouser/Reuters/Corbis; p.105 top to bottom ©Blend Images/Alamy, ©JupiterMedia/Alamy, ©Design Pics Inc./Alamy; p.106 ©Ralf Schultheiss/Zefa/Corbis; p.107 left to right ©Bettmann/Corbis, ©Ramin Talaie/Corbis, ©Bettmann/Corbis, ©Underwood and Underwood/Corbis; p.108 ©Comtock Images/Alamy; p.110 top to bottom ©Nordicphotos/Alamy, ©View Stock/Alamy, ©IGG Digital GraphicProductions

GmbH/Alamy, ©S C Photos/Alamy; p.111 ©BananaStock/Alamy; p.113 ©Photodisc Green/Getty Images; p.114 ©Thinkstock/Alamy; p.116 ©Catherine Karnow/Corbis; p.118 ©Marshall Cavendish; p.119 top ©Indeed/Getty Images, bottom ©Mark Peterson/Corbis; p.120 ©Brian Leng/Corbis; p.121 ©David Hoffman Photo Library/Alamy; p.122 top to bottom ©David Hoffman Photo Library/Alamy, ©John Foxx/Alamy, ©Tetra Images/Alamy; p.126 ©Blend Imges/Alamy; p.128 top ©AFP/Getty Images, top left © AFP/Getty Images; p.130 a ©Steve Murray/Alamy, b ©Holt Studios International Ltd/Alamy, c ©ImageState/Alamy, d ©Atmosphere Picture Library/Alamy; p.133 ©Peter Bowater/Alamy; p.138 left to right ©Marshall Cavendish, ©Graham Light/Alamy, ©Photofusion Picture Library/Alamy, ©Marshall Cavendish, ©Marshall Cavendish; p.140 ©Patrick Ward/Alamy; p.145 ©Andrew Fox/Alamy; p.147 ©Jose Luis Pelaez, Inc/Corbis; p.148 ©Tracey Fahy/Alamy; p.150 ©Jeff Christensen/Reuters/Corbis

Text
p.6 left to right: www.Chevening.com, based on article from www.cies.org, adapted from europa.eu.int; p.13 based on article from education.guardian.co.uk; p.15 based on article from www.ox.ac.uk; p.17b based on chart from www.ukcosa.org.uk, c based on chart from www.atlas.iienetwork.org, d and e based on charts from www.opendoors.iienetwork.org; p.19 based on article from www.bba.org.uk; p.23 © The Economist, May 5th, 2001; p.28 Annual Student Experience Report, 2005 ©UNITE Group; p.31 ©istc.org; p.35 ©gizmohighway.com; p.45 based on article from Washington Monthly; p.58 based on information from www.columbia.edu; p.59 based on information from www.open2.net/modernity ©Open University; p.69 ©Carla Power, Newsweek International, March 2005; p.78 adapted from www.good2bsecure.gov.uk ©HMSO; p.81 based on article from www.ctl.ncsc.dni.us; p.83 ©The Economist, March 11, 2004; p.93 based on article from www.monash.edu; p.95 based on Globalization: Threat or opportunity? at www.imf.org; p.98 based on information from www.eftafairtrade.org; p.109 adapted from 'More Women Cruise to the Top' by Stephanie Armour, USA Today, June 2003 and 'As Leaders Women Rule' by Rochelle Sharpe, Business Week, November 2000; p.114-15 Adapted from 'Smashing Through the Glass Ceiling' by Mary-Ann Stephenson from www.ivillage.co.uk; p.119 adapted from www.uky.edu; p.120 based on www.bbc.co.uk/health; p.122 based on a range of articles from www.newscientist.com; p.124 based on article from www.bbc.co.uk; p.128 Information from news reports in: The Week, August 2003, The Independent, February 2005, The Guardian, January 2004 p.131 adapted from 'Most of the World's Resources Used Up' by Tim Radford, Guardian Weekly, April 2005; p.133 www.news.bbc.co.uk; p.138 based upon 'How I Made My Area Greener' on www.bbc.co.uk/dna/actionnetwork; p.143 ©The Economist, Dec 21, 2000; p.147 based on information from web.mit.edu; p.150 Courtesy of John Kirwan, www.careers.ox.ac.uk.

The authors would like to give special thanks to Simon Ross and all at Marshall Cavendish ELT; Anna Gunn, our editor for her good advice and patience throughout the project; Graham Hart and Cathy Willis; Philip Saltmarsh of Eotvos Lorand University, Budapest; Andrea Liptak; Gerry Loftus; Zhang Tien; Rattapol Panyayutthakan and Mohammad Khalaf – MBA students at the School of Management, University of Bradford, (Unit 1); Jeremy Cushen and Michelle Hind (Unit 2); Dr Pouwan Lei, School of Engineering, Design and Technology and Dr Geyong Min, Department of Computing, the University of Bradford (Unit 4); Canberra and District Historical Society (Unit 6); Dr Steven Picksley, the University of Bradford (Unit 7); Michie Nishiguchi (Unit 12).

Most of all we would like to thank students at the University of Bradford and the University of Buckingham who worked through *Achieve IELTS* and gave us invaluable feedback and suggestions.

For Andrea, Ted and Eva.